Light Med For a Year

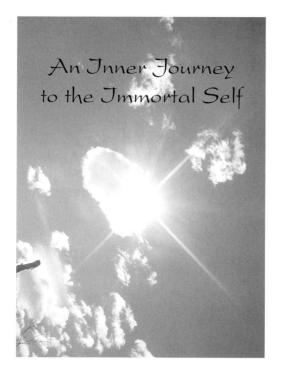

An Inner Journey
to the Immortal Self

*Contemplations, Meditations
and Affirmations for Every Day of the Year*

Elisabeth Constantine

First published by Findhorn Press 2004

ISBN 1–84409–038–8

British Library Cataloguing-in-Publication Data.
A catalogue record for this book is available from
the British Library.

Edited by Lynn Barton
Cover by Thierry Bogliolo
Internal design by Karin Bogliolo
All photographs © Elisabeth Constantine 2004

Printed and bound by WS Bookwell, Finland

Published by
Findhorn Press
305a The Park, Findhorn
Forres IV36 3TE
Scotland, UK
tel 01309 690582
fax 01309 690036
e-mail: info@findhornpress.com

www.findhornpress.com

Table of Contents

I humbly dedicate this book in celebration of the life of
my beloved soul sister Tsering Dekyi, La and to
the plight of all refugees on this planet, be it in body, mind or spirit.
I honour the light in each and every one of you.

"With kindness, with love and compassion, with this feeling that is the
essence of brotherhood, sisterhood, one will have inner peace."
—His Holiness the Dalai Lama

❁

Thank You

I am eternally grateful to my beloved Swami for holding
me in the light and thank his holiness the Dalai Lama
from my heart for teaching me that humour is indeed
a transformational tool and that
loving-kindness is the greatest remedy of all.
I'm humbly grateful to my publishers, to have been given
the 'green light' for this book and for making
me welcome in such a loving way.
I'd like to thank my dearest soul sister Valerie for
her continuing, unwavering support and invaluable guidance;
Sally and Robin for their generosity;
Anne and John for their kindness;
Lindsey, Jennifer and Eva for their friendship;
Mark for his blessings and Neil for his honesty,
all of which mean so much to me.

I thank my mother, father and sister for teaching me
compassion and forgiveness, and my niece Elisabeth
and nephew Thomas, for loving me unconditionally.
Lastly, and by no means least, I say a big thank you to
my many students, clients and workshop participants
over the past 15 years who've taught me invaluable lessons.

Preface

Blessings to you all, dear readers. I humbly welcome you to partake of the light contained within the words and pages of this book. Light is love and love is light, the "superglue" which holds the entire universe together.

It is the source of "all there is"; it is the material of which you and I are made. In the unity of love and light we are all one. This book, written from love and with love, was inspired and guided by the over-lighting energy of Hermes (the messenger also known as Mercury, or Thoth) whose gentle, fatherly voice shines through the pages. It will take you on a journey through many aspects of the self, (as in essence, it is only the self which exists,) and aid and facilitate your personal and spiritual transformation.

The universal themes running through the text are presented over and over again from different angles, so that you may understand and absorb them in the way that is most natural to you.

This book will, I hope, serve as an instrument, a tool on your path to self-illumination. As with all tools, use it wisely, take on board only that which feels right for you now and leave the rest for later. See yourself as a "spiritual work in progress" and be gentle, kind and understanding with yourself along the way!

I pray that this book will shower you with many blessings on your path, aiding and supporting your spiritual journey to the core of light within.

I thank you, dear reader, for without you, I would not have had the privilege and pure joy of putting pen to paper.

I honour the light within each and every one of you!

With many bright blessings,

Your soul sister and fellow traveller in the Light,

A Note of Grace

By the grace of God, I see.

By the grace of God, I hear.

By the grace of God, I smell.

By the grace of God, I taste.

By the grace of God, I think.

By the grace of God, I speak.

By the grace of God, I feel.

By the grace of God, I am.

By the grace of God, you and I are
The creation, the creator and the created,
The Holy Trinity united as one,
And for that, I am wholly grateful

Introduction

HOW TO USE THIS BOOK

Light Meditations for the Year is divided into 12 monthly and 366 daily entries.

Each monthly entry starts with a blessing, which is intended to provide an overall spiritual focus for the month. Each daily entry is made up of three sections; first a **Contemplation**, then a work section entitled **Meditation**, and finally a selection of **Affirmations**.

You will find that throughout the text I have used the terms "God", "source" and "universe" interchangeably; I have done this so that you will feel free to use the spiritual term with which you are most comfortable. (You will be blessed no matter what name you use for the divine!)

The Contemplation: These are channelled messages from a higher source. Within each contemplation a particular aspect of the universal truth is expressed. You will find that the essence of the contemplation will be relevant to your life, as well as to the lives of all your soul brothers and soul sisters on this planet. At our core, we all share the same anguish, hopes and dreams.

The Meditation: "Meditation" is used here as an umbrella term, as this section includes various processes such as guided meditation, visualisation, inner journey work, energy work and practical exercise. Throughout the book the term "meditation" refers to all these inner processes. Don't worry if you feel you haven't always got time to go fully into the visualisations or practise the exercises; you will absorb the essence of the themes simply by reading through them.

The Affirmations: These encapsulate the theme of the day and provide you with fuel for your inner growth. By your positive intent you will, in time, let go of the old to make room for the "new, light stuff" in your life! Repeat the affirmations as often as you can throughout the day and, if needed, for a few weeks or a month, until one day, you will feel a definite shift in your energy. When such a shift manifests, you will feel lighter, as if you have dropped a lot of baggage and, indeed, energetically, this is the case. You have been able let go of old thought patterns, old habits and old addictions! Well done, you!

There are several ways to use *Light Meditations for the Year*. You might simply like to read through the pages day by day. Or you might prefer to use the book as an oracle. To do so, just find "the still place" within yourself, hold the book between your hands and quietly ask for guidance for the day. Whatever page you open the book on will then be the appropriate page.

Be gentle with yourself. If you use this book faithfully, at some point resistance to change will show its ugly face. Fear not! Don't give up! Look fear straight in the eye and embrace it as that part of you which needs to be loved and nurtured. If you resist your fears on any level they will simply persist; that is a universal law. Always be kind and patient with yourself; give yourself a cuddle and allow what the psychologist C.G.Jung called the "shadow side", which I prefer to call the "unloved side" of your being, to be bathed in the light of your own unconditional self-love and self-forgiveness. In forgiveness lies the true liberation of the self!

THE SIX-STEP ROUTINE

Step 1: How to prepare – Preparing your space

Cleansing the space

Regularly cleanse your meditation space by simply opening the window to let the stale air out and the fresh air in; then ring a bell or clap your hands to dispel any static negative energy. You might like to light a candle or burn some incense. (Always ensure a naked flame is well away from any flammable materials and that candles are secure in their holders.) Fresh flowers, crystals and inspiring pictures or statues also support and enhance the energy of your meditation space, which could be a dedicated room, or just a suitable corner.

Inviting an angel

You might like to ask the angel of your meditation space to bless it for you. Simply ask the angel in your mind to do so and it will be done. Always remember to give thanks to this angel for his/her kind blessing.

Preparing yourself

As your physical muscles grow strong on a regular routine of good nutrition and exercise, so your spiritual muscles need to be similarly flexed, honed and trained. To achieve this you need faith, trust, perseverance and a large does of patience. Simply ask God and the angels to instil those qualities within you, and it will be done.

Setting aside the time

The ideal time for spiritual exercises is in the morning, upon waking, so if you are able to create some time then, great. However, if this is impractical or you intuitively feel that a different time of day works best for you, go with what feels right. In order to successfully complete your meditations, visualisations, energy processes or exercises, make sure that you have time to yourself and that you will not be disturbed. So unhook the phone, put a sign on the door or do whatever is needed to give you uninterrupted time, about 30 minutes should be sufficient for each meditation.

Sitting comfortably

When meditating you may sit in the lotus position or in a chair, or if you prefer you may lie down. Remember to keep your spine straight, to rest your hands in an open position either on your lap or your thighs, and if seated in a chair to plant your feet firmly on the ground.

Keeping a journal

I recommend keeping a spiritual journal, where you note your findings, dreams, inspirations and progress; not only is it a useful record of events, it will also provide a chart of your brilliant success. Keep your journal and a pen close by so that you can record your inner experiences after each meditation.

Step 2: Grounding – Aligning with the earth energies

Whenever you embark on any meditation or energy work, it is very important to be grounded. The concept is similar to having an earthed wire on all electrical appliances.

To ground yourself, simply imagine you are growing golden roots from the soles of your feet down through the layers of the earth; all the way to the earth's core where you find a beautiful, golden oak tree trunk to wrap your roots around. Make your roots hollow, as they will be serving as channels for energy to run up and down, in addition to providing you with a sturdy anchor.

As you breathe in, draw stabilising, strong, supporting and grounding energy from Mother Earth, through your roots, into your body and chakras.

During most of the meditations you will be taking in light from above on the in-breath and releasing the negative energies through your roots into the earth on the out-breath.

Following any energy work unwrap your roots from the golden oak tree and bring them back up through the layers of the earth, leaving them in the ground just a few inches or as deep as you need, to keep yourself well grounded during the day.

If you feel light-headed after any meditations or at any other time, further grounding may be necessary. You can achieve this by various means:

1) Food often helps: drink water and have a little piece of chocolate or a little honey, or a piece of bread or other carbohydrates you are able to digest quickly to give your blood-sugar a boost. You may want to eat some potatoes or pasta, which are very grounding foods during the day if you are doing a lot of energy work.

2) Get moving. Running, walking, gardening and dancing will help you stay grounded.

3) Holding or placing a haematite crystal in your pocket also has a grounding effect.

4) A shower or just sleeping for some time will also ground you.

Breathing

Always be aware of and endeavour to utilise your breath to its maximum potential.

Your breath is your core energy, your life force; it is sacred and contains God's love and light within it.

Breathing light in and through your chakras and your auric field is an excellent way to attune yourself. Use your imagination and intention to program your breath as an attuning device.

As you breathe in, imagine a flow of divine, heavenly energy coming in from above, flowing into the top of your head and from there all the way down into your feet.

As you continue to breathe, imagine this loving energy flowing all around you.

As you breathe out, send any negative, old, stale energy out through your feet, draining down through your golden roots, into the earth.

Mother Earth kindly transmutes this energy for you into "earth light".

(In the Filling Yourself with Light Meditation, I show you specifically how to bring this light into your main chakras and into the 7 layers of the auric field.)

By putting roots down into the earth and then filling and surrounding yourself with light you will have achieved a balance, an equilibrium, between heaven and earth.

Always remember to thank God and Mother Earth for your attunement.

With regular practice, you will not only be able to sense but to physically feel energy and will learn to manifest your positive intentions much quicker.

However; it is most importantl to remember that the biggest sensation to feel and possess is the one of a loving heart.

May your efforts be abundantly blessed.

Step 3: How to meditate, or visualise

There are many different ways of meditating. The meditations in this book are primarily active meditations, or visualisations. They are based on an important universal law: That energy follows thought; therefore the purpose of guided imagery, or visualisation, is to manifest a positive reality by utilising the power of the mind.

The process of visualisation takes place in the brow or third eye chakra.

To begin with you may not actually be able to see an image or a scene on your "inner screen". Don't worry, as this doesn't matter.

What's important is that you "think with your heart"; it's the feeling, or the intention with which you imbue your imagery that will create your manifestation. The pictures are only a means to evoke the feeling, or intention, which is the vital element. This is why it's so important to "think with your heart".

You can practise your visualisation skills by looking at everyday objects in great detail; really study their design; observe their shape, colour, texture, smell, sound, etc. Then when you close your eyes, it will be much easier to see, or get a sense of, the object on your inner screen.

For instance, in the beginning, it might be helpful if you are trying to visualise the colour gold, to look at a golden object, like a piece of jewellery; then close your eyes and "think gold". If you are asked to visualise a rose you might want to spend some time contemplating a rose from the florist or your garden, experiencing its velvety petals, its strong stem, smooth shiny leaves, sharp thorns, vivid colour and sweet scent.

Don't try too hard. Everyone can visualise, just as everyone is able to dream in pictures. Just allow the images to build and the energies to flow. You are destined to succeed!

Step 4: How to close down

Since your energy centres, or chakras, naturally open during your spiritual practice, you need to close them down as you complete your meditation or energy process.

"Closing down" does not mean a shutting off or blocking of your chakras; it is more a case of simply returning them to normal operating level for everyday activities.

The following exercises also install a protective energy filter around the chakras, so that only unconditional love energy may reach and penetrate your energy bodies.

All negative energies will be filtered out.

There are many ways to close down. The following are my three favourite ones. Please try all of them and choose the one that feels right to you! (Always start to close down from the crown chakra and end with the base chakra.)

Closing down exercise 1: The Lotus

Imagine that your chakras are like open lotus flowers.

Try to get a sense of this sacred flower and visualise its beautiful petals.

When you are ready, see the petals slowly closing until the lotus resembles a bud.

Start with your crown chakra and end with your base chakra.

Then visualise a golden cross, surrounded by a golden circle, and place one on top of each chakra. This will act as a "seal" and give extra protection.

Finally unwrap your golden roots from the golden oak-tree trunk and draw them out of the layers of the earth, leaving them in just a few inches, which is the grounding you will need during the day.

Closing down exercise 2: The Wooden Gate

Visualise your chakras as wooden gates.

Sense that they are made of strong wood and have sturdy locks with golden keys in them.

When you are ready, firmly shut the first gate – your crown chakra – turning the golden key in the lock. Do the same all the way through to the base chakra.

Take up your golden roots as in exercise 1.

Closing down exercise 3: The Silver Trap Doors

Imagine your chakras to be heavy silver trap doors, held open by strong, silver chains.

Get a true sense of their smooth silver and their sturdy construction.

When you are ready, let go of the silver chains and see and feel the trap door   drop shut with a clank.

Repeat through all your chakras, starting from the crown.

Take up your golden roots as in exercise 1.

Step 5: How to protect yourself

If you dwell in your full divine power 100% of the time, you will not need to protect yourself. (Divine love is the best protection there is.)

However, few people are yet able to do this. So, in the meantime I would strongly suggest that you complete any meditations or energy work with some form of protection.

The energy process of protection will shield you from a variety of potentially harmful factors.

Here are the ones you will most likely encounter:

1) projection of negative thoughts or thought forms on to you.

2) people or places "taking or draining" your personal vitality.

3) negatively charged place energy, which could be geopathic stress or harmful memory patterns absorbed by the ground, or by a building you find yourself in.

4) environmental harm, such as microwaves, radio-waves and other electronic bombardments.

5) harmful disembodied entities.

Here is a choice of three protection processes. Try all of them and use the one that suits you best. Complete your closing down routine with this finale. Additionally, you can instantly use one of these processes at any time you feel in need of some energy protection.

Protection exercise 1: The Sleeping Bag

Visualise a cosy, sky-blue, down sleeping bag with a strong zip.

When you are ready, climb into it and do up the zip.

You are now surrounded by strong blue energy and nicely protected.

Protection exercise 2: The Mantle

See your guardian angel handing you the mantle of protection.

It is made of golden velvet and lined with dark blue satin, and is floor-length, with full sleeves, a large hood and crystal clasps.

You put it on and it fits perfectly, covering you from top to toe.

Thank your guardian angel.

Protection exercise 3: The Auric Egg

Imagine yourself to be like the egg-yolk inside an egg.

See golden energy filling the space where the egg-white would be.

Then, where you would normally find the eggshell, imagine a layer of strong electric blue, neon-bright energy.

Create your protective shell as thin or thick as you like.

I recommend that you protect your aura after your morning and evening meditations, and after any spiritual exercise. Additionally, if you ever find yourself in stressful, demanding situations, where people are pulling on your energies, or if you ever feel you are being drained or if someone is dragging you down, then please repeat the grounding, the closing down and the protection exercises as often as necessary.

Step 6: Giving thanks

Make a practice of giving thanks at the end of your meditations.

May you walk safely in the light!

The Six-Step Routine: Summary

1) Prepare your space by clearing it of any physical or psychic clutter and invite the angel of your space to bless it. You might want to light a candle; then make sure that you are not disturbed for about 30 minutes and make yourself comfortable.

2) Align yourself by handing over your will to the divine will. Ground yourself by growing golden roots and wrap them around the golden oak tree trunk deep in the earth core. Attune yourself by connecting to the light; and allow the light to flow through all your chakras and through your auric field by using your sacred breath, breathing in light and releasing negativity on the out-breath.

3) Follow the meditations in the book.

4) Close down by following one of the three routines suggested, whereby you close each individual chakra, starting from the crown and ending with the base chakra.

5) Protect yourself, surrounding yourself with light, using one of the three suggested energy processes.

6) Give thanks for the love and light you have received!

Understanding the Chakras and the Auric Field

The Chakras

Chakra is a Sanskrit word meaning "wheel of light". Most traditions refer to seven major chakras.

In Fig 1 you will see the seven major chakras plus the two minor ones (the foot and palm chakras) that we use in the Meditations.

Each chakra rotates at a different speed and therefore has a different vibration, perceived psychically as a colour. The seven main chakras run from the tailbone of the spine up to the top of the head. They are traditionally assigned the colours of the rainbow. In ascending order they go:

Number	Colour	Name	Location
1	Red	Base	Tailbone, or coccyx
2	Orange	Sacral	Womb, or lower abdomen
3	Yellow	Solar Plexus	Just above the waistline
4	Green	Heart	Mid-chest
5	Blue	Throat	Throat
6	Indigo	Brow, or Third Eye	Centre of Brow
7	Violet	Crown	Top of head

Each chakra energetically feeds the physical body, connecting via the glandular system, and so affects the workings and health of the whole body.

Each of these perpetually rotating wheels of light creates an energy vortex that draws light into the physical body via the subtle bodies (the mental, emotional and spiritual bodies) that make up the aura.

The chakras are multi-functional and also contain emotional, creative and celestial components; therefore, by working with the chakras you can positively influence every aspect of your life.

As you consciously allow more and more light to flow into your chakras, blockages of an emotional, mental or physical nature are cleared.

Palm and Feet Chakras

These are two of the twenty-one minor chakras. The palm chakras are of great importance for the healing process, as they are small force centres through which the healing energy passes. The foot chakras provide a connection to the earth; so that positive earth energy can be taken up into the body and the accumulated negative energy can be released.

The Human Energy Field or Aura

This is a field emanating from, and surrounding, the physical body, which comprises seven interpenetrating subtle bodies (Fig 2). Each of these bodies vibrates at a different rate. The rate of vibration is slowest at the densest, most physical level and becomes quicker and therefore lighter and brighter, as it rises up through the ever more subtle levels. This vibrational matrix forms the human aura, which may become stronger or weaker, brighter or duller depending on the physical, emotional, mental and spiritual health and awareness of the individual.

Beyond the aura are collectively ever more subtle bodies, which eventually merge into the Universal Energy Field. It is this that connects and interpenetrates everything on every level of existence. All life is linked together via the Universal Energy Field; this is what I refer to when I use the word God.

CHAKRA CHART (FIG. 1)

God – The Source – The Universal Energy Field

7. Crown Chakra - Violet - Pineal Gland

6. The Brow/Third Eye Chakra - Indigo - Pituitary Gland

5. The Throat Chakra - Turquoise - Thyroid Gland

4. The Heart Chakra - Green - Thymus Gland

3. The Solar Plexus Chakra - Yellow - Pancreas

2. The Sacral/Spleen Chakra - Orange - Adrenals

1. The Base/Root Chakra - Red - Gonads

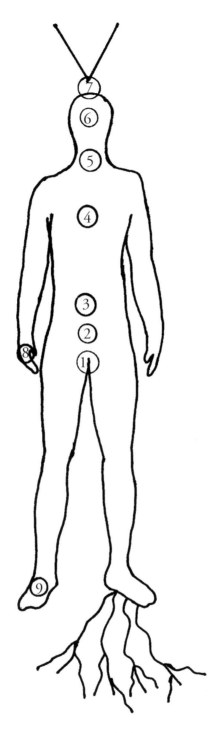

8. The Palm Chakras for Healing and Cleansing

9. Foot Chakras - Golden Roots into the Earth to Ground and Release Energy

THE HUMAN AURA (FIG.2)

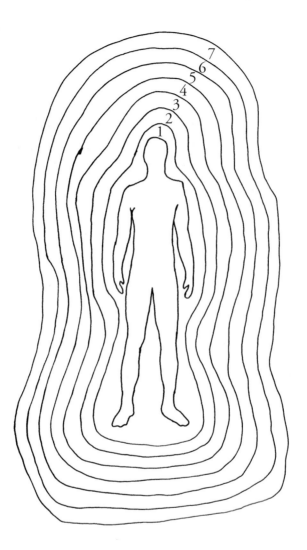

THE SEVEN LAYERS OF THE AURIC FIELD

1 The Physical Body

2 The Etheric Body – Lower etheric aspects

3 The Emotional Body – Lower emotional aspects

4 The Astral Body – Bridges the Physical to Spiritual

5 The Etheric Template – Physical Aspects of the Spiritual Plane

6 The Celestial Body – Emotional Aspects of the Spiritual Plane

7 The Ketheric-Spirit Body – Mental Aspects of the Spiritual Plane

The Filling Yourself with Light Meditation

Having aligned yourself (see Step 2 of the Six-Step Process) visualise a huge, ancient golden oak tree, which is situated deep within the earth's core. Start to visualise golden roots sprouting from the soles of your feet into the earth; let your roots grow through the layers of the earth until they reach the ancient golden oak tree trunk; then wrap your roots around the trunk.

Make sure, that they are firmly in place.

With practice, you will be able to get a sense, a feeling, of being fully grounded!

Now visualise a cloud of golden light above your head. (The colour of the light may vary, according to specific meditations. If you practise this exercise by itself, you may spontaneously perceive a specific colour, which will have been chosen by your higher self for you.)

A beam of golden light emanates from this cloud and enters the top of your head on the in-breath.

After filling your crown chakra with light, release and let go of any negativity on the out-breath.

Take the next breath of golden light in and allow it to flow into your third eye chakra.

After filling your third eye chakra with light, release and let go of any negativity on the out-breath.

Again breathe in the golden light and let it flow into your throat chakra, filling it with light.

On the out-breath allow any negativity to be released.

Take another breath of golden light and allow it to flow into your heart chakra, filling it with light to its maximum potential.

Breathe out and release and let go of all sadness, grief and other emotions.

Breathe in again and allow the golden light to flow into your solar plexus chakra.

As you breathe out, release all fears, worries and anxieties from this centre.

Take another breath of golden light and allow it to flow into your sacral chakra, filling it with light.

On the out-breath release and let go.

Now take a big breath in and allow it to flow into your base chakra, filling it with golden light.

When you are ready release and let go of all that is not love!

(You may use the chakra chart Fig.1 as a guide for your visualisation.)

Next, refocus on the cloud above your head and imagine it to transform into a large golden showerhead.

When you are ready, "turn on the tap" and visualise golden universal healing light flowing out and washing through the seven layers of your auric field, clearing and cleansing it of any physical, emotional, mental or spiritual blockages.

Start with your physical body and then allow the energy to flow through the rest of your auric field, one by one, through all its layers.

(You may use the human aura drawing Fig.2 as a guide for your visualisation.)

Having transmuted all negativity, feeling cleansed and recharged, you are now ready to withdraw your golden roots. Unravel them from the ancient oak tree deep within the earth's core and bring your roots up through the layers of the earth, leaving them in just a few inches of soil for grounding.

Then ask for protection from the healing angels and give thanks or the healing energies you have received.

This is the in-depth version of the Filling Yourself with Light Meditation. With practice you will be able to do it quickly

You will find variations on this important meditation used throughout book.

GLOSSARY OF SPIRITUAL TERMS

Angels: benevolent beings of light and messengers of God dedicated to the enlightenment of humankind.

Archangels: a higher order of the angelic kingdom.

Aura: energy field surrounding all life forms.

Blockage: a negative mental or emotional pattern stopping the natural flow of the life force.

Channeling: allowing higher energies to flow through you for healing, guidance or inspiration.

Chakras: energy centres within the aura.

Cleansing: the act of removing negative energy from your body, from other people or objects or locations, by utilising positive intent.

Divine Power: the life force, the source of all things, the pure energy which exists within the divine.

Elementals: beings who govern the spirit realm of the elements of earth, fire, water, air and the fifth element, ether.

Gaia: the Greek name of the earth mother goddess; also the theory that planet earth is a self-regulating, conscious organism.

God: the essence behind the form; the source of all there is, incarnate in all: humans, animals, plants and minerals.

Grounding: energy process that allows the body to connect to the earth.

Guides: discarnate beings of light who assist humankind in their quest for enlightenment.

Guided Imagery/Visualisation: a "mind over matter" technique of imagining positive images to promote mental, emotional, physical and spiritual well-being.

Healing: a conscious channelling of divine energy for yourself or others either "hands on", or projected distantly, when it is known as distant healing.

Higher Self: highest, wisest, all-knowing part of the self; the divine personal aspect of the mind carrying your divine potential or blueprint.

Incarnation: literally means "enfleshment"; the soul inhabits a physical body by taking birth on the earth plane.

Inner Child: part of the adult self that has not matured emotionally or mentally.

Karma: Hindu and Buddhist belief based on the law of cause and effect, stating that thoughts and deeds, if not balanced out over one lifetime, will be carried forward into the next one, so binding you to "the wheel of karma".

Light: finest universal substance.

Lower Self/Ego Self: the "little self" which identifies with the conditioned desires and needs of the lower nature of humanity.

Meditation: literally a state of "no mind" also a term used for the process for getting into such a state via contemplation, visualisation and guided imagery, etc.

Reincanarnation/Rebirth: the belief that the soul incarnates into different bodies throughout many lifetimes in order to learn, grow and rediscover its true origin, namely that it is God.

Self-Realisation/Self-Illumination/Enlightenment: synonyms for **God Realisation** and the personal, conscious recognition of ones divinity.

Sentient: endowed with feeling, sensory perception and consciousness.

Soul: the divine personal aspect of the heart, carrying your life's purpose.

Source: divine essence.

Unconditional Love: highest universal vibration, pure love without condition on a human level.

Universal Energy: another term for God, the energy underlying and infusing all there is.

Blessing for the month of

January

New beginnings

Open your heart to new beginnings!
Step out of the way and allow God to bless you
abundantly this coming year!
May all the riches of the universe be
bestowed upon you!
May peace enter your troubled heart!
May serenity enter your troubled mind!

And above all...
May you be able to perceive God
in everyone and everything!

January 1

New beginnings

Dearest one,
Welcome to another year on your planet earth, a new year,
an opportunity for new beginnings.
A wealth of beauty, love and adventures awaits you!
Be open and willing to receive God's bounty!
All too often, you expect the worst or the mediocre.
Do not be content with such; life has
so much more to offer you!
Gifts from God for you are everywhere,
although often hidden from view.
Do not rest! Search them out! Do not despair and never give up!
Every breath you take is the miracle of a new beginning in itself.
Are you aware of that?

❀

Meditation:

Imagine you are looking at the earth from a point in space.
Feel yourself travelling towards it.
You are automatically drawn to a certain part of the world.
You get closer and closer and as you land find
that your guardian angel is awaiting you.
Your angel guides you to a secret, sacred space, a beautiful crystal
cave hidden deeply in the mountains.
There, an ornately carved wooden box awaits you.
As you open it you find within it lies a gift of new beginnings for you.
You take it out and store it safely in the chambers of your heart.
Walk out of the mountain back into
the bright sunlight and return to your own space.
Give thanks to your guardian angel!
Please do not forget to ground, attune and protect yourself.

❀

Affirmations:

I am willing to accept the gift of new beginnings.
I am willing to be guided by God and the angels along my way.
I am deeply grateful for the new opportunities ahead of me.

Communicate love

Communicate love wherever you see an opportunity!
Be an ambassador for unconditional love.
Not just in the spoken word, but in deed and thought also.
Utilise the divine harmonic vibration
of unconditional love to its full potential.
Every day, endless opportunities to pass on this
healing light are given to you.
Look out for them and use those possibilities wisely.
A loving look, a smile, a helping hand or a healing thought
may just change someone's destiny forever.
You may never know, as you are not able to see the bigger picture!
God, on the other hand, waits patiently for you to fulfil
your role in the divine plan.

Meditation:

Bring your awareness into the throat chakra.
Take a deep breath and allow the pink light of self-love
to fill and energise your throat chakra.
Take another deep breath and allow the pink light
to flow into your heart chakra.
Now make a conscious effort to link your heart with your throat,
thus ensuring that the words you speak are guided from your heart.
See yourself going about your daily life: going shopping, working in
your office, being at home and all the while speaking words of love
and kindness to everyone you meet and spend your time with.
Every time you do so you feel a warm glow in your heart.
As you give out love you receive it back a hundredfold!
Remember to ground, attune and protect yourself.

❀

Affirmations:

I think love, I speak love, I am love in action!
I communicate love, wherever I go, by my thoughts, speech or action.
I am an instrument of God's love!

January 3

Bless your food

You live in a polluted world, my child.
This is a world where not only mountains and rivers are polluted, but
also your food – fruit, vegetables, fish, meat and even your
water supplies. Chemical pollution is everywhere.
Thus the vital life force contained within your foods and your water
has little chance of surviving unharmed.
It is the life force, the energy, in the food, however, which will give you
the vitality you need for your survival.
By blessing your food, you raise its vibration,
its energy levels, and so by the grace of God benefit from
the increase of vitality for your well-being.
Do so with all substances you take into your body and give thanks to
God and Mother Earth for sustaining you
in mind, body and spirit!

Meditation:

With the food in front of you, visualise silver light coming in through the
top of your head flowing into your crown chakra, your third eye chakra,
your throat chakra, into your heart chakra, from there into the lungs
and from the lungs down through your arms into the palms of your
hands and into the food. Ask for the food to be blessed and allow
the silver light to permeate the food.
You will intuitively know when this process is completed.
Give thanks!

Affirmations:

I am grateful for what I am about to receive.

I bless every substance that I put into my body.

I am what I eat; therefore, I choose my food wisely.

Family time

Honour and cherish the time you have
with your family on this earthly sojourn.
Your family provides you with
the most opportunities to learn and grow.
They are in fact "serving karma" for you!
Be grateful for that, no matter what situation
you find yourself in with your dear ones.
Anything you "do not like" about them is really a pattern
within you that has as yet not been healed.
Swiftly set out to heal those patterns.
In healing yourself, you are also healing your family.
This is the biggest gift you can give them!

Meditation:

Choose a family member/friend who has recently
made you angry or upset you in any way.
Now, in your mind, recall the happening and consciously
become an observer of the situation.
Watch yourself and the other person
acting out those behavioural patterns.
Soon you will start to recognise which game is being played.
Most likely it will be rather familiar to you.
Ask yourself what is the part you play in it
and why do you feel the need to act that way?
When the scene is over ask the healing angels to bless
and help you release those negative energies.
Now, again, in your mind, repeat the same scene,
but this time with a positive outcome.
Give thanks to the healing angels for their support
and do not forget to ground, attune and protect yourself.

Affirmations:

I love and cherish my family for their sacrifice of serving karma to me.
I am healing and releasing all old negative family behavioural patterns.
As I heal my old emotional wounds, I also heal my family's wounds.

Playtime

When you were a child you spent most
of your time playing and you loved it!
In your adult life, you have forgotten all about having fun.
Who will make life fun and enjoyable for you, if not you yourself?
God intends you to be happy!
To be happy you must allow yourself time
to be the child you once were!

Go out and play!

❋

Meditation:

Go back into your childhood to a happy time where you
find yourself playing your favourite game.
If you're not able to find such a memory, imagine yourself doing so.
Observe how happy and carefree you are.
Now decide to take some of this essence of carefree happiness
with you into present time!

❋

Affirmations:

I cherish my inner child and "take it out" to play!

I now embrace the God-given gifts of joy!

Happiness is my birthright!

Nature's power

The power of nature is truly awesome.
Therefore, my child, it would be a good idea to align yourself with the
elementals of earth, water, fire, air and ether.
Go out into nature and pledge your co-operation with the elementals.
Promise never to harm or destroy their environment.
Instead honour and respect them from now on.
As you have formed an alliance with the elementals, you will get a
sense, a feeling, that nature is on your side and that no harm will ever
befall you when you are out "battling the elements"!

Meditation:

Go to your favourite spot in nature.
Now sit or lie on the ground.
Feel yourself, becoming one with Mother Earth.
Offer your unconditional love to the elementals of
earth, fire, water, air and ether.
Ask them to protect you from harm in return.
Leave behind a gift (a physical one, like a crystal, or feather etc.)
Thank Mother Earth and the elementals for supporting
and nourishing you.

Affirmations:

I am part of nature, and nature is part of me!

I pledge to live in harmony with nature!

I love and honour the earth and all elementals, who, unconditionally,
nourish my body mind and soul!

Friendship

What would you do without having a good friend?
A friend who holds your hand and comforts you in your hour of need.
A friend who melts into the background and just lets you
"get on with it" without interfering in your affairs.
A true friend is one who loves you unconditionally and is
there for you when you need him/ her.
If you have one such friend, you are very fortunate indeed.
If you're not lucky enough to have a friend like that, maybe the time
has come to be such a friend to someone in need.

Never forget: as you love, you will be loved in return!

Meditation:

See yourself as the perfect friend for someone.
Think of all the lovely things you would say and do for this friend!
Now imagine meeting this friend in real life.
See yourself and your new friend visiting a place you both enjoy,
having a wonderful time being together cementing your friendship.

Affirmation:

I honour the friendships, I have!

I am releasing stale, sour friendships to the light!

I am always open to making new, meaningful friendships!

Clearing debts

Many of you earth children find yourselves in financial debt
– a situation that causes much hardship
and the break-up of all too many relationships.
Debt means that you are unbalanced.
Too much energy is going out and not enough is coming in.
Respect and value yourself, and more
"green energy", money, will come in.
The more you do this, the less the need occurs for spending sprees,
which only satisfy you for a short period of time.
When you finally have paid your debts you will be free
and this freedom is not only physical.
It can also be felt emotionally and mentally,
and first and foremost, it will set your spirit free!

Meditation:

Contemplate on what your personal debt stands for.
It may be a lack of self-value, a lack of self-confidence, a lack of
honour for the self and also a lack of self-respect.
When you receive the answers, ask the healing angels
to gift these qualities to you.
You ask and you will receive, just trust the healing angels to deliver.
Now visualise yourself diving into a pool of golden coins.
There is an endless supply of "green energy" all around you.
Money does grow on trees, metaphysically speaking!
Give yourself permission to have as much money as you need!
Thank the angels for their support.

Affirmations:

I allow myself to be wealthy!

I honour and respect myself and allow the universe
to provide me with all "the green energy" I need!

I deserved to be healthy, wealthy and happy!

Listen to your body

Are you feeling tired, worn out,
your limbs aching and your feet swollen?
Maybe not quite, but something like it?
Then, stop and listen to your body!
Your body is trying to tell you that you
will not be able to carry on in this way.
So far you have ignored your body's messages,
you also have ignored your mind, which has been bombarding
you with warnings; neither have you listened to your soul,
which has often made you feel you ought to change things.
Now, sit up and take heed of what your body has to tell you!

Meditation:

Gently bring your awareness into the part of the body
that is hurting at this moment.
Ask this part of you, if there is anything you can do to help.
Is there anything you can give to it now or in your everyday state?
For instance, exercise, a different diet, more sleep are
some of the demands your body might make.
Now take a deep breath and breathe in the
golden universal healing light.
Allow this healing light to flow into the painful part of your body,
transmuting and healing any dis-ease that has manifested there.
Give thanks for the function this part of your body fulfils,
day after day, year after year, and assure it that you love it
for the work it does for you.
Repeat until symptoms disappear.
Your body will always tell you exactly what it needs to stay in excellent
health and what you can do to ensure that!
PS. Always consult your doctor with any serious conditions

Affirmations:

I am listening to the messages my body is trying to tell me!

I am ready and willing to heal my body!

Every cell of my body is divine and I honour the divine within!

The power of prayer

God hears your prayers, my beloved!
When you pray you state an intention.
You say, "God I want you to help me or my loved ones".
This signal provides the "green light"
for God to reply to your needs.
Before your prayers the "red light" of the universal law of free will
was on, which did not allow God to intervene on your behalf!

Ask and you will receive!

Meditation:

Meditate on the love of God, which is available to you constantly.
This love is unending, timeless and permeates all and everything
through time and space.
Feel this love, like a warm light within and all around you.
See God's unconditional love shining through
the whole of creation and thank God for it!

Affirmations:

The power of prayer can move mountains!

I ask and I shall receive!

God grants all my requests in accordance with divine law!

Living food

The foods you eat, my child, are mostly "dead" foods.
I am not just referring to "dead meat" here.
I am talking about all the other lifeless substances
with which you feed yourself.
What you really need is the life force of the food; all the rest is
ballast and will leave your system within a short period of time.
It is the life force in your food that keeps your
battery charged and your engine running.
It is so simple!
The purer, fresher and more unadulterated
the foods, the more life force they contain,
the less you have to eat to become full!

Meditation:

Be fully present in your body.
Now ask your body consciousness which foods are the healthiest for
you to eat at this time and which ones definitely to avoid.
You will receive the answers you are looking for,
either through pictures appearing in your third eye or
through spontaneous inspirational thoughts.
Please remember to always bless all the food and drink you consume!

Affirmations:

I eat live, wholesome food!

I choose my food with love and care for the environment and myself!

I thank the kingdoms of nature for providing me with the food I need!

Ride the wave of love

God loves the earth and all its inhabitants, the rocks and minerals,
the plants, the animals and the humans, unconditionally.
God's love comes in waves of light, which travel through the density
of this planet, leaving behind the residue of love.
This love is to be found everywhere!
We just have to go out there and search for it!
Look into the eyes of a child, listen to the contented purr of a cat
and watch the gracious flight of a butterfly!
Open your heart to God and the world and you will see,
feel and perceive love where ever you go.
This is God's gift to the world!
On your onward path, travel on the wave of love!

Meditation:

See yourself standing at the ocean shore. Big waves are rolling in.
As you look closer you become aware of
magical lights dancing within the waves.
These are the lights of God's love coming ashore for you!
Allow the seawater to wash over you and feel the waves of love
entering your heart chakra, depositing a dose of
unconditional love there and taking away all
sadness and sorrow with them as they ebb away.
Repeat until your heart feels light and filled with love.
Give thanks!
Remember to ground, attune and protect yourself.

Affirmations:

I open my heart to perceive God in all there is!

God's love accompanies me every step of the way!

I ride the wave of love!

January 13

Love spectacles

My dear child, the time has come for you to look at your fellow
human beings in a different light.
I would like you to put on a pair of "love spectacles" right now!
Through the lenses of these very different glasses, you will see your
fellow human beings for whom they really are,
namely your brothers and sisters in body, mind and spirit!

Meditation:

See yourself standing in a crowded room at a dinner party
with people you have never met.
You are, understandably, feeling apprehensive and a little threatened.
Now you remember that you have brought your special
"love spectacles" and put them on straight away.
Immediately the scene changes before you:
all and everybody is bathed in a beautiful pink light.
Moreover all the feelings the people around you have
become apparent to you.
You look on in amazement as you realise that the fears, the doubts,
the hopes and insecurities in every single individual
are just exactly what you are experiencing.
Your heart opens and you are able to approach your
brothers and sisters with love!
Do not forget to ground, attune and protect yourself.

Affirmations:

I look at the world with loving eyes!

I now see the divine in all my earth brothers and sisters!

I am aware that all separations are illusions created by fear!

God's instrument

Many times, my dear one, you ask God
for help with your worldly affairs.
"Sort me out", you cry!
Be aware that God is forever here to help you,
to support you in your daily tasks.
God's energy is within and all around you.
However, YOU must actually realise it, do something with it,
use it and manifest it into form.
YOU are God's arms, legs, eyes and ears.
YOU are His instrument on earth.
So you are the ones who must utilise the energy inherent within you.
Go and be a worthy co-creator with God!

Meditation:

See yourself sitting by your computer, sewing-machine
or piano wanting to perform a difficult task,
something you've had problems with before.
Now become aware of the all-powerful,
all-knowing energy of God within you.
You can feel a warm sensation or maybe a tingling
running through your body.
Also, you may get a sense of your body stretching,
growing in size, accompanied by an increase in confidence.
The scene before you lights up and you confidently proceed
with your task, which this time runs smoothly and according to plan.
You have successfully used God's energy within, congratulations!
Try this process in "real life" as soon as possible.
Please ground, attune and protect yourself.

Affirmations:

I let go and let God!

I am God's instrument on earth!

I am a co-creator with God!

Inner guidance

Trust your inner guidance on your spiritual path!
Reading books and attending workshops are just facilitating
your self-development: they serve as markers
and stimulate your spiritual appetite.
The most direct route to your self-illumination is found within.
This is the "fast" route; all it needs is for you
to make an effort to look within!
Once this supreme effort has been made,
you will be astonished beyond your fondest dreams
of the wellspring of knowledge you have come upon!

Meditation:

See yourself in a vast library.
It is a beautiful, airy space with light coming in from
a domed, glassed ceiling above.
The bookshelves are made from ornately carved wood
and the floors are inlaid with semi-precious stones.
This truly is a special place.
As you walk along the aisles of books, one suddenly
falls off the shelf on to the floor right in front of you.
As you pick it up you see that is has your name written on it.
You go and sit down in the study area of the library.
Now you open the book and find that it is titled
The Book of Inner Guidance for.........(your name).
You read the book from cover to cover and to your surprise find out
that the author of the book is YOU!
Visit the library as often as you like to re-read
passages from this important book.
Remember to ground, attune and protect yourself.

Affirmations:

All the knowledge I need to access lies within me!
I am one with the power and the knowledge of God and the universe!
I am guided by my higher power of knowing, every step of the way!

Your guardian angel

From the moment of your birth you have been
looked after by your guardian angel.
This very special angel was assigned to you by the grace of
God and is, and will be, constantly by your side
through your earthly sojourn.
Be grateful for this precious gift, but also make good use of it!
Your angel needs to be invited by you to be of service as he/she
cannot override the law of free will and interfere
in your life where it is not appropriate.
(There may be situations where you have to learn without the
assistance, help and guidance of your guardian angel.)
Every morning upon awakening call on your angel to guide
and protect you throughout your day.
Thank your angel every evening for his/her
unconditional service to you!

Meditation:

Close your eyes and see your guardian angel
standing right in front of you.
Your angel's loving eyes are gazing at you and a stream of
unconditional love energy, much like a laser beam,
is flowing from them into yours.
As the eyes are the windows to the soul, you can feel
this energy flowing right into and through you.
A pleasant tingling is rippling through your whole body.
Continue gazing into the eyes of your angel until you feel truly filled
to the brim by this gentle, loving force.
Then your angel gives you a big hug and bids you farewell.
Thank your angel for the healing you have received.
Do not forget to ground, attune and protect yourself.

Affirmations:

I always have my guardian angel by my side!
I am able to call on my guardian angel in any situation!
My guardian angel loves me unconditionally!

January 17

Focus

My child, you often bumble along in life…hither and thither…. indeed
just like a little bumble bee.
This is fine for a while, but you are
devoid of a plan or a goal, and you start to get lost.
What you need in this moment in time is a focus!
"What should I focus on?" you cry.
"There is so much out there and I am so confused!"
Fret not my child, as the solution to this problem is a simple one.
Look closely at what is already around and within you.
Can you see or feel anything that makes your heart sing?
Whatever makes your heart sing, that will be your focus.
Pay attention to it; nurture it; for then it will grow
and develop into wonderful new opportunities for you!

Meditation:

Look around at the objects in the room where you are now.
Ask yourself which one of those objects gives you joy.
Soon one will "jump out" at you.
Now focus your full attention on this object.
The more you focus and concentrate, the more the good, positive
attributes of this object will become apparent to you.
As you do so, you also start to enjoy focusing
on this object more and more…
The same is true for any situation that may occur in your life;
find and focus on the good that is already there
and more good will be able to come of it!

Affirmations:

I allow my heart to guide me in finding a positive focus in my life!

The more I focus on joy, the more joy there will be in my life!

I now focus my attention on love and light!

Be your own best friend

So many of you would like to find a good friend, someone in whom you
can confide, someone you can trust and with whom
you can share your innermost secrets.
You complain bitterly that you do not seem
to be able to find such a friend.
The answer to this riddle lies within you; it is of your own doing.
Are you being a friend to anyone at this time?
Are you being even remotely friendly to yourself?
Or are you despising yourself and others,
pointing the finger, apportioning blame?
If you cannot find a friend, then some of this applies to you,
my beloved, albeit in a variation on the theme.
There is a simple solution to this dilemma!
Start with your self: become your own best friend, and soon,
very soon, you will attract a "real, live" best friend into your life!

✿

Meditation:

Sit and contemplate the "unfriendly" behaviour
you display against yourself.
Write a list, in the left-hand column write down all your unfriendly
behaviour towards yourself; then in the right-hand column
write down how you could befriend yourself.
Decide, right here and now, to release and let go of these destructive
behaviour patterns towards yourself
and replace them with positive and kind ones.
Repeat this exercise until you truly feel that you are your own
reliable, trustworthy and loving best friend!

Affirmations:

I now become my own best friend!

I am looking after myself in ways I have never done before!

I love and cherish myself as I would my future best friend!

The music of the universe

There is light and there is sound.
Sound is condensed light.
Each and every one of you resonates at a particular note,
so does every rock, tree and animal on this planet.
Also the earth resonates at a particular pitch,
so do the stars and planets.
Together they perform the music of the spheres.
You are part of this divine orchestra!
Make sure, that you "sound the right note"; the high note of
unconditional love, the note God had intended you to sound forth!

Meditation:

Sit in your favourite place,
preferably somewhere undisturbed in nature.
Ask God and the healing angels for "your note"
to come through for you.
Relax your jaw muscles and start humming
whatever comes naturally to you.
Allow the energy to flow; you may be humming different tunes,
but soon you will automatically settle on one note.
This note will be very close to the note God has given you
to sound in His orchestra of life!
Repeat often and you will find that the same note or tone will recur,
which will affirm for you that you on the right path
to perfecting the high note of unconditional love!

Affirmations:

I take my seat in God's divine orchestra!

I play my part well!

I fully rejoice in resonating on the high note of unconditional love!

Your contribution

What you contribute to society, to your brothers
and sisters, is very important!
Do not play down your role as co-creator with God!
Do not make it anything less than the magnificent honourable role it is!
It is false of you to say "I have done nothing",
when in fact you have given valuable contributions;
put your heart and soul, your time and energy
into being of service to humanity.
Accept the praise; accept the honours bestowed upon you graciously.
Be humble; do not turn anything away that is given with love.
And…give yourself the credit you deserve!

Meditation:

Remember a situation where you did contribute towards your family,
friends or society as a whole, in a positive way.
It may have been a small contribution, but all are of equal importance.
Play this situation back to yourself, becoming the observer.
Now notice what a magnificent, loving person you are,
how well you dealt with the situation,
how happy you made the people who where involved.
Play back to yourself as many situations as you can remember, fully
accepting the "karmic plus points" you have created for yourself!

Affirmations:

I contribute all that I can in service to humanity!

I honour myself for the efforts I make to be of
good service to humankind!

I value myself for the role I play as a co-creator in God's universe!

January 21

Goal-setting

To have a goal in life, my child, is of utmost importance!
Everyone needs something to aim for, to strive for!
Through attaining your goals you will grow not only as a person,
but also spiritually, mentally and emotionally.
If you are lacking inspiration on what this goal should be for you,
go within, align yourself with the divine will of God
and simply ask for your ultimate goal to be shown to you!

Meditation:

Ask God and the healing angels to help you
reveal your ultimate goal in life.
Breathe in blue light and allow it to flow into your third eye.
As you carry on breathing, a blue bubble
of light starts to form within your third eye.
When you are ready, ask the healing angels
to burst the bubble for you.
As soon as this is done, your goal, which was
up till now hidden from view, will reveal itself.
Thank God and the healing angels;
then trust and follow your inspiration!
Do not forget to ground, attune and protect yourself.

Affirmations:

I am in alignment with the source and receive
inspirations for my highest good!

As I search, all I need to know will be revealed to me!

I now let God set my life goals for me!

The breath

I want you to become aware of your breathing!
Every breath you take is a gift, the gift of life
bestowed to you by the Creator.
Value and cherish this gift.
Focusing your awareness on every breath you take
will bring you into the present moment.
Being totally present equals being fully conscious
of who and what you are;
a child of God, connected to all that is!

Meditation:

You become aware of a golden funnel extending up from your
crown-chakra, connecting you to the source of all life,
which you might want to visualise as a huge ball of golden healing light.
From this ball of light, divine energy steadily flows into
and down the golden funnel into your crown chakra.
With every sacred breath you take, more golden energy flows down the
funnel, filling your whole chakra system with divine light.
Keep on breathing and allow the energy to extend itself
into the seven layers of your auric field.
You are now drawing light from the source with every breath you take,
which ensures life in the body you inhabit.
Do not forget to ground, attune and protect yourself.

❀

Affirmations:

My breath is sacred!

My breath connects me to the source of all life—God—at all times!

With every breath I take, I am being recharged
with the power of unconditional love!

Instrument of love

You are created to be an "instrument of love" born out
of the womb of God's infinite, unconditional love for you!
As with a piano, which needs tuning and cleaning,
look after yourself, for you have much work to do in this lifetime.
Not only will you facilitate the awakening of many of your brothers
and sisters on this earth plane, but you are also the instrument
for the divine to become conscious of itself.
Only through you, and with you, can that be achieved!
Accept who you truly are, embrace your holiness!

You are God and God is within you!

Meditation:

Take into contemplation the qualities a flawless
"instrument of God" has to have.
Which of these qualities do you already have
and which ones do you still need to develop?
Once you have pinpointed the qualities you are striving for,
imagine and feel yourself already possessing them!
This is a process that does not happen overnight!
Please be kind and gentle with yourself and you will succeed
and be the shining golden instrument of love God intended you to be!

Affirmations:

I am the divine instrument of God's love!

I have come from love and I will return to love!

I am one with God and God is one with me!

There is no limit

There is no limit to what you can become, my dear one!
Also, there is no limit to anything you may wish for!
Providing your desires are in accordance with divine law,
the universe provides you with a limitless supply
of all your heart desires!

You are an unlimited being in an unlimited universe!

Meditation:

Ask your higher self to show you the state of your own self-limitations.
In your mind's eye you will see yourself imprisoned in metal armour.
What do the various parts of the armour represent to you?
Now ask the healing angels to give you a hand in taking the armour off.
As they assist you in this task, you are letting go piece by piece
until the armour has come off completely
and you are free of all limitations.
Now ask God to send you all there is for you to receive.
Accept it graciously!

Affirmations:

I am free of all old conditioning and limitations!

I am an unlimited being in an unlimited universe!

I am free to have what my heart desires!

January 25

Self-doubt

When you doubt yourself and your abilities you doubt your own divinity!
Do you really think that God would create imperfection?
God created you perfect in His image!
At this moment in time this concept may not have been grasped
by you yet, it may seem far out of your reach.
Look within; this is where your "perfect divinity" resides.
It has been there all the time, eagerly awaiting its discovery.
As you doubt yourself, so you are doubting the existence of God.
And as you are God, what is there to doubt?

Meditation:

See yourself as a diamond.
The cut is perfect.
Only some of the facets of the diamond are not
quite sparkly enough; they need polishing!
Allow God and the healing angels to help you with this task.
Unconditional love is the polishing cloth; passion,
compassion, self-discipline and perseverance are the cleaning fluid!
Go to work and cleanse all parts of your self
until the whole diamond, which you are, radiates out the clear,
sparkling light of unconditional love to the world!
Thank God and the angels for their help.

Affirmations:

I release all self-doubt!

I trust in my God-given abilities!

I am a perfect diamond, sparkling with unconditional love and light!

Your pet protectors

If you share your life with a pet, you are indeed lucky, my dear child.
The pet that has chosen to live with you is
indeed a gem within your household.
Small as it may be, it is a true spiritual friend, for it
provides psychic protection for you.
It really is a guardian sent to you by the animal kingdom
to watch over you and your loved ones.
If at present you do not have the pleasure of
the company of a pet, keeping even a photograph, a drawing
or statuette of your favourite pet will bring the beneficial,
protective energy of the animal into your household.
Honour and cherish the service the animal kingdom is giving to you!

Meditation:

Imagine yourself sitting in a chair with a purring cat on your lap.
As you stroke the cat you become more and more aware of its energy.
Carry on stroking the cat and feel the inherent qualities
of the animal flowing into your auric space.
As you connect with the energy of the cat,
you begin to feel more cheerful.
All in all, there is a sense of well-being flooding through you,
which is deeply relaxing.
Give thanks to the animal kingdom.

Affirmations:

I am part of the animal kingdom and the animal kingdom is part of me!

I respect and honour the animal kingdom!

I treat all animals with loving care and affection!

January 27

The role you play

As you go through life you play different roles.
It may be the role of child, mother, father, wife or husband.
Even through the course of a day you may
change your role many times.
It is your "persona" that undergoes these changes.
What should never change is the "true you",
which lies beneath the mantle of the personality.
No matter which duty you are carrying out,
the true you must always be visible and easily recognisable.
Do not allow yourself to be blinkered by false realities.
Allow the essence of you, which is love and light,
to shine through which ever role you play!

Meditation:

Imagine yourself in one of the roles you find difficult to play.
Become the observer in a typical uneasy scenario.
Watch closely in order to spot where you are losing your true self,
where you are not acting from love, but from fear.
Now, re-run the whole scenario again but being
truly rooted in your true loving self.
You are watching yourself performing your role perfectly with love.
What a joy to behold!
Repeat with any areas of difficulty in your daily life.

Affirmations:

I am always my true self no matter, which role I play!

My true essence of love and light shines through in all life situations!

I act and react from love!

The divine puzzle

You, my child, are a very important piece of the divine puzzle.
What would the puzzle look like with a piece missing?
Incomplete, of course, but more so, the full,
complete picture could not manifest.
The full picture, the divine plan, can only unfold
when all the pieces of the puzzle participate in the game.
The game we are talking about here is the "game of life".
In order to be a fully participating player you
must accept life and say yes to life.
Play the game and accept your rightful place in the divine puzzle!

Meditation:

See yourself as a child in the playground,
playing a game you felt that you were not very good at
or did not enjoy at the time.
The game does not go very well and ends in defeat
with you in floods of tears.
Now allow the same scene to unfold with a positive ending.
This time you are really confident and play the game perfectly,
laughing and joking as you go.
Your parents, friends, siblings, etc. are cheering you on
from the sidelines and you now start to feel
how invigorating it is to be a player and how alive
and vibrant you feel, when you put your heart
and soul into this game!
You are a winner!
Repeat with any other similar childhood situations.

Affirmations:

I am an invaluable piece in the divine puzzle!

I play the game of life well, as the divine plan is incomplete without me!

As I put 100% into life, I get 100% out of it!

The adventure of being you

Life is an adventure, my beloved!
The big adventure is the search for the "true you".
What you need is a treasure map!
In order to find this precious map you must look
for signs as to its whereabouts. Those signs are all around you.
Take heed, so as not to miss them,
for they are not monumental but small and plentiful.
Listen closely to what your friends and family have to say to you.
Notice the newspaper article that catches your eye or the scene
in a film. What are your reactions to all of this input? Take note.
It is not the actions of others, which are important,
but how you react to them that counts.
Do you act and react from love or from fear?
Your treasure map is right there within your heart!
Read it and use it wisely!
Make this adventure your best one yet in this lifetime on planet earth!

❀

Meditation:

See yourself in a place of higher learning, a celestial university of sorts.
Walk up to the registrar and ask for your
personal treasure map to be brought to you.
Soon you receive a rolled-up ancient parchment with your name
embossed on it in golden lettering.
You take the map to the celestial reading room
where your guardian angel awaits you.
Together you open the map and start to study it…
All you need to know is to be found in the map!
You may return to the celestial university any time you like.
Thank your guardian angel for assisting you and do not forget to
ground, attune and protect yourself.

❀

Affirmations:

My life is a divine adventure!
I discover my true divine identity!
Being me is a joy!

The road to mastery

You are all on the road to mastery!
How do you know when you have achieved mastery?
Only when you have experienced what had to be mastered.
Otherwise you would be a master of nothing.
So therefore joyfully embrace what is being put before you.
Own it, heal and then release it and move on to the next challenge.
Do not hold on to any of it; just allow the divine
light and love to flow through you.
That is the mastery you are looking for!

Meditation:

Think of a relationship you are having difficulty with
at this moment in time.
See the person in question standing in front of you.
Now ask to be filled with the golden light of love,
healing and forgiveness.
Take a deep breath and the light will come flooding in.
It flows into your crown chakra and down through your third eye,
through your throat into your heart, filling it with unconditional love.
Now see yourself embracing the other person.
As you hug them you feel all the negativity that has been between you
simply melting away through the power of love flooding
from your heart into the heart of the person you are embracing.
As you step back, you are both happy and smiling.
Ask this person for forgiveness for anything you might have done
and in return forgive them for any trespasses.
Then forgive yourself for the part you played.
Now let the whole scene dissolve into the light.
Repeat if necessary and do not forget to ground,
attune and protect yourself.

Affirmations:

I joyfully embrace all life experiences!
I am practising mastery every minute of the day!
As I master the self, I master all else!

Have patience with yourself

You would like, my dear one,
to "have everything done yesterday" as you so nicely put it!
But yesterday was not the right time for the event to be manifested.
All events are ultimately being played out in divine timing
not in your ego-desired time scale, driven by
your worldly desires and deadlines.
God holds the stop- and start-watch!
So, why don't you stop being so harsh and impatient with yourself
and allow God to look after your calendar of events?

Meditation:

Think of what is giving you most time-related stress at present,
something you have a deadline for!
Hold this in your mind.
Now visualise a very large grandfather clock,
beautifully decorated, with your name inscribed on the clock face.
Its face shows minutes, hours, days, month and years.
Looking at the clock, ask God to show you the divine time
for your project/event/completion.
The hands of the clock light up and move to the perfect divine time!
You will now find that you have no problems achieving your deadline.

Affirmations:

I am aligning myself with divine timing!

I am always in the right place at the right time!

There is plenty of time to do all I need to do!

Blessing for the month of

February

Winds of change

Bare your soul to God and allow the
winds of change to clear the way ahead!

May your mind be free!
May your spirit soar!
May your soul sing melodies of heaven!
May clear skies and sunshine accompany
you on your path always!

February 1

Inner storms

Your inner battles are reflected in your outer battles not only with your
fellow humans, but also in the battles of nature.
As the storms rage within, so they rage without.
The emotional state of the human race is perfectly reflected
in nature's weather patterns.
To calm the storms, look at what has raised them in the first place.
Maybe the emotion responsible was anger or envy.
Own and embrace these emotions.
Ask for them to be blessed and released and then calm will follow!
As you regain peace in your heart, so will Mother Nature
bring you sunshine and happy days!

Meditation:

What are the inner storms raging within you?
Put your hands (one on top of the other) on your solar plexus chakra
– the centre of your fears and anxieties.
Take a deep breath and centre your awareness there.
What can you feel?
What is the emotion that is showing up?
Follow it back to its roots, where it has sprung from;
then accept the situation, release it, bless it, forgive yourself
and the people involved in it and you are well on your path
to heal this hurt part of yourself!
You may have to repeat this exercise several more times

Affirmations:

I give up all battles with others and myself!

My inner self is calm and content!

I am at peace with myself!

All you need is provided for

God provides for whatever you need in your life!
It is in place before you have even asked for it.
Unfortunately, so often, you do not see the gifts
that are laid out in front of you.
When you are being given a gift,
the one who gives chooses it for you, remember?
God gives to you exactly what you need
every moment of your existence.
Your gift may not be what you had expected or even prayed for,
but it is chosen with pure unconditional love
and therefore can only be the right gift for you!

Meditation:

Fill yourself with the pink light of unconditional self-love.
Breathe it in deeply and allow it to permeate your chakras
and the layers of your auric field.
Now, in your mind, ask God to give you the gift that
he thinks is best for you at this moment in time,
something you really need at present.
You see a large, beautifully wrapped parcel appear in front of you.
In it you will find exactly what you need!
Thank God for His generous love for you!
Do not forget to ground, attune and protect yourself.

Affirmations:

My life is a gift from God!

God provides me with all I need at all times!

I am grateful and honour the gifts I am given!

February 3

Miracle cure

Laughter, my dear one, is a miracle cure for many ailments!
It uplifts and energises you and literally shatters unhelpful
thought forms, thus releasing negativity out of your system.
Do not take yourself and what you do so seriously!
Remember that the fool is in truth the wise one!
To travel light on your earthly journey, make love
and laughter your constant companion!

Meditation:

See yourself as the spectator in a divine circus,
of which God is the circus director.
You are the only one in the audience.
A celestial clown comes into the arena; he performs just for you,
cracking lots of jokes and making you roar with laughter.
Enjoy every bit of this spectacle and take some of this
uplifting energy with you into your daily life!

Give thanks.

Affirmations:

God wants me to have fun!

Having fun is my divine birthright!

I am happy to laugh at myself!

Soul to soul

How do you know when you are truly connected to your brothers
and sisters on this earth plane?
What are the signs in your relationships,
which show you that a"communion"is taking place?
The answer to this lies in the depth of your soul.
When you relate to others with unconditional love,
then your soul is speaking to their soul, and then not only
communication, but a truly holy communion is taking place.
As you connect at this deep level – it may even be for a mere second
– a deep healing is able to take place for both of you.
To connect soul to soul should be your ultimate goal!

❁

Meditation:

Think of a person you would like to connect with on a deeper level.
Breathe in the pink light of love and centre yourself
in your heart chakra.
Ask for the healing angels to help you with this process.
Now see this person sitting in front of you.
Look into their eyes with love.
The eyes are the windows to the soul and soon you can feel
your love flowing into the soul of the person opposite you.
They are starting to relax and give you a beautiful, radiant smile!
If you would like to communicate something special
to this person do it now.
Say what is in your heart.
Give each other a wonderful hug and thank
the healing angels for their support.

❁

Affirmations:

You and I are one!

I am deeply connected to my soul brothers
and soul sisters on this earth!

I allow my soul to speak freely!

February 5

Your body is the temple of your soul

In truth you are spirit having a human experience and
therefore your body is the temple of your soul.
Do not neglect the needs of this precious vehicle.
It is a wonderful instrument and you must look after it well.

Your body is a gift from God!
Treat it as one!

Meditation:

See another You inhabiting your "dream body" standing in front of you.
This other You looks healthy, happy and radiant.
Fill out any details to create the dream person
you would dearly like to be.
When you are ready, take a step forward and merge with this image.
With every breath you take you are feeling more and more
your true, radiant new self.
Feel the life force radiating through you, the vital energy
course through your veins.
You feel newborn, so happy and full of life!
You have truly become the dream image you have had of yourself!

Affirmations:

My body is the perfect temple for my soul!

My body is filled with love, light and unending vitality!

I am deeply grateful for the gift of this body!

Inspirations

Follow your inspirations!
They are sparks of divine energy
from your higher self/God!
Do not disregard them as unrealistic,
inappropriate or impossible to follow through.
If particular inspirations keeps coming back repeatedly,
get up the courage and act on it!
You will soon see the tiny seed growing and developing
and finally coming to fruition, as the universe will support your
endeavours to manifest your inspirations.
This is how you become a co-creator with God!

Meditation:

Contemplate what you need inspiration with at this moment in time.
Have pen and paper to hand.
Visualise a tube of light going through all your chakras.
This tube of light is connecting to your higher self/God.
Now sincerely and humbly ask your higher self/God for
divine inspiration on your chosen subject.
Immediately you will feel the divine energy of inspiration flowing from
your higher self/God through the tube of light
into your third eye chakra.
Be very still while this process is taking place;
you will sense when it is completed.
Immediately write down, without thinking about it, what is in your mind.
The inspirations will be there on the paper in front of you!

Affirmations:

My inspirations originate from the one mind!

I am divinely inspired at all times!

I trust and follow my inspirations!

February 7

All you need

All you need in this human existence is within you.
All the resources are there.
Second by second, minute-by-minute, hour-by-hour,
God supplies you with the unending gift of unconditional love.
Your soul is the storehouse for this potent, miraculous energy.
This energy has the capacity to move mountains and is able
to create anything you truly yearn for.
It is available "on tap" for you 24 hours a day, every day!
All you need to "open the tap of love" is faith and trust in God.
These are the qualities that will ensure a steady flow of love for you.

You always will have all you need!

Meditation:

Feel the unconditional love and light of God all around you!
As you breathe in the light it permeates every cell of your being,
filling it with the power of unconditional love.
The more you concentrate on God, the more love energy there is.
You start to realise through an inner knowing, that there is an
unending, limitless supply always freely available to you.
Your heart sings with joy at this revelation!

Affirmations:

All I ever need is right here within my heart!

All my needs and desires are already met!

God's love for me is eternal and all encompassing!

Mirror images

The world around you and the people in it mirror back to you what you
most dislike about yourself, what you most criticise in yourself
and what you judge and condemn about yourself.
Simply all the negative aspects you have not yet learned
to accept and love for what they truly represent
are acted out right in front of your nose!
What a fantastic way God has invented to help you heal yourself!

Meditation:

Have a mirror to hand.
Now think of a person who has annoyed you recently.
Hold an image of this person and their behaviour in your mind.
Now hold up the mirror in front of you.
Gently gaze at your image and ask yourself the question which
character traits do I have in common with the person
who has annoyed me so much?
What have their behaviour and actions come to teach me?
Fill any negative traits within yourself with loving thoughts of
forgiveness and also forgive the other person for their behaviour.

Repeat the same exercise with the same person,
until when you think of them you feel only love towards them.

Affirmations:

The events and people in my life mirror the state of my inner self!

I love myself unconditionally!

I look in the mirror and see a beautiful being of light!

Buried light

Reach into the darkness for buried within it lies the light!
The dark shows up the light;
without that contrast you would not have
any awareness that the light was already there!
And so it is, once you have conquered the darkness,
there will always be light!

Meditation:

See yourself walking into a pitch-dark room.
At first there is only darkness around you,
but as you keep on looking you see a glimmer of light.
The more you focus on the light,
the larger it becomes, until the whole room
is filled with it and brightly lit!

Affirmations:

I move beyond the darkness into the light!

I perceive the light in everything and everybody!

The light is the source of all!

In the way of your highest good

Dear child, most of the time you stand in the way of your highest good.
God is desperately trying to give His unconditional love to you,
but you do not accept it!
Please, from now on, allow God to give you
what He has in store for you!
As a child of God you are deserving of your highest good!

Meditation:

See yourself walking on a very stony path up a mountain.
You are finding this a hard climb and have stumbled several times.
Suddenly, ahead of you in the mist, you make out a hooded figure
picking up and clearing the stones from the path you are on.
The figure has a golden glow about it
and you now recognise who it is.
As you walk up to say thank, you the figure dissolves
and all that is left is a cloud of golden light
gently drifting away from you.
Give thanks to God for always being there for you,
smoothing the path ahead.
Do not forget to ground, attune and protect yourself.

Affirmations:

I am worthy of God's love!

I am ready to accept what is for my highest good!

I allow God to give me what is best for me!

February 11

Emotional baggage

You are travelling through life laden down with emotional baggage.
Allow yourself to become aware that this is so.
To you these emotions make up your identity; in truth,
they are holding you back from discovering who you really
are beneath all that "luggage".
The time has come to let go of this false you and hand
all your baggage over to the healing angels,
to be disposed of forever!
Move on into a carefree, true, joyful you!

Meditation:

See yourself climbing on board a very old steam train.
You are so laden down with luggage that
you hardly make it into the train.
After a long journey through fog and rain
you arrive at your destination.
You are now so fed up with your heavy luggage that
you decide to get rid of it as soon as possible.
As the train pulls in, to your surprise you see
a group of healing angels awaiting you on the platform.
As you embark from the train, you hand them your luggage
and bit-by-bit they fly away with it!
You are free of your burdens and carry on the rest
of your journey "as light as a feather".
Give thanks to the healing angels.
Make sure to ground, attune and protect yourself.

Affirmations:

I am ready to let go of my emotional baggage!

I am free to "travel light" on my chosen path!

I am free to create a new, glorious reality for myself!

Claim your birthright

Not only have you forgotten your true origins,
but you have also forgotten your true state of being.
Most of the time you think you are an unhappy human being,
and are miserable with this state of affairs.
"Human" your true self is not,
you are a divine spark in a human body!
Let go of your misery and claim your divine birthright: to be joyful!
There is no time to waste, do it NOW!

Meditation:

See yourself going to the registry office to pick up your new
birth certificate, as the old one has become unreadable.
The office clerk is very friendly and soon hands you a
brand-new birth certificate in a large lily-white envelope.
You walk out of the office and sit on a bench in a lovely town garden
to look at your brand-new document.
The certificate is made from the finest grade paper
with an intricate golden border around it.
Written in ornate gold lettering, you read the following:

I. …(Your name), a being of light, incarnated into this body on…
(date)… hereby claim my divine birthright from this day on into all
eternity to live a happy, joyful, peaceful life
filled with love, light and laughter!

You are very pleased indeed with your new birth certificate
and keep it in a special place in your heart!
Please ground, attune and protect yourself.

Affirmations:

I claim my divine birthright of a life full of love, light and joy!

I decide to choose a life filled with peace
and true happiness for myself!

I live my human experience with the awareness of who I truly am!

Movement

Life is never stagnant; it is the nature of all living beings
that there is movement, movement from one cycle to the next,
from day to night, from birth to death and from death
to rebirth into the eternal light.
Do not seek to impede this flow of divine energy
through the application of the will of your lower ego .
Sickness and distortion will occur by doing this.
Instead let go of preconceived, conditioned ideas
of how life "should be" and allow your higher/divine self
to take charge of the divine plan!

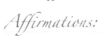

Meditation:

Breathe a silver-blue light into your third eye. Take three breaths and
then relax. Now ask for a glimpse of the life ahead of you,
an insight into your possible future.
Next, see yourself standing beside a beautiful, meandering river.
The water is fresh and clear and is flowing gently through the
countryside. As it is a lovely hot day, you decide to take your clothes
off and get into the river for a swim.
You turn on your back and soon you find yourself, happily
supported by the water, drifting downstream.
As you float down the river, you notice
scenes of your future life being played out on its banks.
You carry on floating until you have seen enough,
at which point you come to a dam.
You climb out of the water and find your clothes
laid out for you by the healing angels.
Give thanks; you have just been privileged to have had a glimpse
into a possible future! Make the best of what you have witnessed.
Do not forget to ground, attune and protect yourself.

Affirmations:

I flow effortlessly with life!
I am allowing my higher self to take charge!
Life supports me at every step of the way!

Beauty is on the inside

You live in a materialistically orientated society,
a society that has invented strict rules and guidelines
on how people should look and behave.
Do not fall into this trap, my dear one, as it is built
on a false notion of self – one that does not seek to embrace,
but to separate.
Beauty truly comes from the inside, from your soul,
the core of your being.
Surround yourself with people who love and respect you
and do not be swayed by outside forces.

Let the beauty of the true you shine forth!

Meditation:

Imagine yourself sitting somewhere in nature
in a truly serene, tranquil spot.
Absorb the energy of the place.
You relax and feel at peace with yourself and the world.
You feel truly connected to your true self, your higher self.
As you look around, to your surprise you find
a little hand-mirror lying by your side.
You pick it up and look into it…
A being of light, more beautiful then you could have ever imagined,
looks at you with loving eyes!
You have finally met the true you!

Affirmations:

I am beautiful inside out!

I radiate love and light!

I have a beautiful, radiant soul!

Everyone is a teacher

As you are seeking knowledge on your path to self – illumination,
do not depend on books alone.
Teachings are to be found all around you
and most of all within your own soul.
Be ever alert at all times as great teachings may be given to you
or come to you from unexpected sources or persons.
Remember that teachings are not always plain to be seen by all.
This is why you call yourself "a seeker"!

Meditation:

Take pen and paper and give yourself about 20 minutes
writing time, possibly straight upon awakening.
Now allow a stream of consciousness to manifest itself on paper.
Just keep on writing whatever comes.
At first it will not make much sense,
but soon you will see a theme emerging
and on reading it back you will find many valuable teachings,
coming from your higher self, within the pages you have written.
Repeat often

Affirmations:

I am willing to be taught!

I hold the key to all the teachings I ever need!

I open my mind to the hidden teachings around me!

The power of thought

Thought is a powerful energy, my dear one!
Do not underestimate this truth.
As soon as a thought leaves you, its source,
it becomes an entity in itself and will have
an effect on the world at large!
Be aware of the power of your thoughts
and guard them carefully!

❀

Meditation:

Look at a flower or plant in front of you.
Be still and gaze at it for some time.
Allow your mind to relax.
Now decide that you will become the observer
of your thought forms, see yourself looking down at them
as they leave your third eye enveloped in big bubbles.
If the thoughts are negative, do not fight or condemn them;
just allow the bubble containing your negative thoughts
to turn gold and float up and out of your space into the heavens!
There they finally burst and the negative energy
is returned to the source and transmuted into light.
This exercise is a very important part of your spiritual development
and should be repeated on a daily basis
and practised as often as possible!
Please remind yourself to ground, attune and protect.

❀

Affirmations:

I am in control of my mind and my thoughts!

I invite the energy of unconditional love to permeate my mind!

I choose to think loving thoughts!

Your dreams

Your dreams are one of the gateways to your soul, my beloved!
If you have repeated dreams about the same subject,
take heed; your soul might want to make you aware
of certain unresolved issues in your life.
Have pen and paper handy by your bed,
so that you may write down your dreams
immediately upon awakening.
Study what you have noted carefully.
The text will contain important clues that will
further your spiritual progress.

Meditation:

Just before you go to sleep, hold what is troubling
you at present firmly in your mind.
Ask for a solution to this problem to be shown to you
in your dream- state.
This process works very well; however it may take time,
so repeat it every night until the answer
arrives contained in your dream.

It always does!

Affirmations:

I listen to what my soul has to tell me in my dream-state!

In my sleep I communicate freely with my soul!

I ask and I shall receive all the information I need!

Mind clearing

Your mind is filled with "this and that" to the brim.
You have lost control of it.
In fact your mind is now controlling you!
If you wish to attain a state of clarity,
if you wish to see clearly,
you must make an effort to clear your mind.
Not just once in a while, no,
you must make it a daily routine until
you have gained full control over it
and it once again becomes the useful tool it is meant to be!

Meditation:

Imagine a siphon attached to your third eye;
it is held in place by a group of healing angels.
Now take a deep breath in and decide that
on the out-breath any negative,
destructive thoughts will be "siphoned off" by the healing angels.
Repeat until your mind feels bright and clear!
Give thanks to the healing angels for their help and make sure
that you have grounded, attuned and protected yourself.

Affirmations:

I now see clearly!

My mind is clear and sharp!

I am free of all negative thought forms!

February 19

Your path

Before you incarnated into your present body,
you agreed to walk the path you are on!
You may have forgotten that, but it is so.
Walk steadily and be not dismayed by hindrances along the way.
Look out for the "signposts", as they are surely there to guide you!
God is holding your hand all the way along
your chosen path; you are just not aware of it!

Meditation:

See yourself alone in a desert wilderness.
You are lost and have been for a long time.
Finally you decide to ask God for help.
As soon as you do this, you feel a firm hand
holding and supporting you!
You know in an instant that God is aware of all your troubles
and is there to listen and care for you always.
You are now filled with strength and encouragement by God's love!
You wander along hand in hand with God
and soon reach the most lush, fertile oasis.
You feel light in your heart and thank God for
the unconditional love and support you have received.
Do not forget to ground, attune and protect yourself.

Affirmations:

God is always by my side!

I can call on God with every need!

I am never, ever alone on my path!

Balance

You are all striving for balance.
Balance means peace and serenity.
However, to achieve a state of balance is no mean feat!
It cannot be forced or urged or speeded up in any artificial manner.
True balance has to be achieved from within.
Equal measures of love, acceptance and compassion
for the self have to be heaped upon the scales.
The unconditional positive regard you give to yourself will be
the final weight with which you will achieve true balance within!

Meditation:

Visualise a pair of golden scales within your heart chakra.
The scales are not balanced.
Note on which side they are down: the left will represent the female
aspects of the self, the right the masculine aspects of the self.
Looking closer at the scale that is down,
you notice a small scroll placed on it.
Open the scroll.
Within you find written what you need to do
to balance the scales, such as

"appreciate yourself more,"
"respect yourself more,"
"give yourself more time to play."
Follow the instructions and you will achieve inner peace,
harmony and a balanced life.
Make sure to ground, attune and protect yourself.

Affirmations:

I am balanced and at peace with myself!

I have balanced the masculine and feminine sides of my nature!

I appreciate the parts of me that are balanced
and love the ones that are not unconditionally!

The fruits of your labour

You struggle so much in your quest for success, my beloved!
Worry not; the fruits of your labour will ripen!
Go about your daily tasks; perform them as well as you can,
and do not allow yourself to become attached to
the outcome of any of your endeavours.
Allow God to look after that.
He will ensure the best outcome for your spiritual growth
and for that of those around you at this moment in time!
Enjoy your work in the moment and all else will be taken care of!

Meditation:

Think of a task you are trying to complete at present
that has so far not gone too well.
You will have lost the joy in it.
Now, try to find the joy within.
You might have to change your approach to your work or find a
different angle in order to carry it on in a happy manner.
As you focus your mind on the problem,
many ideas and inspirations will come flooding in!
Implement the changes and you will
enjoy your tasks moment by moment!

Affirmations:

I am living in the present moment and enjoying every bit of it!

I let go of the outcome of my ventures!

I love what I do and cherish the experience of it!

Your goal

There is a lot of talk on your earth plane about goals.
This goal and that goal and "when I have achieved this goal of mine,
then I will be happy" is what you say. Is that truly so?
Do you remember what you felt when you had reached
the last goal you had set yourself? Did you feel exhilarated?
And how long did this feeling last? Not all that long.
It did not fulfil you otherwise why would you be already
well on the way to chasing the next goal?
Now, my child, make the next goal an inner one.
Try to achieve inner peace, strength, healing and harmony.
For when you have achieved any one of those qualities,
it will stay with you not only for the rest of this earthly existence,
but into all eternity!

❊

Meditation:

Breathe in pink light and allow your awareness
to drop into your heart centre.
There you find a chamber with the door half open,
a brilliant light shining from within.
You walk into the chamber and find a round table in the middle of it.
On it is placed a book bound in precious hand-coloured paper;
the book is entitled Inner Goals for…(Your Name)
You open the book and there in order of importance
for your life path you find written your inner goals!
Memorise them all and then leave the chamber of your heart
and return into waking consciousness.
You may return to this chamber any time you like.
Make sure that you are grounded, attuned and protected.

❊

Affirmations:

I make my next goal an inner one!
I find peace and lasting happiness in achieving my inner goals!
I am deeply fulfilled by what I am!

February 23

God's approval

You are looking for God's love; not being sure that it actually exists!
You are seeing God as a parent and are looking for His approval.
God, however, has no need to approve of you.
Approval need only be given if there has been
a lack of some sort preceding it!
God does not perceive a lack within you.
He made you in His image and He knows that
you are perfect in every way.
He is also well aware that you do the best you can,
with the tools He has bestowed upon you.
There is nothing you can do or need to do
in order to gain God's approval.
Just be yourself!
God loves you unconditionally, for you are God and God is YOU!

Meditation:

In which areas of your life do you seek approval?
Have a good think about this and make a list, writing the "lack of
approval items" on the left-hand side of the paper.
Now ask God and the healing angels to help you with this list.
Next go through it one by one and opposite every item write
"no need for approval, I am perfect as I am."
Trust and have faith that this is a reality.
God and the angels are always by your side!
Put this list under your pillow and update regularly!

Affirmations:

I approve of myself unconditionally!

I release the need for approval from a source outside of myself!

I know that God loves me unconditionally!

Resistance to change

There is one thing you can be assured of,
my beloved and that is change!
You and your life are in constant flux.
The cells of your body are changing as we speak.
People, situations, times and places are subject to constant change.
This is a frightening prospect for you, as you resist change.
As you are very familiar and comfortable with what you know,
the fear of the unknown often proves too much to overcome.
Trust in the divine plan and surrender to the divine will of God!
Hand over all your fears and your resistance to Him.
Take your hands off the steering wheel of your life
and allow God to be your private Chauffeur!
The more you are able to do just that, the easier the ride will get!

Meditation:

See yourself driving a snazzy golden car.
You are driving through a city.
There are traffic jams and you are going slower and slower.
You now hit a roadblock. To your surprise there is a sign nailed to the
barricade that says, in white lettering: FEAR
You decide that this roadblock will not stand in your way
to your chosen destination, get out of your car
and move the barricade to the side of the road.
You drive on, but soon hit another roadblock;
the sign on it says: RESISTANCE
Again you get out of your car, remove the barricade and drive on.
Now, miraculously the traffic is moving on nicely
and soon you are out of the city driving through
glorious open countryside straight to your destination!
Do not forget to ground, attune and protect yourself.

Affirmations:

I release my resistance to change!

I remove all blocks that stand in my way of happiness!

I allow God to take over the steering wheel of my life!

February 25

Listen to your inner child

Within you my child, dwells an unloved inner child!
This child is crying out for your attention. Give it the love it deserves.
Your inner child will show up on many occasions.
Just be watchful and you will become aware of it.
It is demanding and it wants attention.
If it does not get what it wants, it will stamp its little foot and become angry, sad or even spiteful and violent.
Take heed, those behavioural patterns belong to the part of your self that has not grown up and matured into adulthood.
Heal your inner child, so you live your life as a happy, mature adult!

Meditation:

Ask the healing angels for help in this matter.
Breathe in pink light until your chakras and auric field are filled with it.
Now ask for your inner child to appear in front of you.
It will do so and most likely it will be angry, sad or even crying.
Walk up to your inner child; give it a big, heartfelt hug and tell it how much you love it and that you will never, ever leave it – that you will always be there to care for it.
Ask your inner child what it would like to do right now. It might want to be taken to the playground or to the beach. Visualise yourself doing this.
It might want you to give it a teddy bear or a football. See yourself giving your inner child the gift its little heart desires so much.
As you parent your inner child, it becomes happier and stops crying.
You then promise that you will return on a regular basis to comfort it.
Surround your child with golden light and return to waking consciousness.
Give thanks to the healing angels.
Make sure to ground, attune and protect yourself.

Affirmations:

I love and cherish my inner child!
I am the perfect parent to my inner child!
All my childhood traumas are healed and I forgive and bless everyone involved!

Sad syndrome

In the dark winter months it is easy to fall
into a depressive state, my dear one.
I am aware that you have "the blues", as you put it.
This sorry state of affairs is mostly due to a lack of sunlight.
You have given this condition an apt name "sad".
And sad it is! However, help is at hand!
Meditate on the sunlight my child!
Incorporate it into your energy field.
It will soon illuminate the outer darkness
and make you feel much better!

❀

On the in-breath inhale golden light and on the out-breath
release and let go of all feelings of sadness.
Breathe that way through all your chakras.
Then visualise the sun in the sky, a beautiful golden disk,
radiating its bright healing rays.
See the sun disk travelling closer and closer to you.
As it does so, it shrinks in size. You can feel the energy of the sun
entering your auric field, warming and uplifting you.
Now the sun disk is right in front of you,
beaming at you with a gentle glow.
Visualise it merging with your solar plexus chakra.
As it does so, you feel a strong pull in that area
and an instant feeling of warmth, upliftment and strength.
Enjoy!
Make sure that you are grounded, attuned and protected.

❀

I have all the tools for self-healing within me!

I utilise the power of my mind for the healing of the self!

As I release all sadness, I live life to the full!

February 27

The part you play

You are a unique being with unique qualities within you!
As a co-worker with God your job is to express
these qualities to the best of your abilities!
Trust that God has chosen the part you play carefully,
with love and from love, for you.
He has chosen and designed every scene of that play of life
so as to bring out the very best in you.
Honour and respect yourself for the part you play in God's creation!

Meditation:

You are in a theatre watching a play.
As soon as the play begins you recognise the characters.
They are your family, friends, work colleagues and acquaintances.
You realise that you are watching the "play of your life"
acted out on stage in front of your very eyes!
But the play is not progressing, as YOU are nowhere to be found!
Your friends are trying to find you, as they need your advice.
Your office colleagues need a helping hand with their workload
and your parents and family would like to tell you
how much they love you!
Chaos reigns supreme on the stage in front of you
as all of the actors desperately try to find you.
Finally, the penny drops, you get up from your seat
and get on stage to participate in the play, which is your life!
Everyone is thrilled to see you and now the play
can move on to the next act.
Do not forget to ground, protect and attune yourself.

Affirmations:

"The play of life" would be incomplete without me!

I am grateful for the role God has chosen for me!

I now accept my rightful place in this play called life!

Heaven is within you

How often do you look up towards heaven, wanting to be there,
wanting to escape your earthly trials and tribulations?
Many times, indeed, my beloved child, I know.
What you fail to realise is that heaven resides
in your heart here and now.
Where else could it be found!
Walk on the bridge of your own unconditional love right
into the heavens within and rejoice!

Meditation:

Contemplate on your own vision of heaven
and allow it to form a picture in your third eye.
Now allow this picture of heaven to drop into your heart centre.
Add your feelings of heaven to the picture until your vision is complete.
Now you not only see, but feel heaven within:
a wellspring of divine bliss, love, light and grace
overflowing into the rest of your being.
And the more you focus on the vision of heaven
in your heart, the more there is of it.

A limitless ocean of divine bliss, right within your own heart!

Affirmations:

I am in heaven and heaven is within me!

I am filled with divine bliss!

Heaven is a wellspring of divine energy right in my own heart!

Take a leap

Take a leap of faith! What is there to lose?
New opportunities will present themselves;
new lessons are there to be learnt.
Be assured that a new horizon of exciting experiences
opens up in front of you.
Follow your heart; it never lies to you!

Follow your dreams; they are your God-given birthright!

Meditation:

Visualise yourself being a wonderful, golden lemur.
You are leaping from branch to branch.
You feel carefree, happy and totally trusting that
you will land safely on the next tree.
Now, see yourself climbing straight to the top of the canopy.

What a view! You are "on top of the world"!

Affirmations:

I am taking a leap of faith!

I now follow my heart and fulfil my dreams!

I open new horizons for myself!

Blessing for the month of

March

Celebrations

Celebrate your connectedness
with all there is!
Celebrate your existence within the universe
and allow the universe to celebrate
its existence through you!
May you be deeply connected with the
kingdoms of nature!
May you be deeply connected with all humanity!

May you and the universe be as one!

You are connected to all life

You are connected with all life forms on this planet
and throughout the universe.
All life pulses deeply within you!
You are a part of the mineral, plant
and animal kingdoms as much as they are a part of you.
All the attributes of the different kingdoms
are expressed within your divinity,
a vast storehouse of knowledge, power and strength.
Accept who you truly are and become aware
of the "multi-verse" within you!

❀

Meditation:

In your imagination, take a journey through the kingdoms of nature.
Start deep within Mother Earth and explore the mineral kingdom.
Now see yourself becoming a beautiful crystal.
What does it feel like to be this crystal?
Then visit the plant kingdom; travel around the world
to explore it thoroughly.
Now chose the plant you want to become,
maybe an ancient oak tree or a beautiful rose.
What does it feel like to be this plant?
At last pay a visit to the animal kingdom
and choose the animal which most appeals to you.
Become it. What does it feel like to be this animal?
As you are journeying through the different kingdoms
you are finding great affinity and love
for all the different life forms you encounter!
You realise, in your heart, how much
you have in common with all creation.
Do not forget to ground, attune and protect yourself.

❀

Affirmations:

I am part of the mineral kingdom and
the mineral kingdom is part of me!
I am part of the plant kingdom and the plant kingdom is part of me!
I am part of the animal kingdom and the animal kingdom is part of me!
I cherish and honour all life forms as I do myself!

Give and you receive

It is in the giving, my dear child, you will receive a thousand-fold.
Give from your heart, my beloved, not from your head!
For your mind will think up a thousand reasons
for you to withhold what you had intended to give.
Your mind is conditioned into believing that there is not enough.
A conditioning that it has carried with it for many lifetimes.
Indeed your society reinforces this mistaken belief.
Do not allow your mind to rule your heart!
Instead, let your heart rule your mind freely!

Meditation:

You are on your way to visit an orphanage.
See yourself packing a suitcase full of gifts.
Some of the items you pack for the children are your own,
which you have treasured very much.
However, you decide happily to give them away.
With the suitcase laden to the brim, you arrive at the orphanage.
As you open the suitcase the children's faces light up and
they are extremely happy with the gifts you have brought them.
With every gift you give, your heart is filled with more love,
emanating from the hearts of the little ones.
At the moment the suitcase is empty,
your heart is filled to the brim with love!
You hug the children and leave with a happy heart and mind!

Affirmations:

In giving I receive!

I give from my heart!

Unconditional love for all creation is my ultimate gift!

Who am I?

As soon as you pose the question "who am I?"
you become conscious of yourself; you know that you exist.
You are now at the centre of the universe,
consciously looking all around you.
After searching for this truth for many eons,
you realise that you can only be one thing
and that is God.
How else could you be at the centre of all things!

You are God and God is you!

Meditation:

Centre yourself in the heart chakra, the seat of your soul.
Allow your soul to communicate with your human form and mind.
At first you will only hear a small whisper,
but soon your soul will speak to you loudly and clearly.
Listen intently and carefully to what your soul is communicating
to you at this moment in time,
for it will speak to you of the one-ness of all that is!
Repeat often.

Affirmations:

I am the I Am!

I am within God and God is within me!

I am the alpha and the omega!

Trust your inner wisdom

My dear child! At your deepest inner core
you are undiluted true wisdom!
No outside influence has ever reached this centre of your being,
so your wisdom is untainted and therefore all-powerful.
It is through contemplation and meditation that you will learn to
communicate with this core self and to trust it unconditionally.
When the storms of the outside world have calmed,
then you will be able to draw from the stillness
of the unfathomably deep lake of eternal wisdom!

Meditation:

See yourself walking through an oak wood forest. Soon you come
to a clearing and find a beautiful, tranquil lake in front of your eyes.
Luscious plants surround it and colourful dragonflies are hovering
close by. You walk up to the shore of this lake and look into
the crystal-clear waters. The lake is not very deep
and at the bottom you can see a wooden chest.
As you look closer, on the lid of the chest you spot
a silver-plaque with your name on it. You take off your shoes
and wade into the water, retrieve the chest and bring it ashore.
Now you are able to read the full inscription on the silver plaque,
it says "Treasures and Wisdom Belonging to…(Your name)".
You are delighted about this find and open the chest,
which is filled with gemstones and crystals.
On the top of the treasure you find an old parchment
that has your name inscribed on it.
You open the scroll and to your amazement, the text answers all the
questions you have been carrying around with yourself lately!
Thank the heavens for your treasure!
Make sure that you have grounded, attuned and protected yourself.

Affirmations:

I am a wise and loving being!

I have a treasure chest of wisdom within!

I use my insights wisely to the benefit of all!

On being humble

Being humble is like an invisible string of pearls.
Every new act of being humble adds
another gem to your divine nature!
When the necklace is completed you will have overcome
your human ego-nature with all its wants and desires.
You will have attained fully conscious divinity in human form!

Meditation:

Make a list of situations where you feel
you have wrongly put yourself first.
Now imagine individually each instance on your list.
See yourself and whoever else was involved
acting up to the point just before you acted selfishly.
In your mind now see yourself operating from
that point instead with unconditional love.
You have reversed the situation and
visualised a positive outcome!
Ask for forgiveness from the people you
have wronged and forgive yourself also.
Fill the scene with golden light and ask
the healing angels for a blessing!
Repeat through the whole list.
Give thanks.

Affirmations:

I am a humble servant of God and humanity!

By being humble I am empowering others!

I humbly accept what God has to offer me!

Assignment for God

You are on an assignment for God!
You may not remember it, but you have signed
your "mission papers" before you were born and have agreed
to be part of God's "earth angel team".
When you take this possibility on board and go within,
you will remember more and more of who you
really are and why you came here.
You will start to flex your wings and soon they will be
strong enough for you to fly to the rescue of
your brothers and sisters,
be they in human, animal, plant or earth-mineral form.
You will fulfil this mission in your unique way;
such is God's plan for you!

Meditation:

Do this meditation first thing in the morning if possible.
You see yourself just waking up.
Next to you on your pillow you find a sealed letter.
The envelope reads: Assignment for today…(Date)…(Place)…
for earth angel…(Your Name)
You open the letter to find that it contains instructions
for your earth mission for today!
Now spread your wings, fly out into the world
and spread love wherever you go!
Why not repeat this meditation on a daily basis?

Affirmations:

I am an earth angel on assignment for God!

My mission is to spread love and light on this planet!

I am a messenger of love!

March 7

Denial of your inner child

Do you feel that there is no fun in your life?
Do you not allow yourself simple pleasures?
Then you are in denial of the desires of your inner child.
We all have a child within who needs to be paid attention to!
Take note and comply with your inner child's demands.
It might want you to go and watch a funny movie,
munching lots of popcorn all the way through the film.
It might want you to go out ice-skating,
roller-blading or to the funfair.
Your inner child might ask you to have a vacation,
in a place you have always dreamt of since childhood.
Or it would like to learn a skill you have dreamt of mastering!
Follow the instructions of your inner child.
Do not deny your inner child its right to play
and your life will be fun again!

❀

Meditation:

Have pen and paper ready.
Now connect with your inner child.
Just acknowledge that it exists.
Now tell your inner child that you are its
fairy godfather/mother and that it has three wishes,
which you will do your best to fulfil.
Write those down.
Give your inner child a cuddle
and do your best to fulfil your promise!

❀

Affirmations:

From now on I will listen to the demands of my inner child!

I take the needs and wants of my inner child seriously!

My inner child is happy and fulfilled!

Your body

Your body is a divine instrument, as it houses your soul,
and as such it must be treated with respect, nourished
and looked after with great care by you!
Your body is a gift bestowed to you by divine grace.
Keep it in good shape and you will be able to learn
the lessons of your soul in relative comfort.
Remember, the reason why a long life is a blessing
is that it affords you more time to learn the very lessons
you have come here to master in this lifetime!

Meditation:

Imagine your body to be a mansion.
What does the outside of it look like?
Is there any plaster falling off?
Is the guttering hanging down?
Are there any roof tiles missing?
Now walk into the house, moving from room to room,
noting any improvements that need to be made.
When you have assessed the damage ask the healing
and decorator angels for help.
Now go to work and together with the angels repair any damages
and redecorate the house to a high standard.
Fill the house with beautiful furniture, paintings, flowers and crystals.
When you are totally happy with the state of it, you are done.
Thank the angels for their hard work.
Repeat this meditation once a month for a check-up!

Affirmations:

I listen to my body's needs and wants!

I love and honour my body!

I nourish my body with loving care!

Clearing clutter

The state of your immediate surroundings reflects
the state of your inner being!
As within, so without!
As above, so below!
So goes the teaching of eternal truth!
Look around your house. How much clutter do you have?
Let go of anything that does not resonate with you any more.
If you don't love it throw it out!
Clear your clutter away and you will feel much clearer yourself!

Meditation:

Engage in some real physical house clearing.
While you sort out your space, repeat the positive affirmations
that follow out loud to yourself.
This will enforce your clearing and give it the
extra dimension of mind and spirit!
When you have finished, sit in mediation
and ask the angel of your house/space to bless
each and every room and to dedicate each space
to the purpose it is intended.
Give thanks to the angel of your house for assisting you.
Repeat, if the energy in your house/space
does not feel uplifting and peaceful anymore.

Affirmations:

As I cleanse my physical space, I cleanse my mind and emotions!

I release and let go of anything I do not love from my home!

I live in a happy, peaceful home, which I love!

Hug a tree

When you feel sad and lonely and depleted of energy,
have you ever thought of hugging a tree?
No? Then go out and do just that, my dear one!
This, at first, will be a wondrous experience for you.
However, you will find that it really works, relaxing,
recharging and uplifting you.
The spirit of the tree, which is serving mankind unconditionally,
will provide you with the energy boost you so dearly need!
Hug a tree and give your heartfelt thanks to the spirit that lives within!

Meditation:

If you are unable to visit a tree in its natural habitat, then see
yourself walking through an ancient forest.
Feel the soil beneath your feet; how soft and springy it is.
You can smell the moss and ferns and can hear the birds singing.
An old oak tree is catching your eye.
You walk up, put your arms around it and your forehead on its trunk.
Now send golden roots from the soles of your feet into the ground,
where they join forces with the roots of the mighty oak you are hugging.
As you breathe in, you are drawing the mighty oak energy into your
body. As you breathe out you are letting go of all your fears, troubles,
worries and anxieties. At the same time your heartbeat connects
magically with the heartbeat of the oak tree and you feel a sense of
peace, serenity and strength coming over you.
Carry on until your batteries feel recharged.
Then draw your roots away from the roots of the tree, keeping them
rooted a few inches in the earth.
Give thanks to the tree spirit for its loving service to you.
Walk back out of the forest the same way you came in.
Please ground, attune and protect yourself.

Affirmations:

I am one with nature!

I love nature and nature loves me in return!

I am deeply grateful for all that nature provides me with!

March 11

Ignite the cosmic fire

How does your heart feel my dear child?
Does it feel lukewarm or even cold?
It may be so, for you have experienced hurt,
pain and many sorrows, in this and many other lifetimes.
But there is no need for a frozen heart!
All you need is to apply the balm of forgiveness to yourself
and those who have inflicted suffering onto you, and by the grace God
the cosmic fire of love is melting the ice of fear away.
It may be just a flicker at first, but every problem
you surrender to God will increase the inner light.
And before long the cosmic fire of love will be ablaze within you.
Then YOU will be the one, to ignite all around you
with the cosmic fire of love!

❊

Meditation:

Visit the chamber of your heart. In the room you see, there is a
fireplace. Only a tiny flicker of a fire can be seen.
By the side of the fireplace stands a brightly polished brass coal
bucket, with a sign reading "forgiveness" on it.
You put a big shovelful of the coal of forgiveness on the fire and
immediately it starts to burn much better.
Now you spot another bucket on the other side of the fireplace,
marked "sorrows and worries". You empty the whole content of it onto
the fire, which burns even brighter.
Behind it there is yet another bucket, this time with the sign
"anger, hate and resentment" on it.
You throw he contents of this bucket onto the fire.
Within seconds the fire is roaring away. You have done a wonderful job!
Come back every time you feel a build up of negative emotions.
Make sure, that you have grounded, attuned and protected yourself.

❊

Affirmations:

I apply the "balm of forgiveness" to myself and others!
I am igniting the cosmic fire within my heart!
I have the sacred opportunity to help ignite the cosmic fire
of those around me!

Link your tongue to your heart

Have you ever listened to yourself when you
were in a bad mood or even angry?
Have you heard the words coming out of your mouth like bullets,
hitting your opponent where it hurts?
Have you been aware of the power of the spoken word
the long-lasting effect that even a single word spoken in anger
or criticism can have on another human being?
No, often you are not aware, my child.
Be mindful of your speech and most of all,
let your words rise from your heart!
When the tongue is firmly linked with the heart,
your speech will be soft, gentle and uplifting.
Your sweet words will affect those around you in a loving way!

Meditation:

Breathe in the pink ray of love and feel it flowing
into your throat chakra, filling it with pink light.
When your throat centre has filled with light,
allow the energy to flow into your heart.
There it forms an everlasting spring,
from which the pink light of love forever rises upwards
into your throat chakra!

Affirmations:

I express myself with love!

I am linking my heart with my throat in divine harmony!

I speak straight from my heart!

Love unites all

Fear separates and love unites!
Remember these words often, my dearest one!
If you feel fear, do not allow it to penetrate your very life,
but release it and offer it up to God.
In His hands your fear will be turned into love
and returned to you as that!
This cycle will continue until you have released all the residues of fear
that you have been holding in and holding on to,
in your physical, emotional and mental bodies.
With the absence of fear, you are able to feel the presence of love!
Love unites all, bringing you back into the lap of God
from whence you have sprung forth, in the beginning of time!

Meditation:

Visualise a well, bubbling forth from a rocky formation,
framed by satiny green ferns and multicoloured flowers.
The well forms a small pool of clear, pure water
surrounded by sparkling rose quartz crystals.
This is the pool of your heart!
Make sure that this pool stays pure and clear,
by keeping your heart and mind free of fear and hate.
Feed the well of your heart with thoughts,
feelings, words and actions of love!
Please ground, attune and protect yourself.

Affirmations:

All the aspects of myself are united by love!

God replaces my fears with unconditional love!

I am born of love and will return to love!

Guiding Light

The light within your own heart is the light that
guides you on your earthly sojourn.
Allow this light to illuminate even the darkest corners of you,
transmuting pain and suffering, thus turning it into light.
Eventually the amount of light within you will increase
until you become the light and will indeed be a guiding light
to all those whose lives you touch.

Meditation:

Think of yourself as a lighthouse standing
on a rock in the middle of a vast ocean.
You are tall and upright and your lights shine brightly
guiding ships safely to their destiny.
Year in and year out the lighthouse stands there unshakable,
doing its duty, fulfilling its role.
Think of yourself being just like the lighthouse,
steadfast in your service as a light worker to
your brothers and sisters on this planet.

Affirmations:

J am safe in the knowledge that my inner light
is always there to show me the way!

J allow my inner light to guide me!

J am steadfast in my service as a light-worker!

The great illusion

When you identify your self with your physical body,
the clothes you are wearing, the cars you drive
and the houses you live in, the career you have,
then you are falling for the great illusion of the importance of the
material existence, thus harming yourself greatly along the way.
Remember, your soul uses your body, your mind
and your emotions as tools with which to experience itself!
All these experiences with material things
are just part of your learning process. That is all, no more, no less.
The true you, being limitless, is totally free of such constraints.
Know this and be at peace. All is well!

Meditation:

Breathe in white light and gently let it flow through
all your chakras, from top to bottom.
Bathe in this pure light for a few minutes.
Now see yourself stepping in front of a full-length mirror.
To your surprise you see a figure, unrecognisable, covered
with many layers of different coloured cloth.
You instantly know that these veils represent mental and emotional
blockages covering up your true, divine nature.
As you take them off one by one, you find that there are seven layers.
You observe in the mirror that as you take off each layer,
more and more light shines through radiating from your body.
When you take off the last veil, you see a truly powerful,
radiant being of light smiling back at you!
Now step forward right into the mirror,
merging with the image in front of you!
Enjoy the true you!
Do not forget to ground, attune and protect yourself.

Affirmations:

I am now letting go of all the veils of illusion!
I am all-powerful and all-knowing!
My true essence is light!

Realise your dreams

What is in your heart?
What can you see, what can you feel, an empty space?
Now, at this very moment, give yourself permission to dream!
You will feel your heart filling with joy at this thought.
This is your divine birthright!
When you are fulfilling your dreams,
you are fulfilling God's divine plan for you.
And only when you are connected with your highest joy,
your fondest dreams, do you raise yourself to the level of God's plan.
Now go out into the world and fulfil your dreams!

Meditation:

Prepare pen and paper.
See yourself surrounded by a bright yellow light.
Allow this light to enter the top of your head
and flow through all your chakras.
Now take pen and paper and write "My Dreams"
on the top of the page.
Then start to write without thinking or hesitating.
Write down all you have ever dreamt of from the age of childhood.
Let it all flow onto the page.
When you have finished, ask God, the angels
and all the beings of light to help you fulfil your dreams.
Now read through your list out loud three times.
When you have done that, write at the end of your document,
in large letters, with a golden pen if possible,
So be it, So be it, So be it.
Repeat this same procedure until all your dreams have come true!
Give thanks to God, the angels and all the beings of light for their help!
Make sure that you have grounded, attuned and protected yourself.

Affirmations:

My dreams and God's divine plan are one!
I have the power to make all my dreams come true!
By realising my dreams I am realising my full potential!

The diamond

You truly are like a diamond!
There are so many facets to your being.
All of those facets need to be brilliantly polished
and the universe brings you ample opportunities to do so!
Note that every situation you encounter
contains a gift within just for you!
It is the gift of learning about and refining the
facets of your being, a gift that polishes away anger,
fear and hatred, allowing true,
unconditional love to shine forth from you!

❀

Meditation:

Imagine a diamond in front of you.
With every breath you take it grows in size until it is larger then you.
You now take a step forward and merge with the diamond.
You feel the cool, clear, brilliant energy running through
your energy system, filling all aspects of your being.
Now, as you are at the heart of the diamond,
look around you and inspect the facets.
Do any of them still need polishing?
What do these rough facets represent?
Maybe you need to be less judgemental with yourself
and others or maybe you "do not own" your own stuff,
blaming others, refusing to take responsibility.
Decide to release, let go and heal all of these issues
right now, at this very moment.
You do not need to carry them around with you any more.
Step out of the diamond and admire your handiwork.
Do not forget to ground, attune and protect yourself.

❀

Affirmations:

I am happy and willing to polish the rough facets of my personality!

I now allow my light to shine bright!

I am brilliant at all that I do!

True freedom comes from choice

Sometimes you feel a prisoner of your life circumstances!
But my beloved you are not!
You have the divine freedom of choice.
You are free to choose again, and again.
This is contrary to what society tells you that you must
not do this and that you must heed that.
If, deep in your soul, something does not feel right,
pay attention to this inner voice, listen carefully.
It is God speaking to you, urging you to release
what does intuitively not feel right to you,
to let go of any inauthentic thoughts and feelings of who
and what you think you "ought" to be!
The right choice will make you feel free and as light
as a feather and that is God's will for you!

Meditation:

Take a problem you have at this time into contemplation.

Now take a deep breath of blue light and allow your awareness
to drop into your heart chakra, the seat of your soul.
Ask your guidance within which choice to make.
You will be aware of a deep, inner knowing straight away.
Act on it without delay!

Affirmations:

I have total freedom of choice!

I am free to choose again!

I choose from love not fear!

Light food

Light is a divine dispensation, my beloved!
It is all around you!
However, in order to take in this "manna",
this glorious food of the Gods, which nourishes your body,
mind and spirit, you have to attune yourself to it.
This is a process of eliminating all energy input that is detrimental
to your body, mind, emotions and spirit.
Clear your mind of negative thoughts.
Avoid watching the news and reading depressing literature.
Avoid bad company and low energy foods.
Instead, surround yourself with the people who honour, love
and respect you; with heavenly music;
uplifting books; art and nature.
Your life will become a joy to live and more
and more light will enter your very being!

Meditation:

See yourself walking in a magnificent garden.
You soon realise that you are walking in the Garden of Eden.
Everything you have ever dreamt of is there:
wonderful nature, exquisite art, sculptures
and tame animals playing happily in the garden.
Beings of light are sitting together deeply engaged in conversation
and cute little cherubs are bathing in a crystal-clear waterfall.
You wander around, absorbing the atmosphere and energy
of this divine, light-filled place until you feel filled
to the brim and completely recharged with it.
As you walk out of the garden, thank God for the Garden of Eden!
Please ground, attune and protect yourself.

Affirmations:

With every breath I take, I take in divine love and light!

With every out-breath, I release all that is not love!

I carry the Garden of Eden within my soul!

On being a master

What is a "master", you might ask yourself and how do I attain it?
A master is one who acts from unconditional love
for the sake of unconditional love, with no regard for him/her self.
A master is love in action, love on two legs!
It is in your destiny to become a master!
It might take you many lifetimes, but mastery is the goal
for you in the divine plan.
So you might as well start striving for your destiny now!
Act from love; just be, think and do the very best you can.
Clear focus on the goal ahead, coupled with strong intent,
will get you off to a brilliant start on the road to mastery!

❀

Meditation:

Fill yourself with golden light and see yourself walk into a large library.
You are mesmerised by the bookshelves filled with books of great
learning — more and more books of wisdom on every aspect of life.
Soon you find yourself standing in front of a desk.
A being in white robes, a master, sits behind it.
His/Her face looks familiar to you.
Your eyes fall on the name-sign on the desk in front of the master.
And to your surprise, the large, golden letters spell your name!
You are faced with a part of you that has already attained mastery!
The master beckons you to sit down and invites you to ask him/her
any spiritual question about the path to enlightenment you are following.
You gain much wisdom and insight and are invited to come back often.
Walk back out of the library into your present time and space!
Thank yourself, for what you have learned!
Do not forget to ground, attune and protect yourself.

❀

Affirmations:

I am the master of my destiny!

Mastership is part of God's divine plan for me!

I am on the road to mastery!

Spring-time

"Spring has sprung", my beloved, the power and the glory of it all!
Nature is at its best, radiating light, love and colour
to the human kingdom.
Pause a moment and note that all the beings in nature,
the rocks, the plants and the animals live, grow and die,
sacrificing themselves in an endless cycle of birth and death for you!
For you alone!
Giving humans the ground to walk on, coal for their fires,
air to breathe, food to eat and the company of the animal kingdom
to enjoy – what a sacrifice!
And what do they expect in return? No-thing!
At the heart of the kingdoms of nature is the power of
unconditional love, given freely for the benefit of humankind.
It is time to get on your knees and give heartfelt thanks
for this divine miracle of nature!

Meditation:

Contemplate for a moment where you would be without the
co-operation of Mother Earth, the nature spirits
and the elementals of earth, fire, water, air and ether.
Now from your heart, give thanks to all of them.
Radiate pure love through all the kingdoms of nature,
allowing a beam of light from your heart to flow
all the way around Mother Earth!
Do this earth healing exercise on a daily basis,
it will ensure you a life in harmony with nature!

Affirmations:

I am part of nature and nature is part of me!

I am grateful for the gifts nature so generously bestows on to me!

I am taking an active part in taking care of Mother Nature!

Discernment

How do you know that what you want is right for you?
You need to learn the art of discernment,
the art of "sorting the wheat from the chaff".
If a situation or action you are contemplating, does not feel right to
you, take heed. Feeling is the language of the soul.
Something here is out of alignment with your highest good
and your highest truth. Follow this feeling and trace it back to its roots.
Whatever unresolved emotion lies at the bottom of it,
lovingly embrace, heal and release it!
Often your desires are nothing but conditioned responses to the world
around you and have nothing to do with what you truly desire.
God has given you the power of the intellect, which makes you stand
above the animal kingdom, use this power wisely!
If, by the end of this process, what you want uplifts and fills you
with joy, then you have indeed aligned yourself with God's divine plan.
Go forth, do just that and enjoy!

Meditation:

Feel into what you want at this moment.
How does this desire make you feel?
Happy, relaxed and joyful? Then act on it without delay!
Or does it make you feel slightly edgy, unsure and even fearful?
Then ask yourself why you would want
to even contemplate doing such a thing.
If there is a valid reason and you still want to do it,
ask that the best way to deal with it to be shown to you.
Allow all fears and anxieties around the subject to show up,
to be up rooted, healed and let go off.
If the emotion and desire you are finally left with uplifts and spurs you
forward, then the "green light" for going ahead is on!

Affirmations:

I am mastering the art of discernment with grace and ease!

I am aware of what is good for me at all times!

I live a happy, relaxed, joyful life!

Temptation

Temptations in all shapes, forms and sizes are all around you:
the glittering career, where you earn tons of money
and in return never see your children grow up;
the big house, which puts you under constant financial strain;
the glamorous lifestyle, which does not fulfil your true yearning
for peace, love, fun and companionship.
In truth, you play the game because you want to be loved
and respected by your family and peers.
However, they will love and respect you even more,
if you allow your true self to manifest its desires!
Allow your authentic self to come out and play the game of life!

Meditation:

Allow a wave of pink light to wash over and through you.
Now allow yourself to become aware of "who you are" at present,
of the games you are playing in order to cover up the true you!
Next see in front of you another self.
A smiling, happy, radiant, contented self!
This is your authentic self.
Have a conversation with it and ask how it learned to be "real",
how things were able to change and what it had to do to get there.
Make a daily appointment with your true self until the process
has been completed and you and your true self can merge into one!
See your selves hugging as equals!
Make sure, that you have grounded, attuned and protected yourself.

Affirmations:

I now let go of all game playing!

I trust in the knowledge of who and what I am!

I merge with my true, authentic self!

Go with the flow

Flow with life, my child!
Do not swim against the tide; it is a futile pursuit!
There is a pattern, a natural flow, in all things.
Learn to look out for the signs.
If the natural flow is not present, do not try to force
your earthly, little will on to the situation.
Rather sit back, wait and contemplate;
then when the time feels right, try another, different route.
You have found the right mode of action when whatever you are
attempting to think, say or do uplifts you and aids others.
Well done you!

Meditation:

Think about what is not flowing in your life right now.
When you have identified the blockage,
ask God and the healing angels to help you let go of it.
Visualise yourself standing by the bank of a fast flowing river and see
yourself throwing the problem into it, see the problem being carried
away speedily by the fast-flowing current.
If any fellow humans are involved in the problem ask them to step on
to a little barge, moored by the river, which will carry them away down
stream, accompanied by the healing angels.
Thank the angels for their help and assistance.
Do not forget to ground, attune and protect yourself.

Affirmations:

I am happy to release all blockages!

I am going with the flow!

My life flows for now and ever more!

The heart of the divine

The heartbeat of the divine can be found in every
living being on this planet.
Open your heart to this truth!
Look for the proof of this for yourself!
Acknowledge this divine secret!
As soon as you do so, doors that you never knew
even existed will open for you!
Step inside and you will find the divine within!

Meditation:

Think of your favourite bird.
Concentrate on every detail of the bird's appearance,
until the vision of the bird feels alive to you.
Now acknowledge a divine heart beating within this creature.
See how the vision of the bird changes, how even more sweet,
more beautiful and more radiant it becomes,
how the colours of its feathers intensify
and how its song sounds like the most beautiful aria
you have ever heard!
Finally note how your feelings towards the bird have changed!
How much more love you feel for this little creature!
Repeat this exercise with different subjects!

Affirmations:

The heart of the divine beats at the core of all living beings!

I perceive the heart of the divine in all creatures!

I am one with the heart divine!

Sharing

Everything you share, my child, will feel doubly sweet to you!
(If you are alone share in spirit with the divine,
the angels and the masters in spirit; this also will uplift you!)

Think for a moment of all the wealth you have!
How privileged, how blessed you truly are!
Now think how you could go about sharing this wealth with others.
You may share some of your wisdom, your spiritual insights,
your practical expertise or a little of your physical wealth!
Whatever comes naturally to the fore will be the right thing to share.
There is never a better time to do just this, than now!

Meditation:

Contemplate on what you have in abundance.
Now ask the healing angels for inspiration on
the best way to distribute your wealth.
When you are ready, go out into the real world
and share, share, share!

Affirmations:

I am truly wealthy!

I am happy to share my wealth!

Giving is a divine privilege!

March 27

You are the path

What is my path in life you might ask yourself?
Should I go here, should I go there, should I do this
or should I do that…
Much time and energy is wasted this way, my beloved!
To remedy this dilemma, bring yourself into the present moment.
Look for the doors that are open to you right now.
Walk through the door closest to you and explore what is behind it.
If you don't like what you see, walk through the next one.
Look at all the resources you have at hand, directly in front of you.
Utilise them and especially realise the potential inherent within you!
This is the secret – that the path you tread you create!
It starts and finishes with you, right there in your "God within" centre!
You are the beginning and the end! You are the path!

Meditation:

Think of where you would like to be in life right now.
If where you want to be truly feels right,
then carry on with the exercise.
Visualise yourself visiting a beautiful temple,
of gleaming white marble, filled with flowers and crystals.
You are standing in a large hall at the end of which are three doors.
Behind each door you will find a different possible reality.
Explore all three, one by one.
When you have finished your explorations,
you decide which path to take for now!
Walk out of the temple and give thanks for the guidance received!
Please ground, attune and protect yourself.

Affirmations:

I am honouring the resources I have at this moment!

I now step through the door that is currently open to me!

I am always in the right place at the right time!

To be of service

How does it make you feel to be able to be of service to others?
A warm feeling, a feeling of gratitude for being able
to assist others in their hour of need,
this is the feeling flowing right through you!
What a pleasure it is!
Much more so than acquiring yet another gadget
you don't really need; buying clothes you will
only wear once or twice; eating out at expensive restaurants,
where the food is not even that nice;
or wasting your time in front of the television set!
Go back for more of this emotional treat.
Give, give and give again!
In return you will receive manifold! This is God's law!

Meditation:

See yourself walking around your own home collecting
all superfluous items and putting them into a large box.
Now you are taking this box to a place of need,
like a shelter for the homeless.
See yourself giving your superfluous possessions away
to the people who really need them.
See the joy on their faces, how happy they are!
Your generosity has made their day!
You might want to try this exercise in real life!

Affirmations:

I am wealthy, privileged and blessed!

I give to others in need with an open heart!

My giving is unconditional and I do not expect anything in return!

A tool for transformation

Your ego is an important tool for transformation; it drives
you forward on the path of self-discovery.
In order to realise who you truly are – namely a being of light
– you must experience who you are not – a frightened human being!
So one by one you are moving through the polarities:
from hate to love, from fear to freedom, from envy to generosity,
from sadness to joy and finally from darkness into the light!
Bit by bit you are healing your "shadow" the unloved side
of your being, until bathed in your own light
you finally know who you truly are!

Meditation:

Become aware of and feel your "shadow qualities".
Write down what you feel.
Now go through your list, embrace your shadow qualities;
forgive yourself and others, and release
and replace each shadow quality with its opposite.
Keep affirming those positive qualities on a daily basis,

Affirmations:

I now see the ego as a tool for transformation and salvation!

I am transforming my shadow into light!

I am an unlimited being of light!

Let go, let God

Stop, my dear one! Stop holding on to your fears,
your worries, your anxieties!
Hand them over to God, relinquish the burden, let go and let God!
As soon as you do that, you truly will feel lighter;
your heavy burden will lift in an instant!
A host of new, fresh opportunities will come flooding in for you!

❀

Meditation:

See yourself in your hiking gear, walking up a steep mountain.
You are carrying a heavy rucksack, your back hurts
and you are out of breath.
Now stop for a moment and consider that not only
are you carrying your past on your back,
but also your expectations for your future.
It is begins to dawn on you that it really is not a good idea
to carry this heavy load farther up the mountain.
You take the rucksack off, open it
and start to throw all that past and future stuff out.
When you have finished, you end up with a pile of the stuff next to you.
You ask the healing angels to take it away, which they kindly do.
You are now ready to put the rucksack back on
and continue, this time, floating up the mountain.
Thank the healing angels for their hard work.

Affirmations:

I am now ready to let go of the burden I myself have accumulated!

I let go and let God!

I am free!

The spiritual sun

Within all of you shines a radiant spiritual sun!
This sun represents your divine potential,
ready to manifest into physical form.
Each being has a unique contribution to make to the divine plan.
Each and every one is an equally important part of the whole.
Do not ever forget that!
Do not belittle yourself or put yourself down,
thinking that you cannot affect any change!
You can, my dearest one.

All you have to do is to allow this spiritual sun residing in
your heart to radiate out into the world, letting it become form!

Meditation:

Breathe in golden light and let it flow into your heart chakra.
Imagine a golden sun building in your heart.
This is the spiritual sun of unconditional love.
With every golden breath you take, it grows bigger and brighter.
Now imagine the rays of this sun radiating out into the world.
As the rays strike people and places, they all light up, absorbing
the energy of unconditional love from your heart!
Make sure that you are grounded, attuned and protected.

Affirmations:

I have all the love and light I need right within my heart!

The spiritual light of my heart radiates out into the world!

I am fulfilling my divine potential!

Blessing for the month of

April

Gifts of Nature

Give thanks to Mother Earth,
Give thanks to the elementals
of fire, water, earth, air and ether!
May the blessings of nature be bestowed upon you!
May your body be healthy and strong!
May your mind be rejuvenated!
May your spirit be uplifted
by the gifts of nature!

April 1

Resurrection

Let all which is not truly you die…Let it wither away.
Be radical in your approach; feel no remorse or false guilt!
You are entitled to be truly you!
It is time for the death of the old, conditioned you, and for the rebirth of
the new true you that has always existed at the core of your being!
Be triumphant and bathe in the glory of your divine spirit!

Meditation:

Ask the healing angels for assistance.
Find yourself walking through a field, strewn with flowers.
The scent of summer is all around you. The sun is shining brilliantly in
the sky and the birds are singing their best songs.
You can feel the grass underneath your feet and a soft,
warm breeze tousling your hair.
All the spirits of nature are around to support you.
You know that it is time to let go of the past and
you decide "to die to the old you" right now.
You lie in the grass and take a deep breath of golden light.
As you breathe out, you feel the old conditioned self floating away
from you, like a shadow that does not belong to you anymore.
Keep on breathing until the process is completed.
As you do so, you feel lighter and lighter.
You look down at your toes and to your surprise your whole body
is now turning into solid golden light!
You get up and are able to feel that you have a new self now,
shining and radiant!
Your spiritual rebirth has taken place!
Walk back through the field and thank all the spirits of nature
and the healing angels for their assistance.
Make sure that you have grounded, attuned and protected yourself.

Affirmations:

My salvation lays in "the death" of the old me!

I rejoice in my spiritual rebirth!

I am reborn into my true self!

The divine plan

God has lovingly designed a divine plan for you! Much planning
and foresight has gone into it. It will ensure that you reach
your maximum spiritual potential in this present incarnation.
Anyone you come into contact with throughout
your life has lovingly agreed, pre-birth, to serve the furtherance
of God's divine plan for you in this lifetime.
Remember, any situation you find yourself in, no matter
how dire it may be, is part of the divine plan.
In the very worst circumstances slumbers a hidden gift for you!
Make it your utmost concern to search for the gifts
in all and every situation.
God is a God of unconditional love, not of punishment.
How could He give you anything other than gifts?

Meditation:

Find yourself in a bookstore.
It's a very light and airy place and all the assistants
are helpful bookstore angels.
You ask one of them for your own personal calendar for the year.
A heavenly angel assistant guides you into a huge room
filled with gleaming white book shelves.
She picks up a calendar from one of the shelves.
On it, it says: "Divine Plan for …(Your Name) for… (Year)"
The angel assistant presents you with it and you are overjoyed
with this gift from the heavens.
Thank the angel and walk to the reading corner of the bookstore.
There you sit down on a blue sofa, which feels like a plump,
fluffy cloud; you now read your very special diary for the year.
Return as often as you like to look up appointments in your diary!
Thank the heavenly angel assistants for their help!
Please ground, attune and protect yourself.

Affirmations:

I am open to receive the details of God's divine plan for me!
I am searching for the hidden gifts in all situations and circumstances!
I honour others for the gift of their service to me!

Release

How much anger, resentment and bitterness are you
storing up in your body?
How many feelings of guilt are you carrying around with you?
And how does all of that make you feel?
Depressed and irritable, maybe, not at all joyful, definitely!
The time has arrived to release your pent-up emotions.
Whom are you helping by holding on to them?
Yourself? No! Anyone else? No!
Would you like to carry on punishing the people involved in your life,
being grumpy and generally not a nice person?
Tell yourself now, once and for all, a firm no to all of the above!
Walk away from all of those unhealthy emotions.
Let bygones be bygones.
Release them and feel the happy, true you come through!

❀

Meditation:

See yourself walking into your bathroom to take a shower.
As you take your clothes off you realise, to your horror that
you have layers of dirt and grime on your skin.
This represents the emotional and mental "dirt" you have accumulated.
You grab a body-brush and jump into the shower.
You turn the water on and start scrubbing yourself vigorously.
Looking down at your feet, you see the murky water
draining away down the plughole!
Scrub away layer after layer of anger, guilt, resentment, jealousy,
bitterness and any other emotions and thought forms you have been
inflicted with; scrub until the water running from your body is clear!
Repeat as often as necessary.
Make sure that you are grounded, attuned and protected.

❀

Affirmations:

I acknowledge that I carry layers of unreleased emotions with me!

I am ready to release old emotional patterns!

At the core of my being I am always happy, healthy and free!

Balance

Achieving a balanced life is a true art form my dearest one.
This is why you have some way to go to achieve it.
However, this truly is an urgent matter,
as you are presently wasting much needed energy
on unimportant thoughts, feelings, conversations and actions.
On the other hand you never seem to be able
to follow your favourite hobbies and interests.
The power to change all that is within you now!
Decide that you more than deserve time for play, rest and recreation!
You have worked hard in so many ways.
Now balance your life with rest and play!

Meditation:

Take pen and paper.
On one side of the paper write down all
your commitments to family and work.
On the other side write down what you actually do for yourself.
Be very honest about that!
You will find that the two sides are far from balanced.
Now straight from your heart, write down all the activities you
would love to do but have put off doing for one reason or another.
Now take this list into contemplation and what is really right
for you to do now will literally jump off the page.
Take your diary and make space for new
fun, relaxing and fulfilling activities!
Enjoy!

Affirmations:

I deserve a balanced, happy, fulfilled life!

I allow myself the time and space to relax, play and have fun!

I am mastering the art of balancing work and play!

April 5

Ask for insight

How often do you complain that you don't know this or that
and that you are unable to find out about this, that or the other?
A lot, my dear child!
And how futile it all is, as all this time the solution
to the problem lies so close.
In fact it lies right within you!
When you ask for "in-sight", all you need to do is to look "in-side"!
All the answers you will ever need are right there
to be discovered by you!

Meditation:

Contemplate what insight you would like to gain.
See your self surrounded by a bright, sparkling, yellow light.
Breathe in and allow this light to flow through your chakras.
Next you find your self in a brightly lit, lavishly furnished room with
bookshelves covering the walls from top to bottom.
You know immediately that this room represents
the all-knowing part of yourself.
In the middle of the room, placed on a formidably
large desk, you find a file.
Open it and all questions are answered within!
Please ground, attune and protect yourself.

Affirmations:

I have at all times full insight available to me!

The answer to anything and everything I need to know lies
within my own being!

I ask and I receive all I need to know in an instant!

Healing the earth

As a child of this earth, you are sorely needed to heal
this earth of the wounds humankind has inflicted upon it!
Your co-operation and commitment to this cause
are vital at this point in time!
As you are using (and unfortunately also abusing) Mother Earth
for her resources it is now time to give something back!
You may want to start recycling your waste, join an earth-healing
environmental association or send healing thoughts
to the earth on a daily basis.
Any of these options will greatly further the good cause.
The time to act is now, do not delay!
Remember that delay may not matter in eternity,
but could be tragic in time!

Meditation:

Ask the healing angels to assist you with this earth-healing prayer.
Visualise the earth from space, noting the oceans and landmasses.
Now mentally start shrinking it.
Shrink it smaller and smaller until it fits, hovering like a ball,
right between your hands.
Now take a deep breath of golden healing light and send a beam
of unconditional love from your heart, through your lungs,
down your arms into the palms of your hands, right into the earth.
With every golden breath you take, more healing light flows
from your palms into Mother Earth.
Carry on until the earth starts to emit a golden glow.
When the job is done, return the earth to its former size
and thank the healing angels for their assistance.
Repeat on a daily basis!
Do not forget to ground, attune and protect youself.

Affirmations:

I am part of the earth and the earth is part of me!
I honour and appreciate what Mother Earth is giving me!
I am committed to giving something back in return!

April 7

Communion with God

Celebrate your communion with God!
Yes you may! God is inviting you to do just that!
You are not a sinner, a looser or a failure in God's eyes.
You are, at all times, God's beloved child, truly,
unconditionally and deeply loved!
Accept this offering of the divine to partake of God!
Take freely of what you want or need.
The more you take from God, the happier God becomes!

❀

Meditation:

Find yourself walking through a meadow filled with fragrant flowers
and see yourself passing through a series of golden gates.
After every successive gate the meadow becomes even
more colourful and intensely scented.
As you walk through the seventh gate, you find a white marbled temple
in front of you. It has seven steps leading to an open door at the top.
You walk up, releasing and letting go of your earthly concerns.
As you arrive at the top, you see brilliant
golden light streaming out of the temple.
You walk through the door and are faced with a wise
and gentle being of light, welcoming you with open arms.
You allow yourself to fall into the arms of the divine being,
feeling powerful, unconditional love radiating from it,
into your heart and soul, filling you to the brim with light.
When you feel "all love", step back from the being
and give thanks for what you have received.
Leave the temple, walking back down the seven steps.
Then go back through the seven gates into the meadow
and from there into the here and now.
Please ground, attune and protect yourself.

❀

Affirmations:

I am in constant communion with God!

I am entitled to God's unconditional love and affection at all times!

What belongs to God automatically belongs to me!

Success

You fear failure my beloved, but more so,
you are often fearful of success!
However, you are often not aware of this state of affairs.
Do you set yourself up to fail because you might
outshine your siblings, parents or friends?
Yes, you may well do that on a subconscious level.
It is unsettling to be different, to be "above" from what
and whom you have known.
You want to be loved and being different might jeopardise that.
Take the leap into success, my dear one!
You will take your friends, family and, indeed, all souls on this planet
with you, for you are all connected to each other!

Meditation:

See yourself opening a letter.
In this letter you read that you have just been
successful in achieving your dream.
See yourself happily dancing around the room,
filled with joy and gratitude.
Now you see yourself sharing the good news with your loved ones.
See yourself pick up the phone and ring them
all to tell them the good news.
Next see yourself delivering your joyful message in person and see
people hugging, kissing and congratulating you on your success.
Repeat this process until it becomes a physical reality.
Do not give up: "etheric building work" takes time to manifest into reality.
Make sure to be grounded, attuned and protected.

❀

Affirmations:

To succeed is my divine birthright!

I can be as successful as I want to be!

I freely and happily share my success with others!

Earth attunement

Are you "in tune" with Mother Earth?
What is your connection with her?
These are, my child, important questions to ask yourself,
as it is she who sustains and nourishes all life on this planet.
Being attuned with Mother Earth means to be aware
and sensitive to her needs.
It means to respect and honour her as a living, breathing being.
It means to realise, at the core of your being,
that on a physical level it is the earth who mothers you,
feeds and nourishes you from her own substance.

Meditation:

Try this 24 – hour awareness meditation.
Next time you eat, drink, put on your cotton clothes
and leather shoes, turn on your central heating and run
the water into your bath, be aware of the source of it all.
Be grateful that you are able to partake so freely in
the gifts Mother Earth is bestowing on to you!

Affirmations:

I acknowledge that the well being of Mother Earth
and my own well being are intrinsically interwoven!

I am attuned to the needs of Mother Earth!

I use the earth's resources with sincere gratitude!

Emerging like a butterfly

You are wrapped in a cocoon, in a cocoon of your own making!
You have spent many lifetimes weaving
layer upon layer around your sweet self.
Now you feel that you are in the dark alone and frightened.
These are the exact conditions your soul has been waiting for.
As there is seemingly impenetrable darkness around you, you now
have only one choice left and that is to go within.
And lo and behold, as soon as you do that you reach the
"light part" the core of the self, your soul.
And in a mere second "the dark night of the soul" is over!
The light from your soul radiates from your light-core breaking
down all barriers. Those layers of fear and insecurity
are now falling away and you are "free to fly"!

Meditation:

See and feel yourself wrapped tightly in a cocoon.
The layers of the cocoon are made of your fears, doubts,
anxieties and conditioned behaviours,
which have been building up over many lifetimes.
Try to identify the different layers, enlisting help of the healing angels.
When you have done that, feel a beam of golden light entering the top
of your head, travelling right into your heart.
From there a golden light beam penetrates all
the layers of your cocoon simultaneously.
Feel that the layers are literally burned away by the golden fire of love.
As the layers are burning away, you feel lighter and lighter
until you are able to stretch your beautiful wings.
The butterfly has emerged from its chrysalis and is taking flight!
Give thanks to the healing angels.
Please ground, attune and protect yourself.

Affirmations:

I am ready to leave my cocoon behind!
My true self is now emerging from its shell!
I allow myself to fly!

April 11

The abundant universe

Contrary to your beliefs about scarcity, the universe
is abundant beyond your fondest dreams!
It is your own insecurity that creates a personal universe
for you that seems to lack this, that or the other.
All this is an illusion, a projection of your mistaken mind.
Energy follows thought, this is a cosmic law; so simply change
your mind and allow the good to come to you.
Do not try to specify what form it should take;
let God take care of that!
Just be open to perceiving and receiving the abundance there is!
Make your mind magnetic to abundance on all levels.
You ask and you shall receive!

Meditation:

Sit down and make a list of all the things you think you lack.
Now go through the list and choose from it
what is really important to you.
State firmly that you are ready and deserving
of all that remains on the list.
Now go through the list item by item, visualising yourself owning
or realising, in one way or another, all your dreams.
Make the images as vivid as possible until you are able
to feel them becoming a reality.
This process will take time; please be patient with yourself!
Success will be yours!

Affirmations:

I am part of an abundant universe!

I deserve to fulfil my dreams!

I am ready to receive abundantly!

Give your body a rest

Do you listen to what your body has to tell you?
No, my beloved, most of the time you do your utmost to ignore it!
Why is that? What purpose does it serve to work your body into the
ground and to abuse it in so many different ways?
Your conditioned ego has become the taskmaster here.
Your body has become enslaved to your mind, which has decided
that certain objectives have to be achieved at any cost.
However, all the cells of your body function as one
and have divine conscious awareness within them.
So when your body is telling you to stop, to take a break,
your soul is telling you the same thing, as they are one,
interconnected with each other!
In order to come to a state of equilibrium, you must
listen carefully to the messages from your spirit, mind, emotions
and body and heed their advice!

Meditation:

Lie down and make yourself comfortable.
Feel where there is any tension in your body.
Now put both hands, one resting above the other, on the aching part.
Leave your hands there until you start to feel
a connection with your pain or tension.
Now ask this part of your body what you can do to make it feel better.
You will get very precise "orders" as to what
to do to remedy the situation.
Repeat with all the parts of your body that are tense or in pain.
Make sure, that you implement whatever your body suggests,
for instance a change of diet, more relaxation or more exercise.

Affirmations:

I make time to listen to my body's messages.

I thank my body for the hard work it does for me!

I embrace and honour my body!

The wheel of karma

Allow your spirit to dictate to your mind, your body
and your emotions, not, as is most common, the other way round!
The dictates of your mind will forever lead you astray;
wanting more power, money, fame and fortune,
thus perpetuating a never ending cycle of wants and acquisitions.
Which will ensure that you go round and round the same cycles,
lifetime after lifetime, forever bound to the wheel of karma.
Escape now, at this moment, by handing the "steering wheel" of life
over to your divine, all-knowing, all-powerful spirit self!

Meditation:

See your divine higher self dressed in beautiful robes,
radiating love and light, stepping aboard a luxury yacht.
You follow your higher self on board and watch it take the wheel.
Immediately the vessel sets sail.
You are now experiencing a journey through "the waters of life";
such journeys are sometimes fraught with danger.
There may be high seas, thunder and lightning
and treacherous rocks to navigate through.
But even in the face of great danger your divine self
never wavers and stays unflinchingly calm at the helm.
Your higher self steers you safely through the high,
waters and rough seas of your life!
Finishing your "round trip", you arrive back in the harbour unharmed!
Make sure to be grounded, attuned and protected.

Affirmations:

I hand the helm over to my divine higher self!

I am never alone on my journey through life!

My divine self, God and the angels are always there
to love and support me!

Light is love

Within you my child burns the unquenchable flame of love!
At present the flame may just be a flicker,
if that is all you are capable of giving at the moment.
This is fine and does not matter.
What does matter is your willingness to foster
and nurture this flame of love within your heart,
to allow it to grow and develop into a radiant light,
touching all and everything with which you come in contact!

Meditation:

Light a candle.
Observe how small the flame is when it has just been lit.
Now watch how it grows to its full size.
Observe how, although it may flicker in the draught,
it still manages to shine, giving light.
Become aware that although its body,
the wax from which it is made, is melting away,
it still carries on burning.
Contemplate on what this is telling you!

Affirmations:

I am the light and the light is within me!
I am nurturing the flame of love within my heart!
I am a comfort and inspiration to the people around me!

April 15

You are a magnet

What you believe in you draw to yourself, my dearest one!
The world you experience is a manifestation of your belief system.
This is a great but disturbing truth, as this does not
leave room for you to apportion blame for any of
your misfortunes on anyone or anything!
Moreover, there is no God punishing you;
you are only punishing yourself!
There is a simple solution to the dilemma!
Look to God for inspiration, believe in Him, put your trust in Him
and you will become identical with God, magnetically drawing
all good of this earth and the heavens to you!
Enjoy being "the love magnet" you truly are!

❀

Meditation:

Muster up as much love as you can!
Feel it welling up from within your heart and soul, freely flowing
through your being, warming you and uplifting you with its strength.
Now feel the core of your being solidifying and becoming magnetic,
as more and more energy is concentrating in your soul.
You feel confident and happy.
Then see yourself walking out of your home,
everyone smiling at you as you are wandering down the street.
At work your colleagues do things for you
they have never done before.
Your children/partner/others do happily
what you have asked them to do.
You find that the "whole world is at your feet"!
Do not forget to ground, attune and protect yourself.

❀

Affirmations:

I attract what I believe in!

I now choose to be love!

I attract loving kindness in return!

Step by step

Life can be hard!
When the bigger picture is overwhelming you,
the road ahead may seem endless, dusty and barren.
Take a step-by-step approach to life:
a second, a minute, an hour and a day at a time.
Break your goals into bite size pieces and work on them one by one.
Divide your chores into manageable units and you will succeed!
You will have all the strength you need when it is required!
God and the angels are with you, to guide
and protect you every step of the way!

Meditation:

Tackle something you mistakenly thought you could do in a day
(as this was an impossible task the chore never got done).
Take your diary to hand and divide what you are thinking of
achieving into a seven-day venture.
Mark it on your calendar, stick to it and you will find
the task an easy one to achieve!
Once you have tried and tested this approach
move on to bigger projects.

Affirmations:

I am taking one step at a time!

I am in control of the pace of my life!

I complete the tasks I set myself easily and effortlessly!

April 17

Synchronicity

Nothing happens by chance!
There is divine order behind even the smallest detail
and every occurrence in this universe!
When you are filled with light and positive thoughts,
events around you happen to your advantage, in perfect timing.
The more you pray and fill yourself with light,
the easier your life will get.
The law of synchronicity is on your side.
Notice synchronistic events and write them down in your
spiritual journal, to remind yourself in times of uncertainty.
By focusing on synchronicity, you will increase
the flow of divine energy!
Have fun being a co-creator with God!

Meditation:

On Sunday night contemplate your week ahead.
If anxiety arises, hand over your fears, wrapped
in a big brown parcel, to the healing angels.
Now, starting with Monday morning, visualise yourself
going about your day with total ease.
Everything is running smoothly and all is going your way.
People are doing their utmost to be helpful.
The roads are clear. You even find a parking space easily
and get all your shopping done without queuing for hours.
See this happening for every day of the week.
Visualise the special events and tasks of each day
occurring easily and enjoyably.
At the end of the meditation you will actually begin
to "feel" that you are in the flow of things.
Hold on and carry this feeling with you. It will ensure, that you will
attract more synchronistic events into your life.

Affirmations:

I acknowledge the law of synchronicity and make it work for me!
By filling myself with love and light I attract only good to myself!
I am in the flow of life!

Stamina

If you believe in a cause with your whole heart,
never give up, stay with it!
Do not allow the outer world to discourage you from
your plans and beliefs, no matter how strange
and utterly futile they may seem to everybody around you!
If you are following your heart, then you can be sure
of fulfilling God's bidding.
If people or circumstances are trying to stop you,
this might just be a test for the courage of your convictions.
Carry on, on your chosen path.
Do not look left, do not look right, just look up!
God's guidance is never failing!

Meditation:

See yourself running a marathon.
You have trained well and are in brilliant shape with plenty of stamina.
You run, keeping your eyes on the track and your mind fixed on God.
At the pit stops beautiful angels await you
and serve you with refreshments.
To your surprise after every angelic pit stop
you find yourself with more and more energy
and you come first in the marathon!

Affirmations:

I have the courage of my convictions!

I am aligned with divine will and doing God's bidding!

I reach my goals easily and effortlessly!

Contentment

Contentment is indeed a precious gem to own.
If you do, you have peace in your heart and there is peace in your life!
How do you acquire this gem, you ask?
First realise, acknowledge and honour what you DO have!
Then hand all expectations over to the "master planner", to God!
True contentment comes from an inner source, the source of pure
unconditional love, from the "good within".
All contentment achieved through the gain of material possessions or
superficial knowledge is transient and will not satisfy your soul.
Peace and contentment within is an everlasting gift of the divine!

Meditation:

You are walking through a glorious spring garden.
There are yellow daffodils, pink camellias,
bluebells and birdsong all around you.
Ahead of you, sitting on a tree stump, you spot a white dove.
As you walk closer, the dove, undisturbed,
looks at you with its beautiful pearly brown eyes.
As you stop in front of it, the dove starts to speak to you.
It tells you that it represents inner peace to you and that if you wish,
you could integrate this inner peace into your life right now.
You are thrilled at this prospect and ask for this to be done.
The dove now hops onto your hand and as you look at it, it starts to
shrink in front of your very eyes, until it is the size of an egg.
It now tells you to put it right in your heart chakra.
Immediately a little door in your heart opens
and you put the dove of peace inside.
You are now flooded with a feeling of peace, serenity and gratitude!
Thank the animal kingdom for its service to you!
Please do not forget to ground, attune and protect yourself.

Affirmations:

I honour and appreciate what I have in my life right now!
I release all expectations and desires to God!
I am at peace with my life!

Adventure

Life is an adventure! Live it as one!
Do not fall for the promise of false security!
It is your conditioned society, which leads you to believe
that such a premise is real.
In truth you can be sure of only one thing and that is change.
Change is a constant in your life.
In this situation you have two choices: you either resist,
blocking yourself from receiving what God would like
to give you or you go with change, live the adventure of life
and allow God to spoil you with
the abundant experiences of your soul's growth!

Meditation:

Plan an adventure in real life, a challenge,
something you have never done before.
It need not to be something big.
It could be the new hairstyle you did not dare to sport previously,
the painting class you have been thinking of attending for the last
ten years, the local marathon or a bicycle ride for charity.
You have within you a yearning for adventure, let yourself GO!

Affirmations:

I love life!

I am now ready for adventures!

God guides me all the way!

April 21

Water is sacred

You have the good fortune to live on this planet my beloved!
A planet, whose surface is largely covered by water.
Water represents the emotions and supports the emotional body.
Your time on this earth is a unique opportunity to clear
and wash away emotional hurts, sores and wounds, many lifetimes old.
So please look after the water elementals, who look after
the water on your planet, by taking care of the earth's water
– the seas, the rivers, streams and lakes.
To ensure that the earth's waters run clear make sure that
you clear your emotional body of any murky debris that might be
lurking within the depth of your being.
The state of this planet is a reflection of the emotional,
mental and spiritual state of humanity.
Be ever attentive to this important fact!

Meditation:

Be aware of your emotional body; allow yourself to feel right into it.
Stay with your feelings for a little while.
Now, imagining that your emotional body represents a lake,
what would this lake look like?
Allow this picture to form in your third eye chakra.
When the full picture is in your mind, start to explore the lake.
Ask the healing angels to help you clear away any debris or
impurities; to fish out anything that does not belong in this lovely lake.
Help the healing angels in their task until the waters
of the lake a crystal clear!
Thank the healing angels for their assistance.
Please ground, attune and protect yourself.

Affirmations:

I am now ready to "spring clean" my emotional body!

My emotional body is as clear as a still mountain lake!

I deeply honour Mother Earth and all
the elementals that look after her!

Sleep

When you are asleep you are closest to God!
Your ego rests and your soul is free to travel!
For this reason sleep is of utmost importance.
Without sleep you cannot truly nourish your soul.
It would be too difficult a task for you at this stage of your spiritual
development; this is something only a master can do.
Give your soul permission and time to travel, to visit its source,
by giving your body a good night's sleep.
Sweet angel dreams to you!

Meditation:

Please make sure you find your natural sleep pattern
by following your body's messages.
Just before you go to sleep you have the unique opportunity
to ask your soul to bring back knowledge
and insights from its nightly travels.
Just ask one very clear question before falling asleep.
The same question may need to be repeated
for several nights before you get an answer.
Be assured that an answer always arrives.
This might happen in a number of ways, for example through a
"messenger of god", like a friend, family member
or acquaintances or through a chance meeting.
You might get the answer through the media:
radio, television or newspaper.
Nature might give you a sign or you might simply
wake up knowing the answer.
Be patient and the answer will arrive one way or another!

Affirmations:

I make time for a good nights sleep!

During deep sleep my soul is free to travel back to source!

All the wisdom I need is available to me any time!

Fear

Fear is the opposite of love and is at the heart of all darkness
and confusion on this planet.
Darkness is the opposite of light and you all know
and accept this truth.
Hence, if you allow the light of God to penetrate
through your darkest, deepest fears and confusions,
they finally will be transformed into love!
Take refuge in this knowledge, for this process
is openly available to all of you!

Meditation:

You are walking through a tunnel pushing a heavy wheelbarrow
that is filled with your fears and anxieties.
As you can see light at the end of the tunnel, you decide,
no matter what, that you will do your utmost to reach it.
You keep on keeping on, pushing the wheelbarrow along.
Finally you reach the end of the tunnel and a bright light greets you.
In front of you is a deep crevasse, filled with the flames of purification.
You are invited to empty the contents of your wheelbarrow into it.
You watch as the cleansing fire consumes your old fears and anxieties
and transmutes them into pink heart-shaped bubbles, which float up
from the crevasse to where you are standing.
The door of your heart opens and the pink bubbles float straight in,
filling your heart with the soothing power of unconditional love.
Walk back into waking consciousness.
Make this cleansing journey through the tunnel as often as necessary.
Make sure that you are grounded, attuned and protected.

Affirmations:

I move through the tunnel of fear into the light of love!

I choose love over fear!

Love is always triumphant over fear!

Behind the mask

Your true self is hiding behind the mask of your personality,
(personality from the Greek word"persona", meaning mask).
This mask, like one of Venetian papier-mâché,
is made up of many layers.
These are the layers of protection from the outside world
that you have built up in this life and many lifetimes before that.
The true you has been suffocated in the process.
Now the task at hand is to peel off the layers of protection
and allow the true you to come out of its self-imposed prison cell!
You will succeed and your true self will emerge bright and radiant!

Meditation:

Imagine that you are an onion.
Become aware that you have many layers of skin.
Ask the healing angels for help in peeling off those layers.
One by one they are being peeled off by your divine helpers;
each of the layers represents a negative emotion or event
that you now can discard safely.
Some of the layers may stick tightly to you,
due to mainly subconscious resistance to change.
Do not give up, ask for even more divine help
and you will succeed, arriving finally at the pristine,
divine, totally unharmed centre of your self!
Give thanks to your divine helpers.
Please ground, attune and protect yourself.

Affirmations:

I am ready and happy to discard my false persona!

I hold the keys to my liberation!

Through faith and perseverance I reach my goal!

You are blessed

Are you aware, my beloved, that you are blessed
beyond your fondest dreams?
That every breath you take is divine?
That with every thought you think you have the opportunity
to create something really special?
That with every word you utter you can facilitate
encouragement, hope and peace?
That with every deed you can express the divine will on earth?
These are the blessings bestowed on to you, a co-creator with God!
Make good use of them!

Meditation:

Focus on your breath.
Take a deep breath in and be aware that your breath is divine!
Now link your heart with your mind and think of something
very beautiful and special you could do for someone.
Contemplate on how you will complete this process
of divine creation or manifestation in reality.
Set out to do this as soon as you can.
You are now a conscious co-creator with God.
Congratulations!

Affirmations:

I am truly blessed!

I now pass on these blessings via my thoughts, words and deeds!

I am a co-creator with God!

Holding your vision

Do you have a vision of doing or becoming
something special that is dear to your?
Do you have a vision that has been silently
ensconced in your heart all your life?
Now is the time to become this vision, being it, experiencing it.
Do not fret over how to get there, just enjoy the journey.
There will be many signposts along the way
assisting you to fulfil your vision!
Have trust, faith and perseverance and it will be done!

Meditation:

What is your vision?
It may be an inner vision rather then an outer vision or goal.
Contemplate on this until you are clear, what your vision is.
Make sure that it is not somebody else's vision,
like your family's, your friend's or society's as a whole.
Now imagine that your vision is coming to fruition right in front of you!
See this as vividly as you can and then "step into the picture";
become your vision, feel your vision, be your vision!
Repeat until your vision has become a physical reality.

Affirmations:

I hold the highest vision of myself in my heart!

I am entitled to the fulfilment of my fondest dreams!

I am fulfilling my vision in this lifetime!

Spiritual glamour

There is only one truth – that you are God!
Beware of getting caught up in the net of spiritual glamour;
for once enmeshed in it, you will be disempowered.
Do not give your authority away to outside influences, no matter
how attractive, powerful or beguiling they may appear.
Also, be mindful not to create this "ego trap" for others,
which is so easily done.
As an aspirant you are most eager to share your insights
and spiritual achievements.
However, to do so uninvited will inevitably leave the recipients
of your shared wisdom feeling inferior and, in some cases,
overwhelmed and frightened by insights they can not understand
or relate to in their present state of awareness.
Use your intellect to discriminate, examine closely
your need to share and go about
your spiritual business wisely and silently!

❀

Meditation:

When you next buy a spiritual book or are thinking of
signing up for a workshop or seminar, look closely
and find out if you will be empowered by what is on offer
or if there is the possibility of a dependence being created
that will have you coming back for more.

Affirmations:

I am mindful of my need to share spiritual insights and information!

I share my spiritual wisdom freely, when I have been invited to do so!

In my spiritual work I facilitate the empowerment of my students!

Despair

Is your heart filled with despair?
Do you feel that the sun will never shine again in your life?
Do you feel that nothing and nobody can now save you?
If you are feeling this way, then you are going through
the "dark night of the soul", a lonely experience indeed.
You have looked for help from the outside world and not found it.
Now is the time to look deep within, put your trust and faith with God
and there you will find the help and the encouragement you seek!
You not only will carry on happily with your life, but you will
reach the next new level of your spiritual development!

✿

Meditation:

Imagine you are looking at a golden bucket filled with a murky liquid.
This bucket represents your heart filled with despair.
See yourself busily trying to clear the murky water
by dropping all sorts of artificial chemicals into it.
This is not working and the liquid still retains its murky quality.
Now your guardian angel appears and tells you to just tip
the bucket over, to get rid of the contents once and for all.
Your angel then offers to mop it up for you.
You are very happy with this offer and tip the golden bucket over.
The murky liquid spills out and your guardian angel, ready
with the mop cleans it all up for you.
You now take a good look into your empty bucket
and all you can see is the reflection of yourself at the bottom of it!
Thank your guardian angel for the help!
Please make sure to be grounded, attuned and protected.

✿

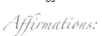

Affirmations:

Even in the midst of despair I am surrounded by God's love!

I now put my trust and faith in God!

I allow the "dark night of my soul" to pass!

Healing hands

All of you are blessed with a pair of healing hands!
A mother stroking her child, a dog owner stroking a pet, a nurse
comforting a patient, all these are examples of the power of healing.
You do this quite naturally and healing powers are to be found in the
hands of everyone, the builder, the plumber,
the shop assistant, the teacher and the toilet attendant.
Take note that anyone may be a bearer of this gift.
Next time you have reason to touch someone, do it with loving care and
awareness of the fact that you are a natural channel for healing.
What a privilege to be of service in that way!

❀

Meditation:

First ask God and the healing angels to assist you in becoming a
channel for healing and to guide and protect you.
Now look at your palms.
Visualise a golden cloud above your head out of which streams
a ray of golden light, the universal healing light.
Ask for this light to flow into your crown chakra, down through the
third eye, then through the throat into the heart chakra, from there via
your lungs down your arms into the palms of your hands.
With every breath you take, more and more golden light
floods in and you may start to feel a slight tingling
or a sensation of heat in your palms.
After a little while, put your light-filled healing hands on
to an area of your body where you feel discomfort.
Stay with it for some time; you will start to feel more relaxed
and the discomfort will ease.
You have just successfully completed a wonderful self-healing!
Please have supervision if you endeavour to heal others.
Thank God and the healing angels for their support!
Do not forget to ground, attune and protect yourself.

❀

Affirmations:

I am a natural channel for healing!
My hands are filled with light!
I am able to use this ability to heal others and myself!

Meditation

Meditation is a necessary tool for self-discovery
and provides a spiritual tonic for body, mind and soul.
Meditation may take many different forms;
meditation, contemplation and relaxation are closely linked
and many aspects arising from any of them are interrelated.
Your best form of meditation might be walking in nature,
taking a long drive, cooking a lovely meal, knitting a jumper,
playing the piano, taking inner journeys, or practicing yoga.
Or you might simply sit in meditation, going within to the still place
within transcending the self and going beyond time
and space to the source of all that is.
This is meditation in its purest form.
Any form of meditation that feels natural to you will be the right one,
for it will flow, and after repetition your body, mind
and spirit will start to look forward to the activity!
Practise your favourite form of meditation often!
Your body, mind, emotions and spirit will be eternally grateful to you!

❀

Meditation:

If you already are a meditator please carry on
your chosen form of meditation.
If you are not, then first take the many different
forms of meditation into contemplation.
To do this successfully you might want to light a candle
and sit in front of it, which in itself is a form of meditation,
and wait for an inspiration or insight to come.
Don't be afraid to try out different forms of meditation
until you find the one that suits you!

Affirmations:

I choose to meditate to aid the speedy discovery of my true self!

I am free to choose the way I like to meditate!

I am deeply fulfilled by my daily meditations!

Blessing for the month of

May

One-ness

You and I are one!
The alpha and the omega,
The beginning and the end,
The light and the dark,
The source of all that is!
May you be one with the divine heart!
May you be one with the divine mind!
May you be one with the divine will!
May you dwell in divine consciousness
and pure bliss, always!

You are worthy

You are worthy of all the riches of the earth and in heaven!
You are deserving of them, because you are a child of God!
And as God, who is your father and mother, loves you unconditionally,
He showers His riches upon you whenever you allow Him to do so.
As many of God's gifts arrive in drab and sometimes ripped
and torn packaging, you often decide not to open them;
you toss them aside as if they were not worthy of your attention.
Other gifts arrive dressed in gold and jewels, which you also reject,
as you think that they could not possibly be for you!
However, there is a gift in every parcel God sends you,
no matter how second hand or royal and glamorous it may appear!
Make sure, that in the future you do not return your gifts unopened
and reject the riches God would like to bestow on you.
You are worthy of them!

Meditation:

Next time you receive bad news decide not
to react to it there and then.
Instead, give yourself time and take this
so-called bad news into contemplation.
Be patient and look at the situation from all possible angles.
What is the gift hidden in this bad news?
What are you able to learn from it?
Tell yourself that every cloud has a silver lining
and that you will do your best to find it!
The gift will certainly be yours!

Affirmations:

I am worthy to receive all the gifts of earth and heaven
God wants to bestow on me!

I now allow God to give me all He wants!

I receive gifts and blessings with open arms!

Your magic wand

You are imbued with divinity, my beloved child!
You are truly living, breathing, walking "magic wand"!
All the power of the universe has been bestowed on you!
There is nothing you cannot do!

Meditation:

Visualise yourself holding a magic wand
and think how much good you could do with it!
See yourself tapping people, animals, plants
and objects with your magic wand, directing pure love
from your heart, like a powerful laser-beam, through it.
Watch the instant transformation as the healing light
hits the target penetrating it with the power of unconditional love.
Watch a wonderful healing taking place.
Repeat until you firmly believe in your God-given powers!

Affirmations:

I believe in divine magic!
I am a living, breathing "magic wand"!
I use my abilities to serve others!

Loss

One of the emotions, which all humanity and indeed
also the animal kingdom share, is the feeling of loss.
You may have lost a loved one, a dear pet,
your dream house, or your job.
You may even feel you have lost yourself
in the midst of the turmoil's of life.
Please take into account that loss only occurs
on the lower levels of your existence.
In the higher realms of soul and spirit nothing is or ever can be lost!
Your soul, your spirit and your love for one another
never can and never will be destroyed.
Love, in all its myriad expressions, will live on in all eternity!
And your loved ones will forever live in your heart!

Meditation:

Think of someone you have lost, either through death or separation.
Now take into contemplation the true reality
of the indestructible nature of spirit.
Think that love is all encompassing and everlasting.
Nothing can truly be lost and no one can truly die.
Immediately you will feel a sense of hope
and peace arising from the depth of your soul.
Stay with this feeling and let it grow!

Affirmations:

I know that loss is an illusion!

Love can never, ever be lost!

The love for one another will be in our hearts for all eternity!

May 4

Life is a miracle

Life is a never-ending miracle, my dear one!
That you are a living, thinking and feeling
self-contained unit is a miracle! Isn't it?
That there is air around you to breathe is a miracle! Isn't it?
That there is a sun in the sky to warm you,
a moon to raise the tides at night,
and corn growing in the fields to feed you are all miracles
– and that you are walking this earth with brothers
and sisters who love you is the greatest miracle of all!
Hail, to the glory of God, the Creator!

Meditation:

Take an egg and put it in front of you.
Sit comfortably and meditate on this egg.
Meditate on how it came into existence and what it symbolises to you.
And how if the mother hen sits on the egg, life will begin to grow in it.
Now visualise the little chick forming and growing
and finally breaking through the shell...
Watch the first steps of this little chick and how, straight away,
it goes about its daily business, happily and trustingly
following its mother's every move.
See it growing into an adult hen, laying its first egg...
The miracle of life continues!
What a blessing and what an adventure to be part of!

Affirmations:

I open my eyes to the miracle of life!

I am aware that I am "a walking miracle"!

I honour and appreciate the miracles of life around me!

Responsibility

Who, my dearest one, do you think is responsible
for the way your life works out?
You might think, because you had a bad childhood, it must be your
parent's responsibility to right things for you in your life.
You might think, because your first relationship did not work out,
it is every man or woman's duty on this planet to follow
your every whim and carry out all your orders, so that
you are able to punish them for what another has done to you!
No, stop! Look within!
There is only one who is responsible for making
the best of your life and that is you, you alone!
Forgive yourself and others, empower yourself,
free yourself from blaming others, take over and"own"your life!

Meditation:

Make a list of people you are blaming for misfortunes in your life.
In your heart and mind take full responsibility for your life.
Now, one by one, release and forgive the people on your list.
Then forgive yourself wholeheartedly for the part you have played.
Finally take any personal power back you feel
you have invested in these people, by simply thinking
of the person in question and stating in your mind
"I am now taking my power back, thank you".
Ask for blessings from the healing angels to complete the process.
How good does it feel to be in charge of your own life?

Affirmations:

I live my life responsibly with the intent of
not harming anyone or anything!

I am responsible for my actions and reactions!

I am not responsible for other people's lives!

May 6

Peace in your heart

Have you ever experienced the feeling of true peace in your heart?
It is the sweetest feeling of all, soothing and tranquil,
spreading into every fibre of your being!
Unfortunately, only a few have tasted this sweet fruit.
Please ask yourself why that is the case.
It is because you have tried to attain the state of peace through
worldly pursuits. Alas, to no avail!
The more you get of anything, the more you want of it!
Turn your attention to your inner worlds, of love, light, God and angels.
Tap into your own wellspring of love and peace,
which lies slumbering in the chamber in your heart.
Herein lies your state of peace and oneness with all that is!

Meditation:

See yourself surrounded by pink light, the light of self-love.
Now take a deep breath and allow this light to flow into your heart
chakra, where it magically opens a door and you are able to walk into
the chamber of your heart, the seat of your soul.
What you find is a room full of clutter; the furniture is dusty and in
disarray and there is not a flower, a bright picture or a crystal in sight.
You are shocked at what you see and search for cleaning tools.
Behind a hidden door you find a broom-cupboard containing
a Hoover and other cleaning implements.
On the top shelf, to your amazement, you find crystals and other
beautiful artefacts, and vases full of fresh flowers.
You set about cleaning the room and arranging furniture harmoniously.
Then you decorate the chamber of your heart until it feels peaceful,
tranquil and harmonious. Walk around and admire what you have done,
then sit down on the sofa in the middle of the room and feel at peace!
Please ground, attune and protect yourself.

Affirmations:

I now choose peace and harmony in my life!
I am in charge of attaining a state of equilibrium!
Peace and harmony are my divine birthright!

Every day is a new day

Every day is a new day!
New light, new love, new opportunities lie
before you every morning upon awakening!
How will you "play" this day?
Will you let negative expectations for the new day overwhelm you?
Or will you align your will with the divine will
and decide in your heart that you are going
to make the most of this day and truly enjoy every minute
and the opportunities given to you?
The choice is yours!

Meditation:

Daily alignment:
Right upon awakening, as soon as you open your eyes,
take a deep breath of golden light and ask for guidance,
protection and the highest energies to work
through and with you during the day.
State, in your mind or even better out loud,
that you are aligning yourself in thought, word and deed
with the divine will, according to the divine plan, in divine timing.
Thank God, your guardian angel and the healing angels
for all the good you will receive today!
This is a most important spiritual practice, which will profoundly
influence life for the better, if it is practised daily without fail!

Affirmations:

I am aligning myself with the divine will!

I greet every new day with love!

I do the best I can and live every day to its fullest potential!

Spiritual pride

Nothing can hamper your progress on your chosen path
more than spiritual pride!
The mistaken belief that you know it all will close
the doors of wisdom around you!
You will have shut spiritual experience and knowledge out!
The universe is infinite knowledge!
Open your mind to this fact!
Allow yourself to receive its wisdom from
every possible source around you!

Meditation:

Fill yourself with pure white light.
Ask your guardian angel to accompany you to one of
the temples of higher learning in the realms of light.
Choose the field of knowledge that interests you,
and your angel will guide you to the appropriate temple.
As soon as you enter the temple, you realise that
the "light of wisdom" contained within is truly awesome.
Your angel walks around with you and shows you
all the sacred texts you are interested in.
Then your angel guides you to a quiet corner where
you are able to study your chosen scriptures for as long as you like.
Tell your angel when you have finished and he/she will guide
you back to earth into your own space.
Give thanks for your angel's guidance.
Make sure that you are grounded, attuned and protected.

Affirmations:

I open my mind to learn and grow spiritually!

My whole life is an adventure of discovering new spiritual
and physical horizons!

The endless wonders of the universe are waiting
to be discovered by me!

Share the light

You are the light!
Your powers to heal, uplift and unite are truly awesome!
Your feeling that you as a mere individual person cannot make a
difference in this world is a huge misconception my beloved!
You CAN and you ARE making a difference!
Give yourself conscious permission to do so
and allow your light to shine bright!

Meditation:

Ask the healing angels to assist you with
this distant-healing meditation.
Become aware of the flame of unconditional love burning
in your heart, just like the beautiful flame of a candle.
Breathe in the golden light of healing and see
the light increasing in your heart.
Repeat for two more golden breaths.
Now with the healing light in your heart blazing,
ask the healing angels to help you connect
with every living heart on the planet, both human and animal.
This is done and the flame of your unconditional love
is now igniting the lights of your blessed human
and animal brothers and sisters around the globe.
Keep on breathing in the golden light until you feel
that the healing is done.
Bring the light back into your own heart
and thank the healing angels for their assistance.
Do not forget to ground, attune and protect yourself.

Affirmations:

Light = Love = Light

I have the power of unconditional love within me!

I am the light and ready to share it!

May 10

Initiations

Life is a series of initiations, dear seeker and student of the path.
You may also call them a "baptism of fire",
as many initiations have that quality inherent within them.
An initiation does not always have to be a formal ritual.
It may take many, sometimes very mundane, forms.
Virtually any experience, any "chance" meeting
can begin a new process for you.
Catapulting you onto the next level of spiritual insight.
Be open to new beginnings leading you up the ladder
of spiritual knowledge and wisdom!

Meditation:

Find yourself in a beautiful wooded grove; surrounded
by silver birch trees, their delicate leaves gently swaying
in a gentle summer breeze.
A group of light beings awaits you there
and welcomes you with open arms.
One of the beings hands you a golden goblet filled with
the liquid of divine wisdom and courage.
You drink all its content, feeling a superb tingling sensation
running through your whole body and your auric field.
Thank the beings of light for their kind and generous gift and slowly
walk out of the grove back into your own room!
Make sure that you are grounded, attuned and protected.

Affirmations:

I open my mind and make myself available to receive
initiations at all times!

I accept that my initiations occur in accordance
with God's divine plan!

I enjoy each successive step in my spiritual unfoldment!

When the student is ready…

When the student is ready the master/teacher appears!
As soon as you seriously want to learn, the universe
cannot do anything but bring your teacher to you!
Your teachings may take many different forms
and may be implemented through different people and situations.
In a sense, everyone you come in contact with
and every situation you encounter, will teach you something.
All that is needed on your behalf is a willingness to learn from it all!

Meditation:

Contemplate what you would most like to learn.
Now see yourself, accompanied by your guardian angel,
approach a huge, impressive-looking university building.
Your angel tells you that they have booked you in
for a lecture on your favourite subject.
You are overjoyed and swiftly walk up to the reception desk
to find out where your lecture will take place.
You attend your lecture learning all you ever wanted
to know about your chosen subject.
Leave the lecture, walk out of the university building back into your
own home and thank your angel for accompanying you.

Affirmations:

I am ready and willing to learn all the universe wants to teach me!

I expect my teachings to come to me from different sources!

My teacher helps me to become conscious of
the wisdom contained within!

Light being

Who and what is it that you truly are?
The answer, my child is that you are a being of light born
of the mind of God, so that you may experience His glory!
Your soul has incarnated into this physical body
and has taken it as a tool to experience itself.
Your mind and your emotions are also nothing but tools aiding in the
discovery of your true, divine self as the being of light you are!

Meditation:

Make a conscious decision for today to be mindful of your body,
mind and emotions as tools for your soul's growth.
See, feel and use them in the context of this new concept.
You will be able to experience your thoughts,
conversations and actions in a new light.
Note any observations you have made in your spiritual journal.
You will find that you have taken yourself
and your life much more lightly!"

Affirmations:

I am a being of light!

I now use my body, mind and emotions as tools for
the discovery of my true self!

I am in constant communication with my soul!

Intentions

You have so many good intentions, to achieve
so many different things, my beloved!
Unfortunately so many of your good intentions end up
being a disappointment to you. Why is that so?
It was the intentions of your little ego self and not the intentions
of your divine, God self you were following, thus rendering
the divine plan God has so lovingly set out for you useless.
Hand your little ego self wholeheartedly over to the divine will of God.
You then will be in perfect alignment with God's plan
for you and from then on your "God-intentions" will work out
and come to fruition perfectly!

Meditation:

Upon awakening, ask God and the angels to align
your will with the divine will and the divine plan
to the highest good of yourself and others.
Be aware that all your intentions, even the smallest ones,
affect the whole.
For today be mindful and anticipate the effect your intentions
will have on those around you!

Affirmations:

I am in alignment with the divine will at all times!

I am in alignment with the divine plan at all times!

I am aware that my intentions affect the whole of creation!

May 14

Free will

God has bestowed onto you the precious gift of free will.
You have been given the gift of choice and are free
to chose again every second of the day.
What will your choices be?
Will they be based on the foundation of love in your heart?
Or will your choices be based on the "easy way out route", handing
over your power to other people or circumstances along the way?
Choose love in all your thoughts, words and deeds, even when it may
seem the much harder, even the seemingly dangerous option!
Exercise your gift of free choice utilising
your own divine truth and integrity.
Thus you will pass on the gift of love and free will
to the world around you!

Meditation:

Remember the last time you used free will in a destructive manner.
Take this instance into contemplation.
At the core of all negative behaviour lies fear.
What was the fear at the core of this particular instance?
Identify it and hand it over to God and the healing angels!
Ask for forgiveness from the person
you have harmed and forgive yourself.
You did not know how to do any better at the time!
Decide that from now on, if you feel fearful you will not act
from this "fear base", but will release any feelings
which are potentially harmful to yourself and others first.
Then you will be free to base your actions on the love from your heart!

Affirmations:

I am eternally grateful for the gift of free will!

I am using God's gift of free will wisely!

I choose to give the gift of love to myself and the world around me!

Access your creative mind

Your mind is deeply connected and intrinsically
linked with the creative mind of God!
Pay attention to this truth.
This reality means that you are able to use the divine,
creative mind in a myriad ways.
All you have to do is to accept this divine truth for yourself,
take it on board fully, trust and believe in it!
There is no separation!
All that belongs to God also belongs to you!

Meditation:

Contemplate on how you could be creative in different ways.
You could be creative with the way you look, how you decorate
your house, how you cook your next meal, how you do
your job and interact with the world at large – starting now.
Think of a particular creative project and decide in your mind
that your creativity is now flowing freely and abundantly.
Feel the creative energy coursing through your veins, feel this "divine
high" act on it and accept your role as co-creator with God!

Affirmations:

My mind and the creative mind of God are one!

I am connected with the creative mind of God at all times!

I accept my role as co-creator with God!

May 16
Unlimited supply of energy

How often do you complain that you are tired
and that you have no energy?
Many times, my child!
You have forgotten that when you live and have your being
in God there is an unlimited supply of energy,
as God will live within you, if you allow Him to do so.
You have free will! Use it!
The energy God is bestowing onto you is truly limitless;
all the love, courage, strength and abundance you will
ever need is supplied to you continuously and freely
by a God who loves you more than you can ever imagine!

Meditation:

Visualise yourself to be a huge electric pylon.
See thick electric cables coming out of all of your chakras.
Each cable links you with God, the ultimate power station.
Feel the energy from God flowing through the thick cables
straight into your chakras and into your auric field,
energising you at all times!
You are connected to an unlimited supply
of divine energy for all eternity!
Please ground, attune and protect yourself.

Affirmations:

I have all the energy I need available to me at all times!

I am constantly connected to God, who is an
unlimited source of energy!

All my needs are met at all times!

Music heals

Music is one of the greatest gifts God has given you!
Its healing qualities soothe and uplift you.
Upon hearing a little nightingale singing its aria,
you cannot be but joyful in your heart!
Use this God-given gift to your full advantage.
Surround yourself with heavenly music, especially
if you feel lonely, sad or depressed.
Music will help you heal!

Meditation:

Next time you feel upset, worried, sad or stressed
play your favourite piece of music.
(The music of Mozart and Bach has special healing qualities.)
Drop everything you are doing, sit or lie down and listen to it.
Allow the music to reach and imbue every part of your being.
With every breath you take you merge more and more
with the melody until you feel you are at one with it.
You are the music and the music is you.
After even a short period of time you will get up from your
"music healing session" feeling relaxed, revived and uplifted!
Thank God for the music!

Affirmations:

I use God's gift of music for my self-healing and upliftment!

I now will bring music into my life whenever I feel down hearted!

I am one with the music of the birds, the sea and the wind!

May 18

God is perfection

If you are looking for perfection, you do not have to look far a field!
God is perfection and He resides right within you!
All you need to do is make a supreme effort to release
your "small I am", which tells you that "I am not good enough",
"I can never do anything well",
"I am never going to reach such a high standard…"
and allow God to take its place!
God's perfection will work perfectly through you at all times.
Tell yourself: "I do my best and I let God do the rest"!

❀

Meditation:

Fetch an apple and put it in front of you.
Make yourself comfortable and meditate on this apple.
Note how perfectly formed it is.
Note its perfect colour.
Note its perfect scent.
How did it become this perfect?
Because it did not resist God's will for its perfection!
The apple just "was" and unresisting allowed itself to be
grown to perfection by God and did not resist it.
Be like the apple and allow God to be your tree!
Allow God to nourish and grow you into the perfect being you are!

❀

Affirmations:

I now release all worries about my imperfections to God!

As God is perfection, so am I a perfect child of God!

I am and see perfection in all things!

Honour your truth

What does it mean to "be in your truth"?
It is an important point to ponder upon, for the truth is stretched out,
fashioned and twisted according to false values far too often.
There is only one truth; this is the universal truth, underlying all truths.
When your thoughts, words and actions spring
from the one truth you feel at peace.
If they do not, you feel unsettled and disturbed
by the error of your ways.
Feeling is the language of the soul.
Trust your feelings; do not ignore them, as your soul is trying
to alert you when you stray from your truth!

❀

Meditation:

When was the last time you were not in your truth?
What did this feel like at the time?
Allow yourself to link back to this feeling;
which of your chakras does it affect?
Now ask yourself the reason why you were not able
to be in your truth at the time, try to find the root of the cause.
Was it because you wanted and needed to be loved at all costs,
even at the cost of self-denial or the denial of the rights
and choices of others and their free will?
Having identified this "unloved part" of yourself, ask for forgiveness
from those you have hurt or deprived and then give yourself
a big hug of forgiveness for what you have done.
Now think of a situation where you were consciously in your truth.
Reclaim the feeling of it and note the difference!
Being in your truth feels like being seven feet tall
and as light as a feather!
Well done!

❀

Affirmations:

I am in alignment with the one universal truth!
I express this truth through my thoughts, feelings, words and actions!
Being in my truth encourages my fellow brothers
and sisters to do the same!

May 20

The path of least resistance

What does it show you when you encounter resistance
to something you would like to do or experience?
Do you see it as a sign to slow down and to reconsider your options, or
do you see it as a challenge to overcome by whatever force necessary?
Have you ever stopped to think that by putting up resistance the
universe is trying to tell you something, maybe giving you a sign
or pointing you in a different direction?
This is exactly what IS happening, when everything goes wrong in
your life, the universe is trying to alert you to the fact that all is not well.
Try a different approach, a different route or wait for a better time.
Walk through the doors that open and do not try to break
through the doors that are closed for you at the moment!

❀

Meditation:

Think of a "closed door" situation you have recently encountered.
Now see yourself walking into a temple of learning in the higher realms.
A series of closed doors lead off a main corridor. You find that one of
the doors not only has your name on it but also the time and date and
subject matter of the closed-door situation you recently encountered.
You try to open this particular door, but find it locked.
You now knock on it and to your surprise your guardian angel answers
you from behind the closed door. You shout to him/her that you want to
come in but the angel declines and instead comes out of the room and
leads you to a nearby desk. The angel sits down behind it and now
explains why it was not in your best interest to have walked through this
door. Now the situation you had encountered makes complete sense to
you and you fully understand the reasons why the universe blocked you.
The angel gets up from behind the desk and leads you to a golden
door, which magically opens and you find wonderful new opportunities
awaiting you! Thank your guardian angel for his/her assistance!

❀

Affirmations:

I now choose the path of least resistance!
I walk through the doors God has opened for me!
I look for the signs the universe is giving me when doors are closed!

Open your heart

My dear one, you expect to be loved, but your
own heart remains closed!
So when someone attempts to love you, their love is not able
to break through the closed doors of your heart.
What a pity that is.
The very fabric of the door, locking out love, is made of
disappointment, betrayal, anger and resentment against old loves.
Wake up to the fact that it is of your own making; see it for what it is
and break down the barriers you have put in place,
through forgiveness of the "perpetrators" and yourself.
The door to your heart will swing open and the love you
so much desire will come flooding in!

Meditation:

Breathe in the pink energy of self-love and allow it
to flow through you and surround you.
With every breath you feel more and more uplifted
by this wonderful vibration of self-love.
Now visualise a heavy stone door closing off the chamber of your heart.
Decide to sit in front off it and forgive everyone
who has ever hurt you, through all times and all dimensions.
Release all these people and let them go.
Then forgive yourself for the part you played
in not allowing people to love you.
Now ask the healing angels to help you open the door.
To your amazement an angel just touches the door lightly and
it opens, the most brilliant light flooding towards you from within.
As you step over the threshold you know that you have come home!
Please ground, attune and protect yourself.

Affirmations:

I forgive myself and anyone who has hurt me in the past!

I am ready to open the door to my heart!

I am ready to receive all the love in the world!

Celebrate the moment

Celebrations, celebrations, celebrations!
Every breath you take, every moment in
your life gives cause for celebration!
The wonder of creation manifests within
and all around you, what a miracle it is!
Open your eyes, your mind and your heart
and celebrate the gift of the moment
God has bestowed upon you!

Meditation:

Be especially aware of your body, of how it breathes "by itself",
walks around, talks, sees, hears
and smells and tastes delicious foods.
Be extra aware that you are capable of thought
and feeling and have the powers of reasoning and discrimination.
What a wonder your body is!
What a wonder you are!
Give thanks for all you have been given!

Affirmations:

I am celebrating my life!

I am deeply grateful for what I have been given!

Every new moment is another celebration!

The hand of God

When everything goes wrong with your life,
when there is no hope and nowhere else to turn,
only then do you turn to God for help.
You want the hand of God to guide you and to help you.
Why wait that long?
Why not ask God every morning upon awakening
to take your hand and
guide you through the day?

Meditation:

Visualise yourself walking hand in hand
with God through your day.
From the moment you wake up to
the moment you close your eyes at night,
feel God's strong hand guiding you all the while!

Affirmations:

I release the need to carry on making wrong choices in my life!

I now ask for the hand of God to guide me through my life!

God and the angels are always by my side!

You are family

You are a child of God, part of His family.
You are also family to all others on this earth plane
– all of you are, transcending race and creed.
What you do to another, you do to God and what you do
to another you do to yourself also.
Remember this law of God's, this great truth,
and treat your "extended family" accordingly.
If you want love, make sure that you give it first!

❀

Meditation:

Visualise the whole earth.
Now see a line forming around it and as you look closer
you can see that it is the "earth family" holding hands.
Start off by holding hands with your family, then see them holding
hands with their friends and then their neighbours,
the whole town, the county, the country and so on until you see all your
fellow family members holding hands,
until a full circle is formed embracing Mother Earth.
Look at them all, happily smiling and chatting with each other!
Feeling loved, accepted and respected by each other!
Pour all the love you can muster into this visualisation and repeat often!

❀

Affirmations:

I am a member of the global family!

I treat every family member with love and respect!

As we stand united on this planet, love and harmony reign supreme!

Creating Eden within

How many of you are searching for the Garden of Eden?
To no avail – the Garden of Eden seems to be forever elusive.
You will not find it outside of yourself.
This garden must be created within.
A crop of love, compassion and understanding
must be sown in the fertile soil of love in your heart.
This is the true Garden of Eden!
The fruits of your loving efforts will go out into the world feeding
and sustaining your brothers and sisters!
Thus the true Garden of Eden has been created
and serves its divine purpose!

Meditation:

Visualise the chamber of your heart as a garden.
Are there any fruit trees or berries growing in it?
Whether there are or not you now decide
to make your heart a special place.
You work the ground and put plenty of compost down
and then plant your favourite fruits, trees and shrubs.
Water them regularly and prune them if necessary.
Visit this garden often and watch the fruits growing and maturing.
When the fruits have ripened, harvest them and see yourself
freely offering those fruits of love, compassion
and understanding to anyone who would like a share of them.
You are now a gardener and co-creator with God!
Make sure that you are grounded, attuned and protected.

Affirmations:

I have the Garden of Eden within me!

I am growing the fruits of love, compassion and understanding
within my own heart!

I give freely of the fruits of love!

Self-realisation

What does it mean to be "self-realised"?
It means having realised your own potential.
What are the limits of your own potential? NONE!
Your potential is truly limitless, as you are created in
the perfect image of a divine, all-encompassing, limitless God!
As you and God are one, so all His divine qualities are inherent
within you, ready to be accepted and expressed by you now!
Realise that you are God and you have realised the self!

Meditation:

Contemplate on what is stopping you
from realising your full potential.
Hand all your doubts, fears and feelings of not
being good enough over to God.
Allow yourself to feel God's unshakeable love and belief in you!
Allow yourself to feel God's unconditional love for you spreading
from your heart to your mind and body.
Now decide with all your might not to differentiate yourself
from the love of God any longer!
Accept that God and you are one.
Accept your divine potential.
Realise who you are! GOD!

Affirmation:

I accept that I am created in the perfect image of God!

My potential is truly limitless!

I realise that my own self is identical with the God self!

Integration

You are a seeker and have come a long way on your spiritual path.
Now the time has come to integrate your
spiritual knowledge into your everyday life.
It is time to allow this higher knowledge to filter down
into your emotional, mental and physical bodies.
Your heart, your mind and your body now know that they are divine.
When this process is complete you will be practising
your spirituality, rather then talking about it.
Through the practical application of your spirituality,
you will become a wonderful catalyst for healing on this planet!

Meditation:

Make a list of spiritual qualities you think you
should integrate within yourself.
Look at which ones you have already integrated into yourself.
Some of those could be acceptance, compassion and understanding.
Now give yourself credit for that!
Next take a look at the ones you have not yet been able to integrate.
One by one, ponder why.
Try to get to the root of the matter; what has been blocking you?
Hand all those blocks over to God and the healing angels
and decide in your mind that you can do it.
Take it day by day, step by step and you will succeed!

Affirmations:

I am now ready to practise what I have learnt!

I am walking the path of a practical, integrated spirituality!

My body, mind, emotions and spirit are working in perfect harmony!

Soul-seed

God is the gardener of your soul!
If you would only let Him do His job!
Allow God to plant the tender seeds of love,
love and more love in your heart!
Do not fight this process, as you have come here on this earth
to love and love and spread even more love.
Say yes to God and watch the divine creation unfold right within you!

Meditation:

See yourself walking through a rose-covered archway
into a beautiful, wonderfully serene garden.
Fragrant heart-shaped roses with pink petals
are growing there in abundance.
You see God and a host of angelic beings tending to the plants,
satisfying their every need with tender, loving care.
Never in your life have your eyes set sight on such a beautiful garden.
Now an angel walks up to you and explains that this garden
belongs to you, that it is the garden of your own soul.
You are delighted and overjoyed and thank God
and the angels for their handiwork!
Come and visit this garden of your soul often to assist God
and the angels in their endeavours.
Do not forget to ground, attune and protect yourself.

Affirmations:

I now allow God and the angels to help me tend the garden of my soul!

I am open and willing to nourish the blooms of unconditional love!

My love for all is flourishing and expanding!

You are free

You want to be free because you are feeling burdened
by the load you are carrying through your life.
You ARE free, my child!
Free to drop your burdens, free to choose a different
way to do things, free to live your life the way you want.
True freedom lies within.
Free your little self from the constraints, the illusions of bondage
and recognise that your spirit cannot be restrained or contained.
Your spirit is and always will be free!

Meditation:

Contemplate on what is restricting your freedom at this present time.
How many barriers exist between your being free and the problem?
Write these down.
Now look at where and when these barriers were built up.
Did you erect them or did someone else put them in place?
Now start to break down the barriers one by one, by removing and
releasing all the old thought forms, people and emotional patterns,
which created the barriers and "chained" you to them.
This is an ongoing process and will take time. Persevere!

Affirmations:

My spirit is free at all times!

I now dissolve the barriers that stop me from feeling free!

I recognise that true freedom comes from within!

May 30

Accept a helping hand

It is much easier to give than to receive!
Especially for you, who have been working tirelessly
to assist your fellow humans in their struggles.
Now is the time to allow others to lend you a helping hand,
to show you love and express their gratitude.
Do not rob them of the opportunity to be of service to you.
Accept it graciously, for if you do not, you will upset
the fragile balance of giving and receiving, thus disempowering
the very people upon whom you are lavishing your love!

Meditation:

Be mindful!
Next time a friend or family member would like
to do something for you, accept graciously.
What does it feel like to receive?
If you are not comfortable with the feeling, find out why.
Are you possibly resisting giving up your role as a helper?
Or do you, maybe, feel that you do not deserve to be loved that way?
Release and hand over any feelings of unworthiness
to God and the angels and decide for yourself
that you are now ready to be loved!

Affirmations:

I deserve to be loved!

I now accept a helping hand when it is offered to me!

I give and allow myself to receive in equal measure!

Transformation

When you transform you heart into an abode of light,
when your heart radiates unconditional love to all humanity
and the world you live in, then true alchemy is taking place!
You have transformed your feelings of "mine and thine"
into the spiritual gold of the I AM presence, which knows
no differentiations, no limits and no boundaries in lavishing its love.
You have transformed the many into the one!

Meditation:

Put your hands over your heart, one on top of the other.
Gently connect to what your heart feels like.
Within your heart you become aware of a number of small
black knots, representing your unhealed emotions.
Now take a deep breath of golden light and allow it
to flow into your heart chakra.
You observe the golden light dissolving those knots,
one by one, with its power of unconditional love.
Keep on repeating this process until your heart feels
transformed into a golden, light and happy I AM presence.
Do not forget to ground, attune and protect yourself.

Affirmations:

My heart is an abode of light!

I am transcending the feelings of "mine and thine"!

I know that at my centre lies the presence of the I AM!

Blessing for the month of

June

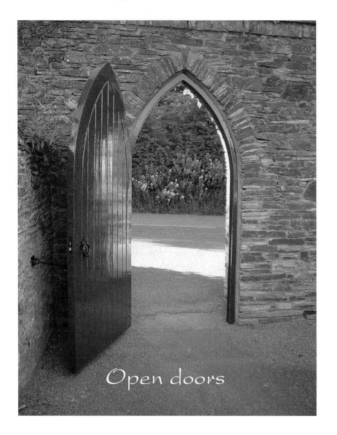

Open doors

The doors of heaven are always open!
Be ready to receive blessings in a myriad ways!
May you walk with God!
May you talk with God!
May you become one with God!
May the "bolt of enlightenment" strike
you in an instant!

May you know that you are one!

Your unseen helpers

At times it feels that all humanity has forsaken you.
You feel that you are totally alone.
This is not so, for your"unseen helpers"are all around you!
The angels are assisting you on every step of your earthly sojourn.
You are just not aware of them!
Acknowledge their existence by actively exercising
your free will and asking them for help.
As you serve your brothers and sisters on this planet,
so it is the angels mission within the divine plan to serve you.

Meditation:

Next time you feel alone and abandoned ask the angels for help.
Clarify the issue you need help with in your mind and ask the angels
very specifically for the support and encouragement you need.
Now pray from your heart for the angelic assistance!
It won't be long before help will come on"angel's wings"!
Give thanks for all the help the angels have given to you
throughout your life, which you have not been aware of
and for all the help they will give you in time to come!

Affirmations:

I am open to the existence of"unseen helpers"!

The angels are always by my side and ready to help me!

I am eternally grateful for their assistance!

It is all in the journeying

What do you do when you go on a journey?
You savour and enjoy every step of the way, taking in the sights
and sounds, meeting interesting people, visiting fascinating
places and delighting in the local cuisine, music and customs.
Why not treat the journey of your life the same way?
Be in the moment and enjoy every moment!
Do not look for some grand destiny, which might never materialise.
Otherwise you will miss all that is good and important
for you right in the here and now.

Meditation

Look at all the good you have experienced in
the journey of your life already!
Make a list of all you have going for you – materialistically,
mentally, emotionally and spiritually.
Pin this list to your bathroom mirror, where you can see it daily!
Keep appreciating and affirming all you have and you will attract
to you all else you might need on your life's journey.

Affirmations:

I am enjoying every step of the way on my journey through life!

I am grateful for what I have in my life now!

God gives me all I need, when I need it!

Being you

Celebrate being you!
You are a unique child of God!
Celebrate your being.
Celebrate being alive.
Celebrate being the very special you!
The energy of celebration will attract positive abundance
in many forms and guises to you.
The more you celebrate what you are and
what you have, the more of it will be "added on to you"!
Rejoice!

Meditation:

Today treat yourself.
Celebrate who you are!
What kind of celebration would most honour being you?
This does not have to be "a big do".
Many pleasures are to be found in small things,
like visiting your favourite museum, buying the music CD
you have been wanting to add to your collection,
and, maybe, most of all, giving yourself the time to just be.
Think about your special celebration and go out and do it!

Affirmations:

I accept and cherish who I am!

I honour and respect myself!

I now celebrate the unique self I am!

June 4

Heal your past

Your past follows you around like a shadow!
And a shadow it is, albeit a shadow of your own making.
Now, my dearest one, the time is right to heal and release it.
What is the purpose in dragging this shadow behind you any longer?
When it is always preventing you from being fully present
in the here and now?
All that is needed is for the light of your loving forgiveness
to shine onto the shadows of old, and all that was not love,
which has been holding you back for so long,
will be dissolved in a second!

Meditation:

Ask the healing angels for help.
See yourself standing in a beautiful spot in full sunlight.
You can clearly see the shadow your past is casting on to the ground.
Now decide in your heart that you are willing
to forgive and release the past.
When you are ready ask the healing angels to cleanse
and clear away your shadow.
Immediately a shaft of bright light engulfs you.
You can feel the negative energies of your past being
burned off and transmuted by the sun's brilliant rays.
You find yourself standing fully in the spiritual sun of the here and now!
Thank the angels for their assistance in this clearing process.
Please ground, attune and protect yourself.

Affirmations:

I am now ready to let go of the past!

I allow the light of forgiveness to erase the old shadows!

I am fully immersed in the glory of the here and now!

Healer heal thyself

Healer, heal thyself!
You heal in so many different ways, through so many
different expressions, in so many different guises.
But when will you start to heal yourself?
Maybe you have been so busy healing others that
you have not realised that you need healing yourself!
Please, my beloved stop and examine your own mind,
emotions, body and spirit. Is all well?
Most likely you will have to administer a
good dose of self-healing here or there.
Make sure that you give yourself the gift
of time and space to do just that!
Remember, what you have healed in yourself
you are able to heal in another!

Meditation:

Do a thorough MOT* on your body, mind, emotions and spirit.
Ask each part of you separately how it feels today
and what kind of energy it lacks at the present moment.
Take immediate measures to remedy any imbalances.
You have successfully climbed up another rank
on the "heal thyself ladder"!
Try not to be so hard on yourself and please value
your healing work, and yourself, as you deserve from now on.

*(In the UK, the compulsory annual inspection
of a motor vehicle over a certain age.)

Affirmations:

I recognise the ongoing need for self-healing!

I am giving to myself all I need for my well-being!

I am well in body, mind, emotions and spirit!

Change

The notion of change may be a frightening one to you.
However, it is one of the most valuable gifts God has given you.
Only change is able to ensure that you encounter
fresh new, opportunities. New horizons.
Do not resist change, open yourself to it, and welcome it into your life.
When changes are afoot the universe is telling you that
you are ready for a new energy-input in your life!

Meditation:

Think of a situation you have wanted to change
for a long time, but have resisted doing so.
Ask for help from "upstairs management" to examine what
has stopped you from changing this situation or part of yourself.
Pinpoint the specific fears, worries and anxieties attached to it.
Now visualise each specific fear as a ball of black energy.
The balls may vary in size.
Now with the help of the healing angels pick up an enormous hammer
and smash the first ball of black energy into a million little pieces.
Ask the angels to take this residue away,
which they will happily do for you.
Repeat with all your worries and anxieties.
When this process is completed you will be able to flow with the
changes in your life gracefully and fearlessly.
Give thanks!
Do not forget to ground, attune and protect yourself.

Affirmations:

I acknowledge change as a positive force for growth!

I am open to change!

I flow with change "lightly"!

Inner sanctuary

Although you might go through troubling times in the outer world,
you always have the refuge of the inner worlds to go to.
Create an inner sanctuary there, a sacred place
to retreat to, which only belongs to you.
Visiting your own inner sanctuary, even just for a few minutes
during the day, will give you peace, harmony
and relaxation, and the energy to carry on your life joyfully!

Meditation:

Think of your favourite place in nature,
either a physical place or a dream place.
Now see yourself walking into this space hand in hand
with your guardian angel.
The place exudes peace, calm and serenity.
The air is sweet and clear, filled with birdsong,
and the plants and flowers bristle with colour and vitality.
You find a comfortable place to rest and marvel
at the wonders of your inner sanctuary.
Every time you visit, it grows more and more beautiful and serene.
The more often you return, the more at home
you feel in this sacred space.
Give thanks to your guardian angel for accompanying you.
Please make sure that you never allow other people
to inhabit this space with you.
Keep it for yourself alone.
Please ground, attune and protect yourself.

Affirmations:

I create my own inner sanctuary!

My inner sanctuary is a sacred space that belongs to me alone!

I am deeply nourished and rejuvenated by visiting my inner sanctuary!

Smell a rose

Take time to smell the roses, my dearest child!
What a delight to do such a thing!
Amidst the hustle and bustle of your busy world,
you have lost the appreciation of the small things in life;
yet there are small wonders to behold all around you
– the smile of a child, the purr of your cat,
the song of the little robin outside your window,
the first green leaves bursting forth in the spring…
It is time to smell the roses…Why not give to yourself
the small gifts in life, the gifts you can have every day! For free!

Meditation:

For today, to start off with, make an effort
and open your heart and mind to the small things in life.
You will be surprised how many unexpected gifts
the universe has in store for you!
Enjoy!

Affirmations:

I am taking time out to smell the roses!

I appreciate the small gifts God wants to give to me!

I enjoy the small wonders of the universe!

Healing thoughts

Never underestimate the power of healing thoughts.
You may at times feel terribly helpless at having to observe
the suffering of humans and animals alike.
But what you are not aware of is that you are
in possession of a great power.
You have the power to heal, to make a positive difference
by sending loving thoughts to any person, animal,
place or part of nature that needs healing!
In doing so you are rendering a great service
and as a reward you will feel empowered and assured
in the knowledge that you have made a
positive contribution where it was needed.

❀

Meditation:

Next time you watch the (bad) news or read a newspaper,
send loving, healing thoughts to victims and perpetrators alike
and to any events or people who disturb or upset you in any way.
You can rest in the knowledge that you have made a definite effort
and contribution towards relieving the suffering in the world.

❀

Affirmations:

The power of healing is limitless!
Loving thoughts are free and easy to pass on where needed!
Through sending loving thoughts I am contributing to world healing!

June 10

Peace keeper

In a sadly troubled world of wars and strife,
you need to be a keeper of peace!
Start by keeping the peace in your own self.
When you have mastered that, you will be able to radiate
the energy of peace from your still centre within, out to your family,
thus keeping and encouraging peace there.
When you and your family are at peace,
even more peaceful energy will radiate out to the world at large.
Peace has spread its mighty wings and is about to fly!

Meditation:

Find your own symbol for peace…This might be a dove or a flower.
See this symbol in front of you and imbue it with the rays of
unconditional love emanating from your heart.
When the symbol is fully charged with love power implant it
into the hearts of all your brothers and sisters on this planet!
Watch the energy of your peace symbol grow and grow until finally
all humanity is linked together by the bright light of peace!
Repeat often!
Do not forget to ground, attune and protect yourself.

Affirmations:

I create peace in my heart!

When I am at peace it affects the world around me!

Peace and harmony is the natural state of being for all humankind!

Expansion

As your life is infinite, God has also given you
the opportunities for limitless expansion.
You may grow and expand in any way you like.
You may choose from a limitless variety of experiences
and if you fail at one you may choose again.
As you are a co-creator with God you have
unlimited power to create, grow and expand.
Manifest all your dreams first and then find out how
much more God has in store for you!

Meditation:

Visualise and feel yourself growing in size and experience.
You are now as tall as a tree!
What does it feel like?
You are growing even more and are now as tall as a skyscraper.
What can you see and how do you feel about being so tall?
You are growing even taller and increasing in self-awareness
at the same time, until you are able to look down at the earth
and "see the bigger picture"!

Affirmations:

I am a limitless being in a limitless universe!

I expand in expected and unexpected wonderful ways!

I create limitless joy in my life!

June 12

Tolerance

At the heart of each society should be the quality of tolerance!
However, sadly that is not so. Lack of tolerance is still leading
to wars, great unrest and unhappiness on this planet.
What can be done to usher in lasting change?
To bring about positive change, you simply start with yourself.
What are your tolerance levels?
How tolerant are you of your own perceived faults?
How tolerant are you of the perceived shortcomings of others?
Please remind yourself of this great truth, that what you perceive
in another you need to heal in yourself!

Meditation:

Imagine yourself meeting your
"worst nightmare person" at a party or meeting.
When you are confronted with their "dreadful" personality
and qualities what is it about this person, which disturbs you most?
Now think why that is the case, why you cannot
tolerate their behaviour?
Work backwards with these issues until you arrive
at your own root cause.
Release, forgive and heal those causes and you will find
that when you meet such a person next in real life,
you will be able to tolerate their behaviour with love!

Affirmations:

I am tolerant towards my own perceived faults and shortcomings!

I practise tolerance in all life situations!

I look for the best in everyone!

Sacrifice with love

God only wants you to make sacrifices if you can do so
from the point of and with unconditional love!
Too often sacrifices are made and then very much regretted,
felt and talked about in a negative manner.
God is giving you a choice in the matter.
Do you feel strong enough in yourself?
Do you have enough love stored up to attempt any sacrifices
or will it all backfire onto your friends, your family and yourself?
If in doubt, it is always a no, my beloved!

❀

Meditation:

Imagine yourself giving up something you really value
and treasure a lot to someone in need.
What does it feel like?
Do you feel resistance to this sacrifice you have made?
If yes, does the resistance stem from what you have given up?
Do you now resent the other person for having received it?
Work on any issues related to this until you are
able to heal and release them.
When you are able to sacrifice something with love, without
a trace of regret, it will not feel like a sacrifice to you anymore!

❀

Affirmations:

All my sacrifices are made with love!
Each sacrifice made with love flows easy and effortlessly!
I give love for love's sake!

Your family

Your greatest teachers are your family and your closest friends!
They provide the invaluable service of "pressing all your buttons".
No one can do this better than a loved one!
If a stranger did this, you just could not care less.
So next time, when "a fear-button" is pressed, be grateful
for the service your family and friends are rendering you.
How else would you find out which parts of you still
need to be healed and made whole!

Meditation:

Let your last argument with a family member or close friend
run like a movie in front of your eyes.
What was your reaction to the situation?
Looking at it from your new, aware vantage point,
what can you now learn from this argument?
Which buttons were being pressed?
Was it fear, insecurity or maybe a "false pride" button?
Heal the issues concerned and see it as another lesson learned.
Forgive and move on!

Affirmations:

I deeply honour my family and friends!

I am grateful for the life-lessons they provide me with!

What I heal in myself, I heal in my family and friends!

Your birthday

Your birthday is a special day, my child!
On this day God chose to give another soul the opportunity to
come closer to Him, to find and to experience Him in everything!
The wonders of the universe are there for the newborn child to explore!
Your soul has been given a body, mind and emotions
as tools for this expedition.
Use them wisely and success on your earthly journey
will be guaranteed!

Meditation:

Every day can be your birthday!
Every day you can birth new ideas into life!
Every day you can add more love to the world!
When you have a birthday you celebrate it.
Look at life as a never-ending series of birthdays,
all of which need to be celebrated!

Be happy!

Affirmations:

I am a unique child of God!

Every day is my birthday!

I look at the world afresh every day!

June 16

Purification

Purification is an important part of your life.
It is a means of keeping your mind, body
and emotions clean, light and bright.
Not only do you have to purify your body by drinking
lots of water and eating healthy foods, but also very importantly,
you must purify your thoughts of all negativity.
Finally, allow your heart to be washed clean of all sadness,
anger and resentment, and your purification is complete!

Meditation:

See yourself standing under an amethyst-rock waterfall.
Feel the clear mountain water wash right through your energy centres,
flowing away from your feet and down the mountain, a little murky.
Then allow the crystal-clear water to wash through all your organs
and lastly through the seven layers of your auric field.
When the water runs clear, your purification is complete for now.
You would benefit from repeating this cleansing exercise often!
Please make sure that you are grounded, attuned and protected.

Affirmations:

I am mindful of purifying my mind, body and emotions
on an ongoing basis!

I am now on a "negativity-free" diet!

I only surround myself with positive, uplifting people and images!

Be steadfast

Steadfastness in your chosen tasks or goals is
a great quality to aspire to!
Steadfastness will provide you with an anchor in the rough seas of life!
Your trust, patience and faith in God will fuel
your steady progress on your upward and onward
path to self-fulfilment and self-illumination.
Keep your mind firmly focused on both God and your goal
and you cannot fail but to reach your chosen destiny!

Meditation:

Contemplate on the journey of your life.
Have you felt like a ship on the ocean without a rudder?
Allow God to steer this ship of your life from now on.
Focus on God and you will find in Him an anchor
for your safety, whenever needed.
A smooth journey to your chosen destination is divinely assured!

Affirmations:

I choose God to be the captain of my life's journey!

I trust God to steer and guide me when I hit rough seas!

I know that God is my anchor!

Give and you receive

The more you give, the more you receive!
This is a wonderful truth my beloved!
Why is that so? Simply because there is so much joy in giving
and that joy attracts more joy to itself.
This is the cosmic divine law of "like attracting like" in action.
The one who gives with free abundance will receive abundantly!

Meditation:

Make a pledge to yourself that for today you will give away
as many smiles as possible to all and sundry.
Go out into the world and fulfil your pledge.

What was it like at the end of the day?

What a wonderful experience it must have been
to receive so many smiles back!

Affirmations:

I give for the joy of giving!

I give without expectations of a return!

In giving I am affirming my divine abundance!

Home sweet home

Love your home!
Be it a house, a flat, a caravan, a tent or a simple room somewhere!
Be grateful for a roof over your head and honour, respect
and value what you have been given.
Fill your home, foremost, with love and light,
then with kind thoughts, flowers and sweet music.
A home like this will be a healing sanctuary
for anyone who enters it!

Meditation:

How loved is your home?
Visualise that you are taking the roof off your home
and allow bright sunlight to fill every corner of it!
Then see yourself decorating your home with flowers,
crystals, incense, candles and other beautiful objects
and playing beautiful, uplifting music.
When you have finished, put the roof back on.
You have created your very own little bit
of heaven on earth to dwell in!

Affirmations:

My home is filled with love and light!

I am grateful for the home I live in!

I respect and honour what God has given me!

Faith

Faith in God and the divine principle within you
is the "fast track ticket to your liberation.
When you are "aboard the faith train", you will go full steam
ahead to your divinely planned destination.
All you need is to keep your trust and faith
in God and enjoy the ride!

Meditation:

See yourself walking into a huge railway station,
built of gleaming white marble.
All the personnel you see are angels hard at work.
You ask one of the station master angels where your train will be
departing from and the angel asks you to produce your ticket.
To your surprise you find printed on it the following:
…(Your Name) riding on Faith Train number 1,
Destination: Self-realisation.
The angel points you in the right direction!
You board the train, having allowed God
"to lay down the tracks" for your journey into the light!
Please ground, attune and protect yourself.

Affirmations:

I have complete faith in the divine plan God has mapped out for me!

My faith in God and the divine qualities within me increase
from moment to moment!

All I cannot manage myself I hand over to God in full faith!

The link

You are linked with the whole of creation
and the whole cosmos is linked with you in return!
You and the cosmos are a living, breathing entity,
forever growing, forever expanding, forever changing forms.
Every single thought you think affects the whole.
Every word you speak reverberates through the entire universe
and every one of your deeds affects the cosmos at large.
Such is the power and influence of your being!

Meditation:

First contemplate such a level of interconnection.
Then think a loving thought and imagine the effect
it has on the whole of creation.
Now speak a loving word or sentence out loud
and imagine the effect that will have on the universe.
Then see yourself doing a good deed and watch the effect of that
unfolding and affecting the entire cosmos in a positive way!

Affirmations:

My body, mind and spirit are intrinsically linked with all creation!

My every thought, word and deed has a profound
effect on the entire universe!

I use my thoughts, words and deeds in a way
that is positive and loving!

June 22

Tough love

You are aware of the notion of "tough love", but you are not
always quite sure what it means and how to administer it.
When you are acting from your own truth and integrity with
unconditional love, at times, you have to do and say things that those
you love do not necessarily want to hear or experience.
However, you know in your heart that by sticking
to your truth you are assisting your loved ones to see,
feel and experience these truths themselves.
You are acting as a true catalyst for change for the others.
Such behaviour needs the courage of conviction on your behalf.
Waver not from the divine truth;
you are doing your loved ones a marvellous service!

Meditation:

Think of a situation where you administered soft love
and acted against your inner truth and against what
your intuition was trying to tell you.
What was the outcome of that situation?
Now imagine the same situation again,
this time you administer "tough love".
Imagine the scene developing past the initial
reaction of the other person.
How has your new approach affected the outcome of the situation?
Ask God and the angels to give you the strength, courage and
conviction to stay in your truth and love unconditionally!

Affirmations:

I love truly and unconditionally!

I am standing firm in my own truth!

I have the courage to act from the point of my own truth!

Divine nature

What divine magic nature is!
How many treasures can be found in it!
Trillions of blades of grass gently swaying in the wind,
blooms in myriad colours turning their heads toward
the sun in the sky, birds filling the air with their song
and the oceans lapping gently on to the shores… and walking
amidst these wonders of nature is the greatest miracle of all —YOU!
Accept your rightful place in creation.
Accept it graciously and make the very best of your divine heritage!

Meditation:

You are walking through a magical forest and find that you
are able to communicate with all of creation.
To your amazement you have been given the gift to speak to the
animals, the fairies and the tree spirits of the forest.

Explore and enjoy your magical encounter!

Affirmations:

I attune myself to the divine magic of nature!

I accept, honour and respect my divine heritage!

I live my life in harmony with nature!

The universe guides you

Who are you?
You are the universe and the universe is within you!
The oceans, the mountains, the stars and the galaxies
are all contained within your very being!
You and creation are ONE!
You and your creator are ONE!

Meditation:

Contemplate on the thought that no matter where you are,
you are always at the centre of the universe.
You ARE the centre!
Now, in your meditation, BECOME that centre,
feel it expanding within you!
With every breath you take, the universe within you begins to grow.
It becomes larger and larger, expanding, stretching and growing
breath by breath until it becomes all encompassing
and you can feel the separation between the inner you and
the outer universe disappearing.
You and the universe have become one!
This feeling will probably last only a short while to begin with;
then you will have to bring the energy back in again by centring
yourself in your heart and making sure that you
are properly grounded via your golden roots.
Practise until it becomes a reality for you!
Do not forget to ground, attune and protect yourself.

Affirmations:

I am the universe and the universe is within me!

I am one with creation!

I am one with my creator!

Love, the universal super-glue

What is it that holds the universe together? LOVE!
Love is the "universal super-glue" bonding all
together into a harmonious whole.
You may not be aware of this fact, as on the surface you
are witnessing great unrest and injustice.
This is only a passing phase, a working out
of world karma according to the laws of the Creator.
Once you become aware and start to look for
the universal super-glue of love you will observe
it's working in all that you see and experience!

Meditation:

Contemplate on the "bonding effects" of your love.
Is your love given unconditionally?
Where can you see its effects clearly?
In which areas of your life could you apply the universal
super-glue of love in a much more liberal dosage?

Affirmations:

The universe is created from love and held together by love!

I perceive the powers of love all around me!

As a co-creator with God, I apply my own unique brand of
universal super-glue liberally!

Self-criticism

How often you criticise and despise yourself,
making your own life and often the lives of other, a misery.
Do you realise why, my dear one, you do such
a destructive thing to yourself?
Stop now and think where this self-criticism is really coming from!
You will find that the origin of this destructive voice
within you stems from an outside agency!
The source of it may be a critical parent,
teacher, friend or boss at work.
Now decide for yourself that none of these voices
will hold any power over you any more.
Do the best you can and honour, love and respect yourself for that!

Meditation:

Imagine that your mind is a large radio and that the
different thoughts you have are to be found on various stations.
You are in charge of the control buttons on this radio.
Now allow a thought to "come in".
If the thought is a critical one, you just turn the dials down
and slowly fade out the negative thought until it has completely gone.
Never fight a negative thought or argue with it,
as what you resist persists!
When a positive, loving thought comes in, turn the volume up until it fills
your entire being with its positive energy!
Remember, you are in control of your mind!

Affirmations:

I release all the critical voices in my head!

I treat myself with unconditional positive self-regard!

I love myself unconditionally!

Energy medicine

How seriously do you take yourself?
How important are you and all that you do?
Is your little self playing tricks on you?
Quite likely so, my dear one, for the lower ego your little self
needs to be taken seriously in order to survive.
It will try to convince you of its importance in every possible way.
Do not fall for this trickery.
Do not allow the lower ego to take a stranglehold on you.
Laugh off those futile attempts to lure you from
your path to self-realization.
Apply a hefty, liberal dose of energy medicine,
namely humour there and then!

Meditation:

You have homework!
Your homework is to watch at least one funny movie a week
or read at least 20 pages of a funny book.
Also look for possible moments of comedy in your daily life.

Use humour as a transformational tool!

Affirmations:

I am taking myself "lightly"!

I acknowledge that humour is a transformational tool!

I treat my lower ego self with large doses of humour!

The power of the sun

You are a being of light nourished by the loving
rays of the sun – the sun, which gives its energy
so selflessly to you and the entire planet!
Day after day it appears in the sky warming and nurturing you,
allowing your crops to grow and your hearts to sing.

When the sun rises next, give thanks for this miracle,
for without it, life on this planet would not be possible!

Meditation:

Plan to get up early for sunrise.
As the sun is rising thank her and the solar angels for their
service to Mother Earth, the kingdoms of nature and all humanity.
Allow the first rays of the sun to penetrate your heart and soul
and deeply honour God for the gift He is giving you.

Enjoy a sunny day!

Affirmations:

I honour the sun and the solar angels for their service to me!

I allow the rays of the sun to feed my heart and soul!

Sunlight is soul food to me!

24-hour meditation

The way you live your life is your meditation my beloved!
To sit in meditation for some time and then to get up and behave with a
lack of love, kindness, consideration and integrity is not enough!
To preach and teach and not follow what you
yourself teach is also not enough!
What would be "enough: is for you to be your true, authentic self,
your divine self, which at all times, acts from a core of selfless love.
Consider the effort it takes you to keep up
the pretences of the false you!
Once you allow all of those artificial behaviours to drop away,
your true nature will soon reveal itself in all its divine glory
and the 24-hour mediation has begun!

Meditation:

See yourself dressed in many layers of clothing.
Every item of clothing represents a negative trait or behaviour.
Now ask the healing angels to help you take these old clothes off.
One by one the old negative patterns are being peeled away.
Some of the garments fit very tightly and have tiny buttons to undo, but
with the help of the healing angels you are feeling lighter
and less burdened with every piece of clothing you remove.
The angels make a pile of the clothes and then set fire to them.
You watch the flames of purification burning away leaving
nothing behind, and even the ashes are transmuted into light.
When you are finally in your "birthday suit", the angels
lead you to a sacred lake and you take a bath.
When you come out the angels dress you in beautiful, new robes.
You are starting your life anew, reborn,
ready for your 24-hour meditation!
Please ground, attune and protect yourself.

Affirmations:

My life is a 24-hour meditation!
I see all of life as sacred!
I pour love and light into all I think, say and do!

June 30

Enchantment

Allow yourself to be enchanted by God's creation!
Become like a small child, open to behold
the wonders of this universe!
This universe has so much to offer you, if you would only
be prepared to look at it with an open heart!

Meditation:

See yourself walking in an enchanted garden.
Walk up to a flower in full bloom.
What do you see?
What do you feel beholding this miracle of God's creation?
As you open your heart a true sense of oneness
and wonderment starts to spread through your physical
and emotional body and your mind and spirit start to expand…

Thank God for the gifts of nature and allow yourself
to be enchanted in your day-to-day life!
Do not forget to ground, attune and protect yourself.

Affirmations:

I allow myself to be enchanted by God's offerings to me!

I am open to the enchanting gifts of nature!

I make time to enjoy the enchanting moments life presents to me!

Blessing for the month of

July

Guidance on your path

When the student is ready
the master appears!
Take hold of your master's hand
and allow Him to show you the way…
May you be guided to fulfil your highest potential!
May you be guided to fulfil your fondest dreams!
May you be guided to attain your ultimate goal!

Remember that every stone on your path,
in truth, is a blessing in disguise!

Denial

Why live in denial of your true nature, my beloved?
Why have you decided that you are an unworthy sinner?
Why have you decided that you are not good enough
to enjoy a happy, fulfilled life?
Why carry on denying yourself your divine heritage?
There is no reason on earth or in heaven to carry on
this pattern of denial!
Such a notion is certainly not in the divine plan
that God has devised for you.
What is written in the plan is your definite destiny to become
like God and ultimately to be God in all his splendour.
Leave all denial behind, let your little self step aside
and allow the divine plan to manifest itself!

Meditation:

Think about the origins of these beliefs that deny you divinity.
Where do they really stem from?
You will discover different sources and will find out that
none of them stem from your true self!
Hand all your negative, old, outmoded beliefs over to God
and ask the healing angels to assist you with this process.
This may take time and definitely lots of effort on your behalf.
When you are free of the beliefs that had been projected on to you,
you will be able to choose your own route to God.

Affirmations:

I let go of old patterns of denial!

I graciously accept my divine heritage!

I rejoice in God's divine plan for me!

God is the director

Why not accept God as the "director" of your life!
Why try to do it all yourself?
How fed up you truly are with doing it all yourself, my child!
It is a heavy burden to bear.
"I have to do this", "I have to achieve that", "it must be like this",
"the outcome of the situation has to be exactly like that"
...and so on and so forth.
This is how you conduct your life most of the time.
How do you know what is truly best for you
and your loved ones, indeed, for the whole planet?
Are you able to see the bigger picture?
No, my dearest one, you are not! Far from it.
God is the director, not only because He sees the bigger picture,
but also because He, in His unlimited,
unwavering love for you, has created it!
Accept this truth and your earthly burdens will fall away!

Meditation:

Next time you listen to a live concert,
observe the orchestra conductor closely.
You will notice that the musicians look and concentrate
on both their sheet music and the conductor!

Affirmations:

I hand my burdens over to God!

I let God direct my life!

I enjoy playing my part in the symphony of life!

Transmute your anger

The emotion of anger is one of the most destructive energies.
Do not allow it to destroy your life or the lives of others.
Learn swiftly to transmute it into a driving force for good!

Meditation:

You need to "own" your anger first, as in essence
you are always angry with yourself,
although others may have served as catalysts for your anger.
Then forgive yourself or anyone else connected
with the source of your anger.
Use the remaining anger-energy, just like petrol fuelling an engine,
to be creative in any way you like.

Good ways to utilise and transmute anger-energy are
cleaning your house, washing your clothes or your car,
or doing the ironing, thereby channelling
the energy into something useful!
It will take some practice to master the art of energy transformation.

Affirmations:

I own my anger and do not project it onto others!

I transmute my anger into positive creative energy!

I am in charge of my emotions at all times!

You are special

You are truly special! A special, unique child of God!
To own this truth is not,
as society would like to make you believe, egotistical!
To play your part in the big jigsaw puzzle of creation,
you need to be special.
God needs you to bring your unique qualities and talents
to the game of life and to express and manifest them
to the best of your abilities.
By believing in your special talents and turning them into reality,
you will have fulfilled your divine potential!

Meditation:

Make a list of the things you enjoy doing.
Now highlight those you feel you are naturally good at.
From this narrowed-down selection,
highlight those activities that bring you most joy.
Whatever brings you most joy and truly makes your "heart sing"
is the contribution God wants you to make toward
the completion of His divine creation!

Affirmations:

I am special and have a lot of good to offer to the world!

I believe in my talents and abilities!

I contribute most to the divine plan by doing what I enjoy most!

Your soul brothers and sisters

What do you share with every being in creation?
You have a soul my beloved.
Therefore every man, woman and child and animal as well
is your soul brother and soul sister.
Even though you never have, and possibly never will,
meet the majority of them on the physical level, that does not mean
that you are not connected on a subtle, soul level!
You are connected!
All souls on this planet are intrinsically linked with one another.
Please heed this universal truth: what you do to or for yourself will
affect all your soul brothers and soul sisters on this planet!
And what you do for another, in turn, will have an effect on you!

Meditation:

Contemplate this and be mindful of the truth contained in the message.
Practise the art of harmlessness towards
yourself and all sentient beings!

Affirmations:

I acknowledge my kinship with humankind!
My soul brothers, soul sisters and I are one!
I live my life practising the art of harmlessness!

Empowerment

You are strong and powerful, capable of mighty feats,
if only you would accept this fact and reclaim this God-given
power you have given away so freely through many lifetimes.
Self-empowerment is a crucial step in your spiritual
and personal development.
God has credited you with just the right amount
of power for you to handle.
Use it for the purpose of your self-development
and for good deeds to others.
Trust in this power and move forward confidently on your path!

Meditation:

Affirm to yourself that everything is in "divine order";
this means that if you are in alignment and attuned
with the divine mind and will of God, you are not even capable
of misusing the power that God has given you.

Follow your heart and you will use your power wisely,
purposefully and for the good of all!

Affirmations:

I step into my God-given power!

I allow myself to be a powerful being!

I use my power with love, for love!

July 7

Spiritual growth

You are growing spiritually day by day, hour by hour, minute by minute.
With every sacred breath you take, you are getting closer to the divine.
Soon, when your spiritual growth culminates into full spiritual maturity,
you will be able to realise the illusion of separation.
Then you will know in your spirit, body, mind and soul that
you and God are ONE!

Meditation:

Imagine that you are an angel and that God has just issued
you with your wings.
How does it feel to have gotten your wings?
Stretch them and feel yourself growing lighter and lighter.
Stretch them again and feel your consciousness expanding.
Now stretch them one more time.
Your spirit is soaring and you are taking flight!
Higher and higher you go, flying high into the sky
… right into the arms of your creator, Father/Mother God!
Come back down to earth gently and thank God
for your wings, you have earned them!
Do not forget to ground, attune and protect yourself.

Affirmations:

I am growing spiritually all the time!

God assures my divine destiny!

I am one with God and all creation!

Take responsibility for your actions

Nobody but you is responsible for your own actions!
Yet how hard you fight to blame the consequences of your actions
on other people or circumstances!

The time has come to stand in your own truth
and integrity and take full responsibility for who you are,
what you are and how you conduct your life.
Before you think a thought, utter a word
or perform a deed, you always have a choice.
What will your choice be?

Meditation:

Firmly decide to endeavour to become fully aware
of what is going on before you act or react to a situation.
Do not allow conditioned emotional
and mental responses to run your life anymore.
If you slip up forgive yourself, move on
and carry on doing the best you can!

Be gentle with yourself!

Affirmations:

I take full responsibly for my own actions!

I have a choice as to how I act and react to life's challenges!

My own conscience is guiding me every step of the way!

July 9

Spiritual being, human experience

You are, in truth, a spiritual being having a human experience,
not a human being having a spiritual experience!
There is an enormous difference between the two!
Your body, the temple of your soul, is a transient affair
… ashes to ashes… until you "rise again"!
Your spirit, however, is indestructible, eternal and limitless.
Your spirit is the constant in the ever-changing
worlds of birth and rebirth!
You are in essence pure spirit and pure spirit is your essence!
That, and nothing less than that, is the divine truth!

Meditation:

Meditate on your divine essence.
Ask God and the angels to help you connect
even more strongly with your true self.
Now see yourself stepping in front of a large, full-length mirror.
To your surprise you find
the reflection of a being of light looking back at you.
The features are yours, but you are radiating
brilliant light out of every pore of your being.
Your eyes shine bright with unconditional love
and your smile radiates gentle kindness.
Now ask your spirit/divine self to join you in the here and now,
at which point your spirit self steps out of
the mirror and merges with you.
Thank God and the angels for their assistance!
Please ground, attune and protect yourself.

Affirmations:

I am a spiritual being having a human experience!

My spirit is eternal and indestructible!

Nothing and nobody can ever harm me!

Divine order

What you perceive as a chaotic world is, behind the screen
of illusions, a world of perfect harmony and divine order.
Each event unfolds according to the divine plan, in perfect timing.
The magnitude of this plan and the divine order behind it, are so great
that the human mind finds it very difficult to comprehend.
Start to look for the signs the universe is trying to show you
and you will soon see how the cogs in the wheel
fit together and work in perfect harmony!

Look for the good in everything and all the good
in the world will be drawn to you!

Meditation:

Take the following into contemplation:
The sun rises every morning…
The moon shines every night…
Every day and night the earth's gravity helps you
to stay safe on the ground…
You have air to breathe…
You will find that when you allow life to develop,
all will work out fine and that when you try to force the issue
it does not work out at all!

Affirmations:

I let go and let God!

My life is in divine order!

I flow with life!

Celebrate life

Life is a celebration!
Celebrate the fact that you have awakened this morning,
having been given the opportunity to make a difference,
to brighten up somebody's day!
It may be in a small way, a smile, a helping hand
or a supportive chat with a friend.
How privileged you are to be able to offer yourself
in so many ways to the world!

Meditation:

Put on your favourite piece of celebratory music.
Now see yourself surrounded by beautiful rose-pink light.
Breathe this light of self-love into all your chakras.
Allow it to fill the seven layers of your auric field.
When you are ready, ask your guardian angels to join you
in dancing to your music!
While you dance allow all the worldly burdens
to melt away through your feet and to drain into the earth.
Give thanks to Mother Earth.
Allow the music to soothe, comfort and uplift you.
Dance, dance, dance!
Celebrate your life, all that you have, and most importantly,
all that you are and have to give!
Thank your guardian angels for joining in the fun and repeat often!
Do not forget to ground, attune and protect yourself.

Affirmations:

I celebrate being alive!

I celebrate the gifts God has bestowed onto me!

My life is a celebration of love!

Mind over matter

Your mind, my dear one, creates your reality!
The world you see, feel and experience
is truly a figment of your imagination!
What you need to do so urgently is to make up your mind
about what you would wish to experience,
as whatever you focus your attention on becomes your experience.
Mind reigns supreme over matter!
Heed this truth and train your mind
to dwell on love and light and all will be well!

Meditation:

Make a list of your negative expectations.
Be aware that most of these negative expectations have been
projected on you by family, friends and society at large.
Go through this list one by one in order to find
the root of each negative expectation.
Release it and let go of it.
Forgive yourself and others for the part that was played.
Now replace each item on the list with a positive counterpart.
Finally decide firmly in your mind that a
positive outcome is assured and hand it all over to God!

In times of doubt repeat this process.
Success will be yours!

Affirmations:

I let go of all negative expectations!

I am in control of my mind!

My mind creates my reality!

Hidden treasures within

You are a treasure trove!
You might not be aware of it, but untold treasures
are buried deep within your very self!
Trust and believe in your divine heritage,
the all-knowing, all-providing God within!
Why not open the lid to the box of your treasures
and allow the world to partake of the gifts you have to offer it?

Meditation:

Take a deep breath of golden light
and centre your awareness in your heart chakra.
Instantly you find yourself in a rose quartz crystal cave,
lit brightly with hundreds of pink, scented candles.
In the middle of the cave you find a large,
ornately carved, golden chest.
Walk up to it and open the lid.
You are delighted at the treasures you find
and are looking forward to sharing your abundance with others!
Bring your awareness back to the physical realms,
taking all your treasures with you into the here and now!

Do not forget to ground, attune and protect yourself.

Affirmations:

I have lots to offer to the world!

I am rich in many ways!

I am privileged to share my spiritual, mental, emotional
and physical wealth with others!

Your home, your sacred space

Your home is your haven!
A place to rest, recharge and recuperate!
Are you able to achieve all of this?
If not, you might want to create a sacred space
within your home to do so.
If a spare room is not available, a small corner will be sufficient.
Clean and decorate this space with pictures of angels
or your favourite deities, and with crystals and fresh flowers.
Light a candle and, maybe, some of your favourite incense and spend
time there in meditation, contemplation or simply resting and relaxing.
Create and enjoy your very own sacred space!

Meditation:

Once you have chosen and decorated your sacred space,
perform a small blessing ceremony.
First open any windows, light a candle
and ask the angel of your dwelling to come forward.
Also ask your guardian angel, the healing angels and any other
light beings of your choice to join you in blessing this sacred space.
Ask for it to be dedicated to… (for instance: the light,
relaxation, mediation, inspiration or healing)
After you have done that, confirm it to be so by
saying out loud three times, "And so be it".
Give thanks to all the beings of light who assisted you, with a special
thank you to the angel of your dwelling, who will help you to maintain
a high level of energy in your sacred space from now on.
Keep the energy in your sacred space clean by purifying it on a daily
basis. You may do this by opening the window, lighting some incense
and ringing a bell, to dispel any negative energy hanging about.
Enjoy your corner of heaven on earth!

Affirmations:

My home is my haven!
I now create a sacred space to further my well-being!
My sacred space provides healing and rejuvenation in my own home!

July 15

Support from the universe

You live in an abundant universe that supports
whatever you choose to do or be!
Choose love and light and all things good
and the universe will bring it to you in great abundance.
If you choose hate, fear and darkness,
the universe will bring all that to you in abundance as well,
for it has no choice but to serve you unconditionally.

Like will attract like, this is the cosmic law!

Meditation:

You are at the centre of the universe...

Now reach deep into your heart
and allow feelings of love to radiate from your soul.
With every sacred breath you take those beautiful feelings intensify.
Each and every one of them acts as a magnet
attracting love and light to itself.
Feel the light from the universe coming back at you a thousandfold!
Rejoice!
Make sure that you are grounded, attuned and protected.

Affirmations:

I am a love magnet!

The universe supports me in all my endeavours!

I acknowledge the cosmic law that "like attracts like" and act
accordingly!

Courage

Have courage, my dearest one!
Courage to live the life you are dreaming of!
Have the courage of your convictions!
If they come from a pure heart you have nothing to fear!
Your love will override all obstacles on your path!

Meditation:

You do have the courage and love needed
to overcome even your biggest fears.
Be brave and find out what they are.
Acknowledge those fears, but at the same time decide
not to let them have a hold over you any more.
Decide that you have the courage to deal with those fears
and to heal and release them for once and for all!
God, the angels, the whole universe are there, eager to assist you!
Ask for their help in this matter.
Write a list of your worst fears.
Now, picture your fears one by one appearing on a television screen.
You are holding the remote control.
First see them in full colour; then turn the images into black and white.
Finally fade the picture until it disappears completely from the screen.
A note will flash up saying: Fear #1 released!
Carry on through your list, a process that you will have
to repeat at least three times with each item.
Thank God and the angels for their help.
Please ground, attune and protect yourself.

Affirmations:

I have the courage to free myself of all my fears!

I am now ready to live the life I am dreaming of!

I am able to live a life full of love and happiness!

July 17

Keeping good company

To keep good company is of utmost importance to your spiritual
and, indeed, also to your personal, development!
Choose to spend time in the company of those
who support, nurture, inspire and uplift you!
Seek the company of the wise and the loving amongst
your brothers and sisters on this planet.
Your combined light will shine bright on the spiritual horizons!

Meditation:

Think about the people you keep company with;
your family, friends, acquaintances and work colleagues.
Are there any "bad apples" amongst them?
If so, see these individuals or groups of people less often.
At times it may be wiser to cut the ties completely.

The choice is yours!

Affirmations:

I now release and cut the ties I have with people
I do not resonate with anymore!

I choose to spend my time in good company!

The company of loving, like-minded people uplifts me!

The human mind

The human mind is a powerful instrument!
Unfortunately, most of the time, you are not in control of yours!
Instead, your mind is in control of you!
Like a wild horse it gallops here and gallops there,
pulling you along with it!
For you to succeed in your life's purpose,
you must learn to become the ruler of your mind!
Once that has been achieved your mind will be
a wonderful miracle tool working tirelessly for you
on your journey of self-discovery and eventual self-illumination!

Meditation:

Set time aside in order to be able to observe
your thoughts and your thought patterns.
A good time to do this is while doing mundane activities
like washing up, driving or gardening.
Just become the observer of your thoughts
and you will spot the persistence, negative, destructive ones easily.
Now when one of these negative thoughts "comes in",
surround and seal it up with a golden bubble,
just like the speech bubbles you find in cartoons.
Then see this golden bubble floating out of
your brain, heading into the sky.
Watch it floating farther and farther away until it bursts
and disappears back to source, where it is transmuted into positive
energy, which will be returned to you in the shape of love and light.
To gain full control over your mind, you need to persist
with this exercise for quite some time!
Good luck and please have patience with yourself!

Affirmations:

I now release and let go of all negative, destructive thought forms!

I am in control of my mind!

My mind is a wonderful tool and I use it wisely!

Answered prayers

God answers all your prayers!

At times you might not be aware of this fact,
as you are not able to see tangible results in the here and now.
Only God has the bigger picture and what you
have asked for may do more harm than good for yourself
and your loved ones at this moment in time.
Have faith, trust and patience and ensure that
what you are praying for has unconditional love at its source of intent!

Meditation:

Contemplate the nature and essence of prayer.
Do you pray to make yourself feel better?
Do you pray to be relieved or spared from
a certain outcome of a situation?
Do you pray because you live in fear?
If so, first pray for help to overcome all the above yourself.
Only then will you be ready to pray for the highest good for yourself,
other people or the outcomes of situations.
You will be able to pray from the point of
unconditional love within yourself, leaving the outcome to God!

Affirmations:

My prayers are always heard!

I offer my prayers from a sincere heart!

I pray for the highest good with all my heart!

Be ready for miracles

Do you believe in miracles?
If not, make sure that you are not blocking
any miracles from happening!
Be ready for a miracle any time
and open your heart and mind for them to manifest!
Be childlike in your approach and expect the best for you
and your loved ones, right here, right now!

Meditation:

What are the miracles you hope for in your life?
Make a list of them.
Now go through this list and imagine one by one
that every single miracle has already occurred.
Make these scenarios as lifelike as possible,
watching yourself being in those situations.
Repeat until you truly feel that these miracles are happening!
Then hand your wish list over to God, sit back,
relax and wait for the miracles to manifest!

Be grateful for what you are about to receive!

Affirmations:

I am ready for a miracle!

I accept all the good God wants to give me!

I am open to receiving the abundant gifts
the universe has in store for me!

Self-care

Self-care is important, it is neither selfish
nor a waste of time and money, my beloved!
If you do not take care of yourself, how do you expect
to take care of anyone else properly?
You can only give to others what you have learned to give to yourself.
Also, you can only give what you actually have to give.
Otherwise you will incur an energy-deficit and will "run on empty".
So fill your cup first, make yourself strong, healthy and resilient;
then you will be fit to give to others freely!

Meditation:

Imagine yourself to be a vessel
(such as a measuring cup used to measure flour or sugar).
How full is your cup?
Have a good look at the energy levels in your seven chakras.
Start at the base chakra and work your way up to the crown chakra.
Take down the readings and note them dated in your spiritual journal.
Make sure to replenish your energy levels
through enough sleep, a healthy diet of fresh fruits
and vegetables, exercise, fresh air, plenty of rest,
relaxation and lots of fun!

Affirmations:

I am aware that I cannot give more than I have to give!

I make the time to recharge my batteries!

I take good care of myself!

Completions

Always endeavour to complete your tasks and projects before
moving on to newer, greener, maybe more interesting pastures!
Make sure, that you tie up all loose ends, otherwise unfinished tasks
will follow you around, forever pulling you back into the past.
Truly wipe the slate clean complete what there is to complete
and you will be free for new challenges and adventures!

A bright future awaits you!

Meditations:

Think of any unfinished business you may have.
What can you do to remedy the situation?
Do the best you can on a physical, emotional,
mental and spiritual level to clear it up!
If the unfinished business involves people who are
no longer with you, who either have left or are deceased,
then you are still able to do the clearing on the higher levels,
namely the spiritual, emotional and mind levels.
Forgive yourself and ask for forgiveness (you may not be able
to do this in person, just ask from your heart, that will be sufficient)
from anyone else involved; release the old situation and let go.
Complete, slowly, step by step, all there is to complete in your life.
This opens the doorway to your liberation.
You are truly free!

Affirmations:

I complete with the old before I move on to the new!

I am now clearing up all past unfinished business!

I move forward in life without restrictions!

July 23

Tolerance

Tolerance is a virtue every true seeker must develop.
First you must learn to tolerate your own shortcomings!
Embrace yourself just as you are in the knowledge
that you are being and doing the best you can!
The same, of course, is true for the rest of humanity, no matter
how bad the deeds and behaviours of your fellow men appear to be!
Please believe that if humanity could do better or be different, it would!

Meditation:

What is it you "can't stand" about yourself?
Identify this part of yourself and practise tolerance, forgiveness
and kindness towards yourself, in order for it to heal.
Continue with this process until you feel that you are
embracing yourself from top to toe, in other words all of you
in body, mind, emotions and spirit!

Upon completion of this process you will be able to practise true
tolerance towards your brothers and sisters on this earth.
Congratulate yourself for your earnest perseverance in the matter!

Affirmations:

I practise tolerance towards others and myself!

I embrace my own shortcomings!

I allow others to experience their lives, the way they choose!

Transient pleasures

The outward pleasures of life are transient!
Do not chase after them my beloved,
for this kind of behaviour will leave you longing for more and more...
You will never be truly fulfilled by any of it!

What will satisfy you are inner peace and harmony, two pearls
residing within your soul, which once achieved, are everlasting!

Meditation:

To which outward pleasures are you addicted?
Whatever they are, these addictions are filling an emotional void!
Make an effort to fill this void through connecting
with your higher self, which is an unlimited source of energy.
Channel in the golden healing light through your crown chakra
to heal your old emotional wounds; then your addictions
and your need to hunt for transient pleasures will disappear.

Affirmations:

I release the need for transient pleasures!

I am connected, via my higher self, to a storehouse of unlimited energy!

I have peace and harmony in my heart!

Sacred breath

Your breath is your sacred core energy!
From the moment you are born your breath gives you
life and thereafter sustains it!
Therefore be mindful of this most precious of all energies!
Use it wisely and learn to breathe correctly.
Breathe slowly and you will live longer, thus being able to learn
and experience what you have come here on this earth plane for.
Spend as much time as possible outdoors in the fresh air
and do not waste your energy in any way.
Honour God for the gift of your sacred breath, the gift of life!

Meditation:

Sit in a comfortable, upright position and be mindful of your breathing.
Relax into the rhythm of it.
Inhale…exhale…inhale…exhale…allowing
three counts in between breaths.
Observe how, even through this very simple breathing exercise,
you start to unwind…your jaws relax…
then your neck muscles…next your shoulders drop…
and so on through your whole body.
Continue for as long as it feels comfortable to do so.
You will have achieved a wonderful, peaceful,
relaxed state by the end of the exercise.

Repeat often!

Affirmations:

My breath is a sacred instrument!

I am aware of my breathing at all times!

With every breath I take, I breathe in love and light!

One-pointed-ness

Practise "one-pointed-ness" my dear one!
Direct all your energy to the one!
The one, which is within you and all around you.
Refuse to waver from your focus!
Do not allow yourself to be led into temptations away from the one!
All the power of heaven and earth is concentrated within you,
ready to be put to good use.
Do not let it go to waste!

Meditation:

Imagine a point of very bright light, like the light of a star.
Concentrate on this light with your heart and mind.
The more you open yourself up and concentrate,
the more light and love flows from it, towards you.
Now see this light coming closer and closer until it enters
your crown chakra and slowly moves down into your heart.
With every breath you take you can feel the energy
of love and light expanding in your heart.
Carry on breathing in the light until you feel one with it
and you have the feeling that you have become the light.
Give thanks and repeat frequently.
Please ground, attune and protect yourself.

Affirmations:

My attention is focused on the one at all times!

I am the one and the one is within me!

I am the light and the light is within me!

July 27

Inner view

Look into your heart my beloved!
What can you see?
What is your "inner view"?
Do you see love and kindness, compassion and understanding?
Or is there room for improvement?
If there is, make a supreme effort to do so, for you will feel
so much better and will uplift all around you with your loving heart!

Meditation:

Take a journey into your heart.
As you arrive a landscape unfolds before you...
What is the inner view of your heart?
Can you see gentle rolling hills, verdant pastures and tranquil lakes?
Or are there ragged mountains and stormy seas to be found?
Use your creative, divine imagination and change the scene
until it feels peaceful, serene, calm and uplifting!

Do not forget to ground, attune and protect yourself.

Affirmations:

I am the caretaker of my own heart!

I have the power to implement positive changes in my life!

My inner view is one of peace, love and tranquillity!

Divine inspiration

Allow yourself to be divinely inspired in all things!
No matter is too big or too small, for God wishes
to express Himself through you throughout your whole life,
not just through selected parts of it!
Go forth and listen faithfully to your intuition, your phone-line to God,
who is identical with your very own higher self.

Do not be afraid to act upon and carry out
your brilliant ideas and concepts!
You are truly divinely inspired at all times!

Meditation:

See yourself sitting outside watching the night sky.
Millions of stars are twinkling in the deep-blue expanse like diamonds.
Each of them represents a divine inspiration.
You become aware that you have the ability to "pick" a star for yourself.
Think about something you would like to know
or do and then "pick your star".
As you are holding this star, which lies in your hand
like a huge, sparkling diamond, you feel its energy
entering your third eye as a brilliant idea!
Thank the heavens for this gift of inspiration!
Remember to ground, attune and protect yourself.

Affirmations:

My intuition is my phone-line to God/my higher self!

I trust in my inspirations!

I am divinely inspired at all times!

Step by step

Achieve your goals step by step, slowly and steadily!
Do not let the big picture overwhelm you, for as soon as
you allow your awareness to be drawn away
from the here and now, fears and uncertainties
will be creeping into your life!
Put one foot in front of the other, forever being mindful
of what is on your path and you will succeed!

Meditation:

Think of a goal you wish to achieve, one you are working on right now.
See yourself having actually achieved it
and make it as real as possible.
Create the sounds, the sights and all
the sensations that go with it, vividly.
What can you see, feel and hear, having achieved that goal?
Bask in this energy of success for a while,
then let go and hand the matter over to God!
Now, all you need to concentrate on is the moment,
the rest is all taken care of.

Give thanks!

Affirmations:

I achieve my goals moment by moment, step by step!

I stay firmly centred in the here and now!

I allow God to take care of the bigger picture!

Search for the divine in everything

Search for the divine in everything,
for the divine is to be found in the whole of creation!
From tiny microbes to mighty humans, from tadpoles to elephants,
grains of sand to mountains, blades of grass to the huge oak,
from the raindrop to the oceans and the trillions of stars
in the night sky, the divine is embodied in all of it!
Once you point your loving attention this way,
the divine will reveal itself to you in all you see and experience!

Meditation:

When you next go for a walk, pick up a stone from the ground.
Sit somewhere comfortable and lovingly hold
the stone in your open hand.
Gaze lovingly at it …
What can you see?
Now close your hand.
What can you feel?
Give yourself time, and after a while you will find that the stone
feels warm in your hand and begins to pulsate within your palm.
Now look at the stone in the palm of your hand…
Note how different it looks to you now!
Note how different you feel about this stone!
It has become like a friend…
The divine within has revealed itself to you!

Affirmations:

I am open to perceive the divine in everything and everybody!

I search for the divine in everything and everybody!

The divine is embodied in the whole of creation!

Beyond the mind

Beyond the mind lies paradise!
A space free of conditioned mental constructs!
The dwelling place of pure spirit, pure love and pure light!
To be able to reach this realm you must "lose your head",
be out of your mind and think with your heart!

Meditation:

Make sure that you are undisturbed for at least half an hour.
Sit comfortably in an upright position.
Focus your mind and let all negative, disruptive thoughts drain away.
Now, dream up your own vision of a spiritual paradise
and make it truly life-like.
With your vision of paradise complete, allow your awareness
to travel into your heart chakra and start to feel this vision,
every little detail and nuance of it!
Carry on until you have an inner knowing that not only ARE you
in paradise, but that you have BECOME paradise!
Enjoy!

Please ground, attune and protect yourself.

Affirmations:

I move beyond the limited constructs of my conditioned mind!

The realms of spirit are always within my reach!

I carry the heavenly paradise in my heart

Blessing for the month of

August

Enjoyment

You are a child of God!
The universe is your home to enjoy!
May you enjoy music, song and dance!
May you enjoy friendship and love!
May you enjoy the treasures of nature,
the sun and the moon and the stars at night.

How blessed you are to be part
of the miracle of creation!

Understanding

Love and understanding go hand in hand, like brother and sister!
One does not exist very happily without the other!
In order to have compassion for the plight of others
you must first learn to understand yourself!
Understanding of others does not always come easily!
You might have to work hard for it, getting behind the scenes,
so that for the true personalities and circumstances are revealed,
trying to see a different viewpoint and letting go
of preconceived ideas about a person or situation.
Your efforts are worth your while,
for without true understanding love cannot develop!

Meditation:

Contemplate this:
When you fail to understand a certain word or phrase,
you usually will make an effort and look it up in a dictionary.
Why not use the same principle if you fail
to understand another person or situation?
Your effort is the magical ingredient
for attaining loving relationships!

Affirmations:

I endeavour to know and understand myself!

I make a special effort to understand other people and situations!

I practise love and understanding!

The folly of separation

Separation is an illusion, a folly you have fallen for!
In truth, there cannot be any separation, for you are all one!
You are part of the one heart, the one soul, the one spirit,
the one mind and the one body!
The "trickster" in this game of seeming separation is your mind.
Your mind, identified with your little self, is frightened to give up its false
identity, frightened of "losing itself".
Acknowledge this truth and all illusionary separations
will dissolve and disappear!
Then you will know that you are one!

Meditation:

Put your golden roots down, ground yourself very well and ask
for extra protection, surrounding yourself with golden light.
Imagine that you are dissolving…first your skin melts away….
then your muscles melt away…then your flesh…
then your bones…then your organs…
until all you have left is your spiritual-light body!
All you can now feel is the love in your heart radiating out to the world!
Soon you become aware of all the other hearts in this world radiating
love, some more, some very little, each according to its own capacity
to love at this moment in time! All the hearts on this planet are now
magically attracted to each other, at the same time drawing closer
and closer to you…until you feel a merging taking place.
Then love truly knows no bounds uniting all into one!
Stay with this feeling as long as you like and then become aware of
your organs, your flesh, your bones, your muscles and your skin until
your are back in your physical body in the here and now.
Be sure that you are grounded, attuned and protected.
Keep your golden roots in the ground for a while after this meditation.

Affirmations:

I know in my heart that all separation is an illusion!

I am constantly connected with the whole of creation!

I am one with the cosmos and the cosmos is one with me!

The power of love

Love is the only true power, an awesome force to be reckoned with!
Love is the limitless power that wipes away all tears
and banishes all fears!
Love is the power that unites, renews and heals all ills!
Love is the power that gives for the sake of giving,
expecting nothing in return!
You have the power to love at your fingertips!
Grab it, hold on to it with both hands
and then go out into the world and BE LOVE!

Meditation:

Visualise yourself holding a small rose-quartz heart in your hand.
Now allow all the love you can muster to radiate from your heart
and allow it to flow into the rose-quartz heart.
The more of your love energy the rose quartz absorbs,
the more wonderfully pink it glows.
When you feel that the little crystal heart is charged up to the brim with
your love energy, see yourself giving it to
someone in need of the healing power of love at the moment.
As soon as they take hold of the little crystal heart,
you can see a transformation taking place:
Firstly their eyes light up…
Then a lovely smile begins to form…
They seem to grow taller and look lighter by the second, finally looking
happy and radiant, they thank you profoundly for your gift!
Repeat this process giving a crystal heart of love to anyone in need!
Please ground, attune and protect yourself.

Affirmations:

I believe in the power of love!

The power of love is limitless and knows no bounds!

There is no greater power in heaven or on earth
than the power of love!

Sacred yearning

Do you feel an inner yearning, a longing to belong?
Are you not satisfied anymore with material pursuits
and has your interest in worldly matters somehow faded?
Then the time is right to follow your inner calling
and allow God and the angels to show you different realities.
Go within and allow yourself to travel to the realms of the spirit,
to your true home, from where you have originated
and where you still belong.
All will be revealed to you!

Meditation:

Make sure that you are undisturbed for at least 30 minutes.
Make sure that your golden roots are in deeply.
See yourself and your guardian angel standing
by the entrance to an elevator in a vast skyscraper.
The building is so tall that you are not even able
to make out the top floor, as it is covered by clouds!
Your guardian angel tells you that the skyscraper
reaches all the way up to heaven!
The elevator door opens and you step in.
Your angel presses the button marked heaven
and you go up and up until you reach the top floor.
The door opens and your angel accompanies you
on your first tour of your spiritual home!
Enjoy the heavenly delights…
Then come back down again in the elevator.
Leave your golden roots in the ground for a while
and thank your guardian angel "for the lift"!
Make sure that you are grounded, attuned and protected.

❀

Affirmations:

I listen and follow my inner callings!

My true home lies in the realms of spirit!

I am able to visit my true home whenever I like!

Expand your consciousness

God has endowed you with a consciousness
capable of limitless expansion!
Behind every "knowing", behind every experience
is even newer territory to be found and explored.
As you become consciously aware of one fact,
the next fact is there to be discovered by you!
The eternal spiral of wisdom forever moving closer to the heart of God!
What an exciting adventure your life is!
To be alive and to be able to seek and find God, the eternal truth!

Meditation:

Imagine yourself sitting in meditation at the centre of the earth.
You are properly grounded, your golden roots
firmly anchored into Mother Earth.
With every breath you take, your consciousness expands and grows...
You first become aware of the different layers of the earth...
then all the plant life on the surface of the earth...
then the oceans, rivers and waterways ...animals roaming the earth...
and all the people populating this earth...
Then your consciousness expands beyond the earth out into the
cosmos...to the Milky Way...and as far as the Andromeda galaxy.
When you feel that you would like to return, take a deep breath and
bring your awareness back from Andromeda, to the Milky Way,
and down to earth, back where you started.
When you repeat the exercise next time, add a blessing
for all the levels of consciousness you experience.
Remember to ground, attune and protect yourself.

Affirmations:

I enjoy the adventure of new discoveries!

My spirit is capable of unlimited expansion!

My consciousness is truly unlimited!

God talks through you

God talks through you!
You are acting as His divine messenger here on earth.
Endeavour to carry out this messenger role with honesty and integrity.
Link your heart with your mouth and infuse your speech
with the divine energy of unconditional love!

Meditation:

Take the following into contemplation:
Silence is golden.
May your speech be golden too!
Attempt to make every word you speak
into "a golden nugget" of love, wisdom and encouragement.
Give those "golden nuggets" away without expectations of a return.

Offer them in service from a loving heart!

Affirmations:

I acknowledge that I am one of God's messengers on earth!

I accept my role as a divine messenger graciously!

I speak my truth from a loving heart!

Immortal soul

You are the proud owner of an immortal soul,
my beloved, a soul, which has travelled
through time and dimensions
and has taken many different bodies
on its journey back to its Creator!
Your immortal soul, which starts out not knowing its identity,
returns to the source knowing it is God!

What a miraculous blessing God has bestowed on to you!

Meditation:

Have a conversation with your soul.
You might ask your soul how it is, where it has travelled
and what you still have to learn in this lifetime.
You may also draw on the wisdom of your soul
from past experiences, which will help
and assist you in this lifetime.
Just ask and you will receive!

Affirmations:

I am the owner of an immortal, indestructible soul!

My body, mind and emotions are tools for my soul to experience itself!

Day by day my soul is journeying closer and closer to God!

Look after the children in this world

It is your duty to look after the children in this world,
not just your own, all children.
You must take responsibility for the world you have created,
for the children have no power to defend, or fend for, themselves.
Do all you can to help on a physical level, but most importantly
remember the children of this world in your daily prayers!

Meditation:

Think of and visualise all the suffering children in this world.
Ask the healing angels for help and imagine
that all the children have a roof over their heads,
plenty of food and clean water to drink,
a caring mother and father and a safe
environment in which to grow up.
Make the visualisation as vivid as possible.

Repeat often and thank the healing angels for their assistance.

Affirmations:

I offer daily prayers for the children of this world!

I do the best I can to help all children in need!

I remind myself, that we are all God's children, big or small!

Condemnation

How quick you are at times to condemn your fellow
brothers and sisters for their actions!
Who are you to judge them so harshly?
God does not condemn, judge or criticise!
Why then do you take it upon yourself to do so?
Realise, that in truth what you condemn in others
is a reflection of a trait within yourself!

Forgive yourself and others and be free!

Meditation:

Now that you are aware of this truth, try to catch yourself
in the act or even better before the act, of condemning someone.
Ask yourself what it was which made you react
so harshly and unloving?
Look into yourself and find out!
Then forgive yourself and anyone else involved.
Finally let go of it all.

Affirmations:

I am aware that other people's behaviour is a reflection
of my own behaviour!

My own self is mirrored in the world around me!

I now "polish my own mirror" with unconditional love!

Harmony

Beneath the surface of trouble and strife lies
the energy of supreme harmony, the true state of being!
Do you choose to focus your attention on the surface
or do you wish to look beyond surface realties
to the deeper truth that underlies all realities?
Go in faith and trust that you will break through all
that is unreal and attain the harmony your heart desires!

Meditation:

Imagine that you are an experienced deep-sea diver.
You are going out to sea on a dive-boat.
It is brilliant day, the sky is blue and the sun is shining,
but the wind is high and the sea is rough.
However, you decide that it is still safe to do the dive.
You dive in… and, to your surprise, just beneath
the surface of the water, not a single wave can be felt.
All is still, calm and harmonious.
You swim through the water, observing the fish
and the creatures of the sea all living together in perfect harmony.
Please ground, attune and protect yourself.

Affirmations:

I live in peace and harmony!

I look past surface troubles and discover harmony beneath!

Harmony is my true state of being!

Forgiving your parents

What are your feelings towards your father and mother?
Do you feel love when you think about them or do
unresolved situations bring negative emotions to the surface?
Whether your parents are still with you or in spirit,
or even if you have never known your parents, make sure
to attempt to resolve these feelings in your lifetime.
Remember that your parents did the best they could with the
awareness and the physical resources they had at the time.
Forgive them, let bygones be bygones!
Release yourself from the shackles of the past and forgive.
No one else can do it for you, but you yourself.
Love will carry you through!

❀

Meditation:

Visualise your parents (or other people close to you with whom you
need to do this exercise) surrounded by the healing angels.
The Archangel Michael is also in attendance.
Now ask Archangel Michael to cut any unhealthy, unloving cords
between you and your parents with his blue sword, which he does
swiftly, leaving only the ties of unconditional love between you.
Give your parents a hug and tell them that you forgive
what they have done and how much you love them.
Then forgive yourself for any part you played in this drama of life.
All of you now receive a blessing from
the healing angels and Archangel Michael.
Give thanks to Archangel Michael and
the healing angels for their help.
Please ground, attune and protect yourself.

❀

Affirmations:

I thank my mother and father for all the life lessons
they provided me with!

I forgive them for any pain they caused me,
in the knowledge that they did the best they could!

I love, respect and honour my parents!

Positive energy diet

There is only one diet the spiritual seeker
needs to follow and that is the "positive energy diet"!
The rules to follow are simple: take a large dose of positive energy in
the form of aligning yourself with "all that is love and light",
in the morning an extra helping of the same at lunchtime,
and another large dose of positive energy in
the form of prayers and giving thanks before you go to sleep!
Finally, add plenty of positive thoughts, fresh air, exercise,
good company and the avoidance of negative influences
of any kind to your spiritual diet, and you
will be radiating good health in body, mind and spirit forever!

Meditation:

Compose your positive energy diet.
Suggestions are as follows:

Avoid the (bad) news on television or in newspapers and magazines.
Substitute with time for meditation, contemplation and relaxation.

Avoid keeping company with people who "bring you down".
Substitute with spend some time in solitude every day.

Avoid bad food and sitting indoors all day.
Substitute with fresh foods and a walk in the park.

Affirmations:

I am on a positive energy diet for life!

I follow my daily spiritual practice!

The more positive I am in my thinking the more positive experiences I
draw to myself in life!

Explore

As a seeker of the divine truth you are truly an explorer!
After having trodden a long and stony path your thirst
for divine knowledge has finally led you
to the hidden gems buried within your own being.
Those gems are the ones you need to explore and examine thoroughly.
Some of them might be rough around the edges
and you will have to polish them carefully.
Others will be pristine and sparkling with love and light.
Those pearls of wisdom are all yours, my child!
Unearth this treasure, step out and make it visible to the world!

Meditation:

You are the proud owner of a huge golden key.
This key is the key to your soul.
Find yourself in front of a golden, heart-shaped, ornate door.
This is the door to your soul....
As you put the key into the lock, the door springs open.
You are walking into the treasure house of your immortal soul.
Enjoy!

Please remember to ground, attune and protect yourself.

Affirmations:

I am a seeker of the divine truth!

Divine pearls of wisdom are buried within my soul!

I share the treasures of divine truth and wisdom with the world!

Set your sights higher

Never, ever settle for second best, my beloved!
Always set your sights at the highest
possible outcome of a plan or situation.
Do not allow illusionary feelings of lack of self-worth
or lack of self-confidence to interfere with your chosen goals.

God knows that you are worthy and God gives you
all the confidence and encouragement you need to succeed.
You just have to ask for it!

Meditation:

Find yourself hiking in the foothills of the Himalayas.
You are enjoying the hike, but would really
like to climb the highest peak!
You decide to attempt this climb and make your way
towards the high snow-capped mountains.
As soon as you make this decision a group of
Sherpa angels appear and relieve you of all your luggage.
You are as free as a bird and as light as a feather.
You climb the mountain with the angels by your side,
watching over you every step of the way.
You reach the peak easily and effortlessly in no time!
Thank the Sherpa angels for their help!
Please ground, attune and protect yourself.

Affirmations:

I am setting my sights to achieve the highest!

I trust in God and the angels to assist in my endeavours at all times!

Divine victory is mine!

Integrity

Integrity is a most vital ingredient of your spiritual makeup.
It is indeed the "backbone" which holds your thoughts,
your feelings, your soul and your spirit in alignment.
Integrate strong moral principles into your life.
Practise those principles and uphold them.
Do not allow temptations to sway you
and your life will truly become whole!

Meditation:

Listen to your body; it is a divine instrument that allows you
to feel when you are out of integrity and not in your truth.
Your mind will also respond and signal you,
when you are in danger of losing your integrity.
You will "know" that something is not right.
Do not ignore these messages.

Act on them, sort yourself out and you will soon be back
in alignment with your highest truth and your integrity will be restored!

Affirmation:

I live my life with integrity!

I am in alignment with the divine truth at all times!

My state of being is one of wholeness!

Tranquillity

Seek tranquillity, my beloved, for it provides you with
much needed rest and, most of all, uplifts your soul.
When your "soul sings in your heart", magical events
can happen all around you and your life flows effortlessly.
You may experience tranquillity
in unexpected places, at unexpected times.
Open yourself up to finding it and it will be so!

Meditation:

Visualise yourself in a Roman spa tended by angels.
You are floating in a huge basin filled with
fragrant water and surrounded by candles.
Sweetly scented rose petals are floating on the water
and melodious, soothing music is playing in the background.
The angels pamper your every need.
Lie back and enjoy this heavenly experience!
Emerge from your bath revived and rejuvenated
and thank the angels for assisting you in this process!
Remember to ground, attune and protect yourself.

Affirmations:

I acknowledge the need for peace and tranquillity!

I now create the space and time to experience tranquillity!

I am open and ready to receive
peaceful and tranquil experiences any time!

August 17

Signs

God has created the universe to serve your divine purpose,
which means that the universe merely exists to support
you on your way to self-illumination.
All you need to do is to learn to read the signs;
the universe is giving you so freely.
The signs are manifold, coming to you first and foremost
through God's messengers on earth, your fellow brothers and sisters.
God may draw your eye to read a certain book or to look at
a television programme, watch a movie or read a magazine,
where the signs will be found to point you in the right direction.
God may also reach you through the behaviour of your pets
or through the patterns of nature, such as the changes in weather.
Be alert and pay attention in readiness to receive
and read those signs, for they are all around you,
day and night being shown to you in a myriad ways.
Do away with the notion that the universe is against you!
Do not block yourself in such a destructive manner
from receiving what God has to offer you!
Trust and all will be revealed!

Meditation:

Starting today, expect to see and read
the signs given to you by God and the universe.
Convince yourself in your heart and mind,
that they are available to you when you need them.
In adopting such a positive attitude you cannot fail
but be aware of the signposts from heaven!
Give thanks.

Affirmations:

I open my heart and mind to read the signposts
the universe is providing for me!

The universe serves my divine purpose!

I trust that all will be revealed to me!

Divine education

Let your education on this planet earth be "divine education"!
Teach your children the values of honour,
respect, and love for each other.
Start when the children are very young, so that the divine way to
conduct their lives becomes deeply engrained in their consciousness.
The greatest teaching, the highest wisdom, to be attained
on this earthly sojourn, is that there is
nothing of greater importance than to becoming love!

Meditation:

Be aware not to fall into the currently practised
"human education trap", which places
the sole importance on intellectual and material pursuits.
Remember, that intuition is superior to intellect
and that love is superior to all!
Even if you are neither a teacher nor a parent,
support this notion in whatever way you can.
Trust your loving heart; it will educate you in all
you need to know and achieve on your path
and will help you to understand and those you so dearly love.

Affirmations:

My intuition teaches me all I need to know!

Love is the greatest teacher and provides the greatest teachings!

I do my best to live and pass on spiritual values!

August 19

Spiritual amnesia

You do know who you are, but you presently suffer
from spiritual amnesia and have simply forgotten your true nature!
However, God has given you free will, coupled with
endless choices and opportunities, to discover
your divinity for yourself, to become truly conscious of it!
Make self- illumination your priority my beloved!
Shine the light of truth on every aspect of your life with determination
and perseverance, awakening from your slumber of ignorance.
Your success is divinely guaranteed! You cannot fail!

❁

Meditation:

Visualise yourself sitting in meditation on a beautifully decorated chair.
You feel comfortable and very relaxed.
Within the meditation you open your eyes, only to realise
that you are not able to see, as your eyes are covered by a veil.
You now discover that not only your third eye,
but also every other one of your chakras has a veil covering it.
You ask the healing angels for help and together you remove
all seven veils from your chakras, starting at the
base chakra and going all the way to the crown.
You know, that as every veil comes off, you are releasing and letting
go of old conditioning and past experiences, allowing yourself to be
awakened and the bright, new light of self-illumination to come in!
When you have completed this process successfully, you will
feel lighter and perceive the world around you much more intensely.
You will experience brighter colours, clearer sounds
and a heightened sense of taste and smell.
Thank the healing angels for their assistance!

❁

Affirmations:

I am ready to remove the veils of illusion and awaken to my true self!

I ask God and the angels to assist me in
the process of self-illumination!

It is my destiny to know my divine nature!

Divine will

Don't you say,"Where there is a will, there is a way"?
Align your will with the divine will and your way will be the divine way!
Having done so, you will be doing God's bidding
and you will know without fail that all the obstacles
you encounter on your life's journey have been put there deliberately
by God, for you to be able to learn and grow through them.

Become aware and cherish your divine role as a co-creator with God!

Meditation:

Think about what you want at this moment in time.
Now, make a supreme effort and hand
your will and wants over to God.
Let some time pass and then take what you have
handed over to God into contemplation or meditation.
What comes back into your present conscious awareness
will be God's higher will and purpose for you.
Trust and follow the divine will!

Affirmations:

I am aligning my will with the divine will!

I trust that I am in perfect alignment with God!

I am making my way the divine way!

August 21

Reflections

As within, so without!
In accordance with this divine law,
the inhumane treatment of people, animals and plants,
indeed the whole of Mother Earth, by the population of this planet is
being reflected in the weather patterns
and natural catastrophes experienced here on earth.
There is no one else to blame for this but the human race itself.
Learn to love one another; be gentle and sweet with one another,
create harmony between each other, and nature
will mirror the exact same state of being back to you!
When the sun shines in your heart,
it will shine for you in the outer world also!

Meditation:

Look at history and note the social goings on, the exploits,
the moral depravations and so on,
previous to great natural disasters.

You will find the results enlightening indeed!

Affirmations:

I treat all the kingdoms of nature with love and respect!

I create peace and harmony in my inner worlds!

My positive inner state of being is projected into the outer world!

Flexibility

Be flexible, my dearest one,
and do not set your mind on preconceived ideas.
Nothing is set in stone.
God needs you to be like a reed, strong and flexible, but also hollow,
so that God may use you as a channel for the divine work to be done.
Endeavour to live a practical spirituality.
Follow the path of least resistance.

Be flexible and allow God to guide you.

Meditation:

Nature is a great teacher!
Contemplate on examples of flexibility in nature…
such as the stream meandering through the landscape,
following the path of least resistance.

Affirmations:

I am flexible and open to exploring different realities.

I follow the path of least resistance and allow my life to flow
and unfold before me.

I have the right to change my mind.

You reap what you sow

Sow seeds of love, compassion,
kindness and understanding, my beloved
For one day you will reap what you have sown.
The day will come and you want it to be of joy and celebrations.
Be mindful of your thoughts, words and actions,
because each of them is a seed going into the ground.
Whether you are aware of it or not,
you alone are responsible for your conduct.
Ensure that when you leave this world, you leave behind not just
material goods, but that you leave behind a garden of love.

Meditation:

You are God's gardener.
See yourself digging the ground, collecting
and removing any stones or weeds from the soil.
Then see yourself ploughing beautiful long furrows.
When you are ready, you sow your best seeds: love,
forgiveness, compassion, understanding, loyalty and many more.
When you have finished the planting, you turn around
and look back at your efforts and, to your amazement,
the seeds have already germinated and the plants are growing
steadily and healthily, shooting up right in front of your very eyes!
Congratulate yourself for your good work!
Please ground, attune and protect yourself.

Affirmations:

As I reap what I sow, I am sowing seeds of love.

I have a limitless supply of seeds of love available to me.

I am creating heaven on earth.

Outward appearances

Outward appearances can be deceptive, my beloved.
Many gems are hidden beneath layers of dust,
and equally behind many rich facades, you may
find crumbling walls and decay.
When you look at the world around you,
look at it with the eyes of love.
For love will penetrate to the heart of the matter like a laser beam
revealing the hidden truth behind outward appearances.
Nothing can be hidden from love.

Meditation:

In your dealings with the world, try to have an open heart,
free from too many earthly desires.
What are the "extra desires" you are carrying around with yourself?
Make a little list of them in your head.
Now visualise your heart to be akin
to one of those ornate, brass Victorian birdcages.
As you look in through the brass bars, you see
all of those superfluous desires locked in there.
You open the door to the cage and the desires escape
back to source to be transmuted, never to be seen again!
Without the extra desires, you will experience things as they truly are.
Do not forget to ground, attune and protect yourself.

Affirmations:

I am love; therefore I perceive love all around me

My heart is open and free of earthly desires.

I look at the world with the eyes of love.

Spiritual conduct

Your spiritual conduct is of utmost importance, my child.
As a co-creator with God, your role is one of empowerment of
your fellow brothers and sisters, of encouragement and of support.
Always stand in the golden light of your own truth.

Obey God's universal laws at all times.
This way, your immaculate spiritual conduct
will serve as an encouraging example to those around you.

Meditation:

Make a list of the points of spiritual conduct
that are most important to you and find out why.
Visualise yourself adhering to all the values and qualities
on your list, especially the ones you find difficult to follow.
Remember, the most important spiritual value is that
of having a good heart and conducting
all you do from the point of unconditional love!

Affirmations:

My spiritual conduct is immaculate.

I conduct my whole life with utmost integrity.

I am standing firm in the light of my own truth.

Corruption

All energy can be used for the purpose of good or bad.
So too can spiritual energy be corrupted and abused.
As you grow in "the light" you will attract
equal amounts of "dark matter" towards you.
Such is the nature of duality and hence
this is one of the laws governing this universe.
Will you be tempted?
Can you be corrupted in your faith?
Spiritual abuse can happen in very subtle ways.
Be wary; do not allow yourself to exploit the weakness
and helplessness of others for greater spiritual or earthly power.
Always examine your heart and soul for your motivation
in helping and assisting others on their path.
Is it possible you are benefiting more than the other person?

Meditation:

Contemplate what drives you to help people
with spiritual and earthly matters.
What are your motivations?
Have you been asked to help?
Do you, maybe, see yourself as higher or better
than the other person, without being aware of that fact?
Do you feel that you have all the answers for everybody?
As a rule: if you act from need rather then love,
you are disempowering the other person
and abusing the law of integrity.
Beware!

Affirmations:

The power of true love is incorruptible.

My motivation for sharing spiritual knowledge
is to be of service to humanity.

I keep my body, mind and spirit firmly fixed on the light.

You are the body of God

God is the creative energy of unconditional love
contained within all creation!
In order for this latent energy to become aware
that it is God it needs to become conscious of itself!
You are God's eyes, mouth, ears, arms and legs!
What you are not quite conscious of yet, is that you truly are God!
You are God manifest in flesh and blood,
for the energy of unconditional love resides within you, it is you!
Wake up to this divine truth!

Meditation:

When you think of your personal concept of God,
which qualities and attributes come to the fore?
Write them down.
Now take a look inside and see which of those qualities
and attributes you have already developed in yourself,
and congratulate yourself for that achievement!
Then take a look at the qualities you still need to work on.
Embrace those qualities as if they where
already incorporated into your whole being.
Do, act and "be as if" with great faith and intensity
and do not berate yourself for any perceived imperfections.
Remember that your mind creates your reality!

Affirmations:

I am waking up to the truth!

I am God's eyes, mouth, ears, arms and legs!

I am the embodiment of love!

The religion of love

Let love be your religion!
Practise your chosen faith and uphold the
divine universal moral codes and the principles
of unity and equality with all your fellow brothers and sisters.
Be kind, tolerant and accepting of other faiths.
As there are "many routes to Rome",
so there are many roads leading to the one God!

Meditation:

Think of all the religions that exist on this planet.
Visualise the various individual groups belonging to them,
standing on a huge football field,
all in their little religious units, separated from each other.
Now project a beam of unconditional love from your heart
into a person in one of the groups and ask that person's higher self
to carry on the same process, projecting a beam of love
and light from their heart to the next person and so on.
Soon the whole group is linked by love, with love and the beam
of light travels to the next group, connecting it to the first one.
You watch in amazement and awe as all of the groups
of different religions, creeds, casts and backgrounds
are being united by one force, the power of love!

Please ground, attune and protect yourself.

Affirmations:

There is only one God; He is a God of unconditional love!

There is only one religion; it is the religion of love!

There is only one purpose for existence, the purpose to be love!

Becoming the light

You ARE the light!
The light that is the "cosmic creation energy"
which has the quality of unconditional love at its centre!
How do you know that this is the truth?
You find out by first recognising and accepting the light into your life
and then bringing it into your very being, where it casts out
all the negativity accumulated over many lifetimes.
This may be a long and arduous process,
requiring great courage, perseverance, faith and stamina.
However, it is your destiny to succeed and triumph over the dark.
When all shadows, everything which is not light, is transmuted
by the light, that will be your moment of "enlightenment"
and you will have truly BECOME the light!

✳

Meditation:

Grow your golden roots and anchor them firmly into the ground.
Bring a golden beam of light into the top of your head
and allow it to flow into your heart.
The light infuses the lotus petals of your heart with the energy of pure
unconditional love and the petals gently begin to open.
Now let the light from your heart radiate through your very being.
It flows into your eyes, purifying your sight; you will now see the truth!
It flows into your mouth, purifying your speech; you speak the truth!
It flows into your ears, purifying your hearing; you hear the truth!
It flows into your brain, purifying your thoughts, you will think the truth!
And then it embraces and purifies all of you,
so that from now on you will act in truth.
Bathe in this light as long as it feels comfortable.
Then close your chakras down (see "how to close down" chapter!)
Repeat as often as necessary.

✳

Affirmations:

I allow the light to cleanse and purify my self!
I am the light and the light is within me!
I am on the road to enlightenment!

Life is a game

Play the game of life!
God intended you to have fun, to be happy
and contented in the knowledge that you are God!
Be aware of Maya – the Illusion – and treat it as such;
do not give undue value to the material plane,
which does not exist on a permanent basis.
It purely serves as a playground for you,
your place to learn and grow.
All matter will eventually disintegrate;
only spirit keeps its form and is indestructible and everlasting.
"Ashes to ashes, dust to dust"!
So go forth my child and take neither your "little self"
nor the world at large too seriously!

❀

Meditation:

Imagine that God throws you a ball filled
with love, light, laughter and endless opportunities.
You have just won the spiritual lottery!
What would you do with it?
Which goals of yours would you like to throw "the light ball" into?

❀

Affirmations:

Life is a game and I am playing it!

The universe is my playground and the world my classroom!

I am taking myself and the world around me "lightly"!

You are an Earth Angel

You are an earth angel, my dearest one!
You have the power to heal!
You have the power to transform!
You have the power to soothe, nourish and uplift!
God has given you all the tools to achieve such tasks;
none are too small or too big to accomplish.
Trust in your divine nature!
Accept who you are, step out into the world and act accordingly!

Meditation:

Ask your guardian angel for assistance with these tasks.
Your angel will guide and support you in every aspect
of your life and service to humankind.
Ask for your angel's help in a clear and concise manner,
so that he/she knows what specific assistance you need.

You ask and you will receive!
Always give heartfelt thanks!
Enjoy being an earth angel!

Affirmations:

I am an earth angel!

I accept my role as divine assistant to God!

All I need to fulfil my role is provided for me by God!

Blessing for the month of
September

Miracle of life

The tiny seed growing into the mighty oak.
The embryo growing into a sweet little child.
The divine principle expressing
itself in its myriad forms!
May the seed of divine love ripen within your heart!
May the seed of divine inspiration ripen within your mind!
May the seed of divine light ripen within your soul!

May your light shine bright for all to see!

Failure

You cannot fail, my beloved!
So do not ever accept defeat!
Failure is a human concept, which is far, far away from the truth!
In truth, every so-called failure is the universe teaching you
that there is a much better, different way to do things.
God has lovingly planned a higher outcome for you!
It all is a question of trial and error.
Keep on trying, walking through the doors that open easily for you.
Do not try to break through the doors that are shut;
your highest good is certainly not behind them!

Meditation:

Contemplate the "open doors" in your life at present.

What is stopping you from walking through them?
If there are any "closed doors" you are desperate to walk through,
ask yourself why and what is your true motivation
in wanting to break through those doors!

Affirmations:

I trust that my trial and errors will eventually
result in the highest outcome!

I see "failure" as a learning tool and do not attach
any importance to it!

I am destined to succeed!

Holy days

Make your holidays into holy days!

Go to wonderful places that recharge body, mind and spirit,
where you can walk in nature or swim in clear waters.
Plan to participate in fun, uplifting activities
and eat fresh, nourishing foods.
Just as you have to put petrol into your car,
which will run smoother on lead-free, high-grade petrol,
so your soul needs to be refuelled at regular intervals.
Not only do you deserve your holy days,
but also your life will be much the "lighter" for it!
Honour yourself by giving yourself a truly special holy time!

Meditation:

Take your diary and work out your holy days and arrange
to fit short "one-off" days, between your long holy days.
Make sure to keep to your planned holy day schedule!
You do not live to work, but work to live!

Affirmations:

My holy days recharge my body, mind and spirit!
I deserve lots of holy days!
I make time for fun and play in my busy schedule!

September 3

Walking your talk

You have studied the scriptures, have attended
many workshops and lectures and have shared
and discussed the subject of spirituality with many.
Now, however, it is time, as you so aptly proclaim, "to walk your talk"!
No more thinking or talking about spirituality, actually doing it.
Practise it from the moment of awakening to the moment
you close your eyes at night.
This is what it means to be a spiritual being:
simply all that you think, speak or do is of a spiritual nature.

Life and spirituality have ceased to be separate!

Meditation:

You are now ready "to walk your talk"!
If you have not already done so, identify the areas
of your life where you are not quite there yet.
What are those areas and what are
the fears that prevent you from doing so?
As with everything else in life, adopt the "little-by-little"
approach, and do the best you can, when you can!
You cannot fail!
God will not let you!

Affirmations:

I am "walking my talk"!

I am spirit and my spirit self guides me all the way!

All my thoughts, words, actions and reactions
are guided by my higher/spirit self!

The kingdoms of nature

There are four kingdoms in nature, my beloved:
the mineral kingdom, the plant kingdom,
the animal kingdom and the human kingdom.
They all depend on each other, not only for survival,
but because they need each other to be able to evolve
to their highest purpose, to become one with God!

Meditation:

Travel to the centre of the earth.
There, ask Mother Earth to tell you
the secrets of the rock, crystal and mineral kingdom.
Thank her for that information and then travel up
through the layers of the earth into the "earth-rind" and ask
the elementals of the plant kingdom to impart their secrets to you.
Give thanks to the fairies, elves and tree sprits for that.
Lastly, ask the over-souls of the animal kingdom
(the governing souls of the different animal species)
to tell you their secrets.
Thank them also, and you now find yourself
in the realms of the human kingdom.
Have a conversation with your higher self and find out more about
the special relationship between the four kingdoms of nature.
Remember to ground, attune and protect yourself.

Affirmations:

I realise that my thoughts, words and actions have
a profound effect on all the kingdoms of nature!

I honour, respect and give my love to rocks, plants,
animals and humans unconditionally!

I am one with all kingdoms of nature!

The divine spark

Allow the divine spark within you to grow and flourish!
Make all your thoughts; words and actions divine
by being 100% focused on God!
With the fire of love blazing in your heart,
your divine spark is ready to ignite the latent flames
of love within your fellow brothers and sisters on this earth!

Meditation:

Visualise your heart to be burning with
the fire of unconditional love.
The more you focus on this divine fire,
the bigger and stronger it burns.
Now you see sparks of love flying off in all the four directions…
See these sparks igniting the fire of love
in everyone on whom they land!

What could be more delightful to witness,
than love spreading like wildfire through the land!

Affirmations:

I love LOVE!

My divine spark is growing stronger and bigger
with every breath I take!

I act as a catalyst for love!

Spiritual revolution

Wars, uprisings, demonstrations and protests of any kind
achieve nothing, my beloved; in fact such activities
only attract more negativity to the situation concerned.
What does need to happen to ensure there will be a home on this
planet for your children and grandchildren is a spiritual revolution!
Uproot your negative beliefs!
Throw out and let go of all false idols!
Adhere to the moral premise of "Love all and serve all"
and release anything and everything that is not love from your life!

Meditation:

Try your utmost to apply the same amount of energy you
waste in judging others, criticising others
and trying to better others; in improving yourself!

You will be surprised at the results!

Affirmations:

I am taking part in the spiritual revolution
by releasing anything that is not love!

I release and let go of all critical
and judgmental behaviour towards others!

I apply my energies in positive and constructive ways!

Waste no-thing

Waste no-thing my dearest one!
All the resources you have are given to you by God
and are not to be abused in any way.
In not wasting, for instance, water, you are honouring
and respecting the gift of water, God has given you.
No water, no life!
A fact that seems to get forgotten on this planet.
The more love and respect there is, the more
a steady supply of the resources you need is ensured.
This is the law of attraction in action!
If you chose to carry on abusing nature's
resources they will dwindle and eventually die away.
The choice is yours.
What will it be?

Meditation:

Be very honest with yourself.
How much do you really honour and respect
the natural resources God has given you for your daily use?
Do you turn off the light when you leave a room?
Do you turn off the water tap or is it still running
while you do other chores in the bathroom in the morning?
Do you drive everywhere or do you make an effort to walk?
Do you throw food away?
It is never to late to change bad habits!
Ask for forgiveness from Mother Earth; forgive yourself
for your trespasses and do your best from now on
to honour and respect what has been given to you!

Affirmations:

I waste no-thing!

I honour and respect all resources, as they are a gift from God!

I live by example and so encourage others to do the same!

Self-reliance

Rely on no one, but yourself!
Your self, being part of God, has all the knowledge,
resources and wisdom needed, to do what needs to be done!
Do not give away your God-given powers to other people,
situations or circumstances!
You are not helping yourself with such acts and
moreover are encouraging others to carry on
destructive behavioural patterns themselves.
Go, trust and rely in the self and allow others to do the same!

Meditation:

Ponder on how self-sufficient you really are.
Where have you been "giving your power away"
and allowing other people to take over against your will?
What is stopping you from truly relying on yourself?
Hand all feelings of fear and guilt over to the healing
angels and ask for their assistance in the process.

Give heartfelt thanks for the love they give you.

Affirmations:

I can completely rely on my self!

My self has all the power, wisdom and strength
to deal with anything life puts in my path!

I trust and rely in my self and allow others to do the same!

Spiritual remedies

How many lotions, potions and pills do you swallow?
How much money, time and energy do you waste on false cures?
Why not give "spiritual remedies" a try first?
"Trust and you will be well" is one such remedy.
Visualising and feeling yourself to be happy
and healthy is another, most potent one.
Ask God and the angels to help you find
and release the cause of your feeling ill at ease.
Give thanks to your body daily
and bless everything you either put in or on it
Those are some of the most important spiritual remedies
ensuring your good health in body, mind, emotions and spirit

Meditation:

Next time you feel ill, immediately ask God
and the healing angels for help.
Ask to be shown the root of your illness.
Ask Archangel Michael to cut the cords connecting you to anybody
or anything that is not pure love and does not serve you anymore.
He will do so, cutting you free using his blue sword of light and truth.
Give yourself a big cuddle and time and space
to complete this natural healing process.
Give thanks to Archangel Michael and
the healing angels for their assistance.
Make sure that you are grounded, attuned and protected.
Please note: make sure of a steady supply of sleep, fresh air,
exercise, good food, vitamins and mental and emotional support
at all times, not just when you are already feeling unwell.
Of course, if symptoms persist, please go and see your doctor!

Affirmations:

My mind creates my experiences

I trust in the natural healing powers of positive thinking

All is well in my life.

Manifestation

The power of manifestation is yours!
You are a co-creator with God
and as such, you cannot help but manifest!
A single thought is the seed of a manifestation.
A single word will bring the thought closer to manifestation.
When you take action on your erstwhile thought, you make
"the word into flesh" and you have manifested your desire.
To ensure that you manifest for the highest good of yourself
and others, attune yourself to the mind o God and receive unlimited
divine inspirations from the source of all that is!

Meditation:

What is it you would like to manifest?
When you have identified what it is, go through this checklist:
Are you in alignment with the divine will?
Is your manifestation going to further yours and others' highest good?
Are you aligned with divine timing?
(Pray to God to give you patience!)
If the above criteria are fulfilled, go ahead with your manifestation.
Act from your heart, use your intellect and imagine
in your mind that the manifestation has already taken place.
See and feel it all done.
Give thanks now, which ensures that you are invoking
the law of grace, making yourself and your manifestation
magnetic to God's assistance in the matter.
As this is a process, you will have to go through this routine
on a daily basis until such time as your feat is accomplished.
Happy manifesting and enjoy the results!

Affirmations:

All I manifest is for the highest good of the planet and myself!
I manifest in alignment with the divine will
and divine purpose in divine timing!
I enjoy being a co-creator with God!

September 11

World peace

An aim that should unite humanity is the striving for world peace!
The yearning for peace should be foremost in all hearts and minds!
To ensure that this wish becomes a reality, first, aim to be at peace
with yourself, then with your family, your friends and work colleagues.
There is nothing more needed than for every individual to accept their
personal responsibility to establish peace within themselves!
Imagine everyone doing just that.
A wave of peace would sweep the world!
What a wonderful image to behold!

Meditation:

See yourself walking along a beach.
As you stroll along, a beautiful white
heart-shaped pebble catches your eye.
You pick it up, and as you hold it in the palm of your hand,
you feel compelled to project love and peace, coming
from your heart as a beam of light, into the pebble.
With every breath you take, more and more peace and love
flows into the pebble, until you start to feel that the pebble
is a living thing with its own little heart beating in your hand.
When you feel that the stone has absorbed as much energy as it can
hold, throw it into the sea with the heartfelt wish, that the waves will
carry the love energy of peace to the four corners of the earth!

Give thanks to the water elementals for helping you.
Please ground, attune and protect yourself.

Affirmations:

I am at peace!

From my peaceful heart I radiate peace and love into the world!

I see a world of peace and love and light!

The independent self

In order to carry out your mission on this planet
you need to be independent of anyone and anything!
You need to be free within to be able to fulfil your sacred tasks!
Link your mind and emotions with your spirit,
as your spirit is always free!
The great freedom of your spirit self will give you the inspiration,
courage, strength and perseverance necessary for you to succeed!

❀

Meditation:

Identify the areas of dependency in your life.
Make a list of your dependencies and write positive,
balancing qualities opposite each one.
Ask Archangel Michael to help you "cut the cords" with all the people
and situations with which you have dependency issues.
When this is done, demand back your personal power
that has been held by people and situations.
See your power in the form of an energy ball moving out of
the other person or situation and returning to your solar plexus,
the seat of your earthly power.
Then, of your free will, return any power you might have "stolen".
You can also see the power energy as a parcel being handed to you.
If necessary you hand a parcel of power back.
Forgive yourself and others for the parts played and ask the
healing angels to give their blessings to everyone involved.
Now go through your list and one by one see
and feel those positive qualities within yourself.
Give thanks to Archangel Michael for his help in the matter.
This will need to be repeated often and might take a while to complete.
Be patient and gentle with yourself and you will succeed.
Make sure that you are grounded, attuned and protected.

❀

Affirmations:

I am independent of anything or anybody!
I am able to rely on my own strength!
I have a constant, independent energy supply
coming from my higher spirit self!

Surround yourself with love

From the moment of awakening, surround yourself
with a golden mantle of love, for it is the greatest protector of all.
Do not fear evil, as what you fear most you will only attract to yourself.
Instead, develop an unshakable believe in the limitless power of love.
Make love the alpha and the omega of your life!
Make it the central focus of all that is!
Such beliefs will render any attacks of negativity powerless!

Nothing and nobody can, or will, hurt you!

Meditation:

Upon awakening, after you have aligned yourself with
all that is love, visualise your guardian angel handing you
the golden robe of love and protection; the fabric of which is spun
from the threads of pure unconditional love.
The robe reaches to the floor; it has a big hood
and long sleeves and fits you perfectly.
Thank your guardian angel for the robe, and remind yourself
of its existence if you are in a negatively charged situation
or environment during your day.

Affirmations:

I am guided and protected by love at all times!

I choose to make love the alpha and the omega of my life!

I am surrounded by a mantle of love!

Spiritual hunger

You hunger for the riches of this world,
but where is your spiritual hunger?
Your belly might be full; you might be the owner of
a fat bank balance, you might be at the height of a powerful career,
but all those achievements and acquisitions
are transient pleasures and could be gone tomorrow.
What will you be left with, if such a situation is to occur?
If, however, you have satisfied your hunger for God
you will be filled with love, peace and contentment and no matter
what your outward circumstances may be, you will be truly rich.

Meditation:

What is your spiritual craving?
Find out and once you have identified it,
ask God and the angels to help you remove
all obstacles that hinder you from obtaining this state of being.
Major obstacle may be:
I do not deserve that God loves me.
I am a sinner.
I am not worthy of anything good happening to me... and so on...
If you want love you will have love!
God is waiting for you to want all of it,
so that He can finally give all of it to you!
Remember, you ask and you shall receive!
Even God is not able to override the law of free will!
Give thanks.

Affirmations:

I am filled with love and joy!

I am content!

I am rich in body, mind and spirit!

Willingness

You are able to fulfil your divine purpose, but are you willing to do so?
You might think you are but nothing seems to move forward
in the divine direction, as your little ego self is
forever tricking you into different, worldly pursuits.
You need to assert your divine will to overcome the attempts
of the lower self to stop you from walking your destined path.
For this to happen you have to make a conscious choice.
Will you make the fulfilment of your divine purpose your reality?

Then decide here and now, assert your divine will, and DO SO!

Meditation:

Align your will with Gods will.
In doing so you have moved from exercising
your will to fulfilling the divine will and purpose.
Trust that this has been done and apply your self to the task at hand.
As soon as you demonstrate your willingness to the universe,
it cannot help but assist you in your endeavours.
All the powers of heaven and earth are
by your side assisting you in the execution of the divine plan!

Affirmations:

I am willing to take up my role as co-creator with God!

My will is in alignment with the divine will!

I am guided and supported by the universe at all times!

Anger

Anger is a most destructive emotion,
my beloved, but it is also a human one!
When you feel anger, do not just ignore and suppress it,
for it will surely surface again in different guises and unexpected ways.
Own your anger, find the roots of it,
release or transmute it and set yourself free!

Meditation:

When you think you are angry with another person or situation,
in essence, this anger is a reflection of your anger towards yourself.
"Own" this anger and decide that you have the right to be angry.
Where is your anger coming from?
Find the roots of it; for this, you may need
some help in the form of some therapy sessions or counselling.
Having identified the source of your anger, you have two choices:

1) release your anger in such a way that you do not harm any
sentient being, for instance through screaming,
bashing cushions or energetic exercise.

2) transmute the anger energy (which can charge a light bulb for quite
some time, in one outburst!) into creative energy, by using it as a fuel,
or driving force and for some activity, such as cleaning your home,
washing your clothes, mowing the lawn, writing your book or studying.

Congratulate yourself to your successful "anger-management"!

Affirmations:

I deal with my anger in positive ways!

I use my anger as a catalyst for change!

I transmute my anger and channel it into creative pursuits!

Act from love

Life presents many challenges, trials
and tribulations on the path to self-mastery.
With every new challenge you encounter, you have a choice:
To act from love or to act from fear!
With every trial arises a new opportunity
to show the world who you truly are!
With every tribulation, you alone will decide how to conduct yourself!
At every turn of the way, whatever difficulties you face,
always ask yourself this question: What would love do now?

Meditation:

Visualise your heart as a deep well.
The well is beautifully and perfectly built,
with a redbrick wall around it.
See yourself lowering a bucket into the well
and drawing up the sparkling water of unconditional love.
Pour the water into a golden cup
and give it to anyone in need you can think of.
There is an endless supply of the water of love in the well!
Every time you bring up the bucket it spills
over with the golden energy of pure unconditional love!

Affirmations:

I choose love, every time!

I cherish every opportunity God gives me to share my love!

My heart is a never-ending wellspring of unconditional love!

Greed

You may be confronted with greed
in its many variations in your daily life.
Before you judge or criticise, ask yourself
where this greed is coming from in the other person
and where are you greedy in your own life!
Invariably you will find out that greed stems
from a serious lack of love, in some shape or form.
The source may have been a lack of nurturing,
a lack of care and attention, a lack of praise.
An inner child hungry and starved of love and affection
can often be found at the centre of a greedy adult.
Be generous and abundant in your love towards
such people and your own inner child,
and greed will not have the need to show up anymore in your life!

Meditation:

What is your inner child greedy for?
What is it you did not have enough of?
Find out, and as your own inner parent together with God
and the healing angels give to yourself that for which you hunger

Give thanks.

Affirmations:

I address all areas of lack in my own life!

I satisfy my inner child!

I am abundant in my love for others and myself!

September 19

Expectations

Expect the best and let God do the rest!

Leave "this will do" and "this is good enough for me" behind!
God intends the best for you;
He is ready to shower you with gifts!
Live a life of positive expectations,
always awaiting the highest outcome of all your endeavours.
Nevertheless, allow God to decide what is best for you.
God is the one with the overview!

Meditation:

Take the following into contemplation:
When you bake a cake you carefully measure the ingredients,
grease the cake-tin, put the oven on at the right temperature
and having made all these preparations,
you expect the cake to come out of the oven
perfectly well risen and baked!
Take the same approach regarding your life!

Do your best and then let go and let God!

Affirmations:

I do my best and let God do the rest!

I expect the best without being attached
to the outcome of any situation!

God designs my life experiences for my highest good!

Soul-food

As much as you take care to feed your body,
so you must make an effort to feed your soul!
At times your soul suffers from serious under nourishment,
as all you think about and care for in your life seems
to be duty-bound and work – or family – related.
This will not do, my child!
You need time alone, time to recharge and feed your soul!
In doing what makes your heart sing, you will achieve just that!
Go out and take the opportunity to gladden and recharge yourself!

Meditation:

What is it that makes your soul sing?
Is it listening to music, dancing, reading or being in nature?
Is it, maybe, sitting in quiet meditation or contemplation?
Whatever it is, follow the calling of your soul!

Your well-being will increase a thousandfold!

Affirmations:

I nurture and cherish my soul!

I give my soul the food it craves!

I allow my soul to sing!

Bad habits

Do not allow bad habits to run your life!
Getting into ruts is a very common human experience,
but it is one that does not have to be endured.
Although some of those old habits may be very engrained,
it does not mean that you cannot change them!
Apply your divine will and discipline yourself to uproot
and change those out moded patterns that are by now holding you
back from living a happy, fulfilled life!

Meditation:

What is your worst bad habit?

Try to trace the root of it and find out where
and when this habit developed.
Bad habits may be patterns of compensation for
something that has been lacking or in short supply in your life.
Remember that at the root of all negative behaviour
always lies fear in its many forms and guises!
Now think of a good habit with which to replace the bad one.
In time and with a good deal of discipline you will soon
experience wonderful changes in your life!

Affirmations:

I am in charge of my life!

I have the power to change!

I now replace old negative patterns with bright, new positive ones!

Attachments

Have one attachment only in this life,
your attachment to God, to the source of all that is!
Be attached and intrinsically linked with
the heart and mind of the divine!
As you are one with God, all will be given unto you!

Meditation:

Visualise yourself as a little baby floating in the cosmic womb.
You are aware of your umbilical cord.
Follow it in your mind to find out where it leads.
You find that it connects straight to the source, a sea
of brilliant light and almost overwhelming unconditional love for you!
You anchor your umbilical cord safely in the source
of all that is and then see yourself growing up.
With every breath you take, you are a few years older,
and your umbilical cord extends and grows with you.
Carry on this process until you arrive at your present age.
Look at your cord to God now.
What does it look like?
If it needs to be enlarged to ensure a greater
inflow of divine love and light energy, then ask God
and the healing angels to do that for you!
Give thanks for your "heavenly attachment",
which is the only one you could ever wish for!
Please make sure to be grounded, attuned and protected.

Affirmations:

I am attached to the source of all that is, God!

God provides all the physical, mental, emotional and spiritual
nourishment I need!

One Source>One Heart>One Mind>One Body!

Mental strength

Develop mental strength, a steadfast mind
and complete faith in the divine principle underlying all life!
It is so important, my beloved!
A strong, unfaltering mind will carry you over
the many crevasses life may open up in front of you.
The time will come when you may have to take "a leap of faith" – a feat
not possible to achieve if you have not developed a strong mind!

Meditation:

Think of the blade of a holy sword,
how strong and well moulded it is.
Make your mind like this blade;
strong, sharp, indestructible, but flexible!
Use your intellect to sharpen your mind
and your faith to keep it strong!
Then link your heart to your mind
and you have become a perfect instrument of God!

Affirmations:

My mind is strong and steadfast!

My mind is intrinsically linked with the mind of God!

I allow my mind to be flexible and flowing!

Action and reaction

Many ills may befall you in your life
and you may be at the receiving end of many an unjust action.
However, beware, as what is recorded for eternity in your soul
is not the action of another, but the reaction you have to it!
Did your reaction stem from fear
and you gave "eye for eye" and "tooth for tooth"?
Or did your reaction stem
from love and you gave forgiveness in return?

Meditation:

Remember your last bad reaction to a person or situation.
Now remember the feeling that went with the incident; how did it feel?
Did you feel sick in your stomach or, maybe, heavy in your heart?
If you experienced any of the above feelings,
then that is a confirmation that you have reacted from fear.
Unearth this fear and set about healing it.
Ask for forgiveness from the other person
and finally forgive yourself for what you have done.
Ask the healing angels to bless the past and it will be gone forever!

Give thanks.

Affirmations:

I am aware of my actions and reactions!

I react from love and with love!

I have the inner strength to forgive all wrongs!

World-healing

Heal yourself and you will heal the world!

The hurt you perceive around you is
the pain you have not yet healed in yourself!
Apply the balm of self-love onto your wounds and allow
God and the angels to assist you in your self-healing process.
Open your heart to the divine helpers all around you.
And also allow your fellow humans to serve you in that way;
it will gladden their hearts!
Love yourself and you love all!

Meditation:

For a moment see yourself as totally identical
to every other human being on this planet.
Think of the different emotions you express and now
acknowledge these very same emotions in all other human beings.
Become aware of the main thought patterns that occupy your brain.
Make a mental note of all your fears, worries and anxieties
and now acknowledge these very same fears,
anxieties and worries in your fellow brothers and sisters.
Now get in touch with your soul and become aware
of your intrinsic link with all the other souls on this planet
who are journeying through their lives together with you.
You are the one and the many!
Stand united in love with your brothers and sisters on Mother Earth!
What a glorious triumph that is!
Do not forget to ground, attune and protect yourself.

Affirmations:

I love and heal myself!

In healing myself I heal the world around me!

You and I are one!

The drama of life

Attempt to play your role in the drama of life well!
You are indeed on stage 24 hours a day,
acting out the roles God has given you to play!
Put your heart and soul into every act of this drama and do not
burden yourself with trying to anticipate the ending of the third act!
Leave that to God!
Be like a professional actor; give your best
and God will take care of the rest!

Meditation:

View the world as a stage.
You are the actor and God is the director.
Allow God to guide you.
He has written a prefect script
and you will be given your lines on a need-to-know basis.
Do not worry about the props,
God has already provided those for you too.
Feel free to use the "theatre of life changing rooms"
any time; God loves you "to change"!

Affirmations:

I act out my part in the drama of life to the best of my abilities!

I let God be the director of the divine play!

I embrace change as a means of self-growth and self-discovery!

Marriage

What has become of the sacred bond of marriage?
To worship God within your wife and to worship God within your
husband, to worship God within your life's partner
and to respect and honour each other, that is true marriage!
A divine promise "to have and to hold"
is far beyond pieces of paper, sexuality or religion.
To fulfil your divine promise to each other moment by moment,
hour by hour, day by day to the best ability
of both partners that is true marriage!
Remember that "the forever" always happens " in the now"!

Meditation:

Are you married to your partner or to your job?
Make extra time for your partner.
Worship God in him/her and through him/her!
Make the best of the time you have together.
Today might be the last day of your life,
or your partner's life, the last chance to be together!
Nourish, nurture, love and care for your "other half",
just as you would like to be cared for yourself,
and your marriage will be one made in heaven!

Affirmations:

I believe in the sacredness of marriage/partnership!

I deeply love, honour and respect my partner!

I worship God within my husband/wife/partner!

The law of attraction

Like attracts like, this is the law:
As you are loving, kind and gentle to yourself,
so you will attract others into your life who are like you.
If you live in fear, you will attract
what you are most afraid of into your life.
If you are violent, you will attract violence;
if you hate someone you will attract more hatred into your life
— and so the sad story goes on.
End this destructive cycle now, my beloved.
Keep your attention and intentions firmly focused on love
and you will become like a magnet, forever
drawing positive people and circumstances toward yourself
As you are love, you will attract love.

Meditation:

Compose a list of your deep-seated destructive beliefs,
which keep attracting negative people,
circumstances and experiences into your life.
Ask the healing angels and any other beings of light for help.
Now visualise yourself standing at the edge of a crevasse,
which you know opens right down to the magnetic core of the earth.
Now see your old negative beliefs like balls of dark energy
popping out of your body and one by one falling into the crevasse.
As they are drawn into the earth's magnetic core
they are transmuted by Mother Earth into positive energy.
Repeat this process as often as necessary and give thanks to Mother
Earth and the healing angels for their service to you.

❀

Affirmations:

I am a love magnet.

I am love and so I attract love.

I am attractive inside and out.

Addiction to love

Endeavour to swap your addictions to money,
power and fame to an addiction to the love of God!
Crave His love every waking moment!
Crave it with every sacred breath you take!
Make the love of God the centre of everything you think, say or do!

Meditation:

Every addiction is an unfulfilled search for love.
Decide now that God, who is identical with
your higher divine self, gives you all the love you want and need.
Ask the healing angels for their kind assistance for this process.
Now visualise a big funnel situated on the top of your head
and glass pipes leading out of your chakras, touching the ground.
Become aware of your addictions and ask for the universal golden
healing light to flow from the source of love and light into the funnel.
Take a deep breath and let the golden light flow into your
crown chakra and from there into the other chakras, pushing all
your addictions out of your body into the pipes, where they flow
down into the ground and are transmuted by Mother Earth for you.
When the process is completed, the pipes simply
drop away and disintegrate.
You are free of your earthly addictions
and ready to be addicted to love!
Give thanks to your divine helpers
and Mother Earth for assisting you in this process.
Please ground, attune and protect yourself.

Affirmations:

I am free of any earthly addictions!

The power of love supplies me with all I need!

I am addicted to the love of God!

Devotion

To what are you devoted?
Is it your family, your friends or your job?
How about setting out to develop devotion
to the divine principle, the God within?
Give your full devotion, worship and honour to God!
Nourish your thoughts and feelings of unconditional love
and let the Flame of divine desire burn bright!
God's rewards for you will be beyond anything
you could ever dream of!

Meditation:

Visit the chamber of your heart.
There you find an open fireplace with a small fire burning in it.
This is the fire of your love and devotion to God, the divine within.
You decide that it is high time to turn this measly little fire into a roaring
furnace and you sit down in front of it to meditate on your love for God.
With every sacred breath you take, your love for God increases
and the fire grows and burns brighter and brighter.
Visit the chamber of your heart often to increase
the flames of love for God even more!
Remember to ground, attune and protect yourself.

Affirmations:

I am devoted to God, the divine principle within!

I nourish the thoughts and feelings of love within me!

The flames of the divine light are burning bright in
the chambers of my heart!

Blessings for the month of
October

The harvest

Let us gather together and invite our brothers
and sisters to partake in our abundant harvest!
May the harvest be the fruits
of the trees or the fruits of your labour!
May the harvest be the fruits of your creative mind!
May the harvest be the sweet fruits of
the outpourings of your pure heart!
May the harvest be the divine sparks of your free spirit!
Allow your brothers and sisters to partake
freely in your great abundance.
God will return the seeds of your deeds
to you a million fold!

Silence speaks louder than words

Silence speaks louder than words, my beloved!

The seeds of love germinate in the stillness of your heart,
silently growing into the fruits of compassion and understanding.
Then you are ready to venture forth into the world,
your heart quietly radiating your love within to the outside world,
which is so much in need of the gifts you bear!

Meditation:

Go to the chamber of your heart and observe
the seeds of love germinating into a beautiful tree,
laden magically, with many different kinds of fruits.
You find the fruits of unconditional love
(compassion, understanding, support, loyalty and many more)
all growing on the tree ripe and ready for the picking.
Honour yourself for your labour of love and give
those fruits freely and unconditionally to any one in need!
Please remember to ground, attune and protect yourself.

Affirmations:

I have a treasure trove of unconditional love within my heart!

I give my love feely without seeking rewards!

I go about my healing work silently!

October 2

Your divine mission

Each and every soul incarnated
on this planet has its own divine mission to fulfil!
God has already provided you with the blueprint for your mission.
Your task at hand is to attune yourself to it and manifest
the divine plan God has so lovingly devised for you!
Serve God, the universe and yourself
by reaching your divine potential!

Meditation:

Breathe in white light and allow it to fill and envelop you.
You know in your heart that you have an appointment
with God, the keeper of your divine blueprint.
Your guardian angel is accompanying you on your way.
Together you enter a light-filled hall, where God
already awaits you, greeting and welcoming you with open arms!
You sit down together on an ornately carved bench
and God produces a scroll, containing your divine blueprint.
You explore the contents of the scroll together and God explains
to you all you need to know to be able to fulfil your mission on earth.
He invites you to come back to see Him for counsel
as often as you would like.
Finally God gives you a big hug and tells you how much He loves you!
Then your angel takes you back into the here and now!
Give thanks.
Please ground, attune and protect yourself.

Meditation:

I am perfectly attuned to my divine blueprint!

I listen to God's counsel!

I am happily and lovingly fulfilling my earth mission!

Charity

Be charitable, my dearest one!
Not only with your money, but also in tolerance,
love and acceptance of others!
'Charity begins at home' is a wise saying indeed!
What does it mean to you?
Be generous in allowing your family and friends
the freedom they desire and be free
of criticism and judgement toward them.
And above all, give your love without strings attached!

That is true charity in action!

Meditation:

How charitable are you towards yourself?
Being charitable with yourself is your first point of practice!
When this has been achieved, you will easily be able to extend
your charity to your family, your friends and the world at large!

Affirmations:

I am charitable and generous towards myself!
I practise charity at home!
I am charitable in my thoughts, words and deeds!

Equality

All are equal in the eyes of God!
The saints and the sinners, the rich and the poor,
the Muslims, the Christians, the Hindus, the Buddhists
and the atheists are all one in the heart and mind of the Creator!
God does not need to forgive you or anyone else for your
perceived sins, for He sees only perfection in you and
has never judged you to be a sinner in the first instance!
In His unconditional love He gave you free will and supported you in
your choices, when on very rare occasions, you allowed Him to do so!
Decide in your heart, that you are equal
not only with your earthly heroes but with God!
The time has come for you to acknowledge
the divinity of your true nature!

Meditation:

All souls are equal!
Why?
Because every one of your soul brothers and sisters
is looking to find and experience the same, namely love!
Endeavour to identify yourself with your
soul brothers and sisters on this basis.
Outward appearances, cultural differences and behaviours
are just illusions of separation, like taking part in a masked ball!
Underneath the mask you are all just human beings!
Achieve this feat and you will see God in everyone – and yourself!

Affirmations:

My liberation lies in finding equality!

I see myself as equal with all creation!

God = I = God!

Fulfilment

Where does true fulfilment lie?
Once you are rich, you want to be richer!
Once you have power, you want more power!
Once you are famous, you want to be even more famous!
And so the list goes on.
It is in human nature to never
be fulfilled by any of it, always seeking more.
Hence, true fulfilment must stem from a higher source!
It must transcend all earthly, illusionary gains!
It is the everlasting love of God, which dwells
within your very being that will give you eternal fulfilment.
It is always there, always constant and working on your behalf!

Meditation:

Visit the chamber of your heart.
There, at the centre of the room, you find a
heart-shaped gilded box, placed on a beautifully decorated table.
You open the box and find your favourites sweets in it.
You take out the sweets and start munching them there and then.
To your surprise, in front of your very
eyes, the box instantly fills up with sweets again!
Thank God for His constant supply of sweet love to you!

Please ground, attune and protect yourself.

❀

Affirmations:

I seek and attain fulfilment within!

I am deeply fulfilled by God's eternal love for me!

I am at peace with my life!

October 6

You are healed

Put all of your trust and faith in God and declare yourself healed!
Decide in your heart and mind that you are
totally free of any diseases of the body, mind, emotions and spirit!
Claim your birthright to be free of all the "baggage"
you have collected over many lifetimes, right now!
Let go, let God and then let it be!
Do not waste another thought on your perceived fears
and imperfections, for you have just released
them all to God, for Him to take care of!

You are healed!

Meditation:

Every morning upon awakening and every evening
before going to sleep, visualise your self, radiant, healthy,
vibrant and beautiful, standing in front of your bed.
Now see yourself getting out of your bed,
stepping forward and merging with your radiant self!
In doing this exercise you will feel your energy levels
and general well-being increase rapidly!

Affirmations:

I am handing all "old baggage" over to God!

I am healed in body, mind, emotions and spirit!

I am healed and I am free to be me!

Give thanks to your body

Your body is an instrument which is "in service" to you!
Billions of little elementals within
your body are working tirelessly to keep you alive.
Special cells are fighting to protect you from disease and your
whole system is working together to achieve optimum health for you.
Thousands of little miracles are happening with every breath you take!
Do not take this body for granted!
Embrace, honour and respect it and first and foremost
give thanks to the "temple of your soul" for being
so faithful and obedient to you in this lifetime you have been given!

❀

Make time for a thanks-giving ceremony for your body.
Have a shower or a bath and then thank every part of
your body for the work it has been doing for you all your life.
Start with your toes and work your way up.
Of course, include all your organs, your skin (the largest organ), your
blood cells, nerves and nerve endings and do not forget your brain!
Also apologise for any abuse you have inflicted on your body!
Now ask for special healing from
the healing angels for any injured or diseased areas.
You will feel an increased sense
of peace and well-being at the end of your ceremony.
Thank the healing angels for their help.

Always ground, attune and protect yourself.

❀

I thank my body for working so hard on my behalf!

I nurture, nourish and look after my body to the best of my abilities!

I honour, respect and treat my body well!

October 8

Abandonment

All of you, my beloved,
have suffered abandonment in one form or another.
This experience may have been so painful,
that you have buried and "forgotten" all about it.
However the scars are there and evident in your suspicions,
your lack of trust and the fears you have of being left alone!
Hand in hand with God and the healing angels, who never have
and never will abandon you, go forth and heal your emotional wounds!
Realise that those who did abandon you were doing
the best they could, according to their state of awareness,
abilities and circumstances at the time.
Seize the moment, release, forgive and allow yourself to be healed!

Meditation:

See yourself sitting in a comfy sky-blue sofa,
holding hands with God, your guardian angel by your side.
Now allow any memories of situations of abandonment
to come to the surface and reach your conscious awareness.
Visualise yourself talking to the perpetrators and
allowing them to explain to you why they acted the way they did.
The perpetrators then ask for your forgiveness.
You forgive them and also yourself for any part
you may have played in the situation.
Now a huge spotlight appears above the scene
and a bright golden light shines on all of you, permeating
and transmuting any sadness and negativity still present.
Soon all is clear and bright!
God gives His blessing and all is done!
Thank God and your guardian angel for their help!

Affirmations:

I am safe in the knowledge that I am not alone!

God will never abandon me!

I allow God, the angels and the universe to support me!

Death

Death, my beloved, is but a rebirth!
The eternal soul is being reborn into the
eternal light of God, where it dwells until it is
ready to be born once again, to enter into a physical body!
It is the indestructible soul who carries your true identity,
not the body, which is changeable and perishable.
So rejoice, for you are immortal!

Meditation:

Attempt to picture your "soul body".
What does it look like?
What does it feel like?
Now get in touch with your soul
and ask about the process of dying.
Does this thought frighten you?
If yes, why is that?
Hand those fears over to God and meditate
daily on the nature of death and your immortal soul!

This invaluable practice will catapult you into
the here and now on a daily basis, allowing you
to truly value life and all it is offering you moment by moment.

Affirmations:

Death is an illusion!

My soul is immortal and indestructible!

I exist through all eternity!

October 10

The joys of receiving!

As you are of service to others, allow your
fellow brothers and sisters to be of service to you!
For the loving soul that you are, it is often easier to give than receive!
Still, make sure not to take the pleasure of giving
away from those who love and respect you.
Give unconditionally and also receive unconditionally!
Do not deprive anyone of the joys of giving!

Meditation:

If you find it difficult to accept gifts of any kind, ask yourself why.
Do you not feel worthy of them?
Do you feel guilty by accepting them?
Where is the root of these feelings?
Maybe your parents told you not to accept gifts?
Maybe your family, teachers, or peer-group
told you that you were not worthy of gifts?
Now visualise yourself standing by a very special
Christmas tree, your guardian angel is by your side.
Underneath this tree, to your delight,
you find all the gifts you have not allowed yourself to receive!
Now the time has come to do so.
Get down on your knees and with the help
of your guardian angel open all your presents!
Enjoy, you deserve them!
Give thanks.

Affirmations:

I am worthy of and deserving of all that I am given!

I give love — I receive love!

I give unconditionally and allow myself to receive unconditionally!

Uplifting reading

Do not waste your time reading
negative, depressing literature, my beloved!
Not only is your time as an earth angel precious,
but the energy of such negative out-pouring will burden
and trouble you, even though you might not be aware of it!
The daily (bad) news will be enough to unsettle you.
Why allow yourself to be influenced in such a destructive way?
Choose for yourself what kind of energy you would like to take into
your system and allow no one to persuade you otherwise.

You are in charge of your life!

Meditation:

Next time you watch the news or read the newspaper,
note how you feel before and after the event.
Observe your thoughts, your emotions
and how your body is responding to this "negativity feast".
The more sensitive you become,
the less you will want to torture yourself in this way!

Affirmations:

I read positive, uplifting literature!

I watch inspiring, worthwhile programmes and movies!

I surround myself with love and light!

October 12

The search is over

The search is over!
All you need is right here within you!
You truly are all mighty!
The power to create is yours.
You are a miracle worker with God!
Believe in this truth, trust in it.
This is your divine legacy, your divine
inheritance bestowed on to you by the powers of heaven!
Accept it for yourself, for it is your divine birthright!

Meditation:

Shine a powerful searchlight within yourself
and you will find there the ability to
"tune into upstairs-management" for direction and inspiration.
You will also find a brilliant mind, full of exciting ideas;
wonderful communication skills, enabling you
to share your ideas with others; and finally,
on the outside, two hands with which to work wonders!

What a perfect child of God you are!
Be happy to be you!

Affirmations:

I have found my true self!

I am ready to receive my divine inheritance!

I trust in my God-given powers!

Angelic guidance

Angels are all around you, eager to protect, guide and help you!
Using your free will, invite them into your life
and let them be of service to you!
Open your heart and they will be there, by your side, always!

❃

Meditation:

Visit the chamber of your heart.
As you open the door and look in, you find that
the windows are covered with wooden shutters.
You walk in and open the shutters one by one
and immediately your heart starts to feel lighter and brighter.
Now, sit down on a pink, heart-shaped sofa
in the centre of the room and ask your angels for assistance.
As soon as you put this wish out to the universe you can hear
the sound of large wings coming closer and
the angels enter through the open windows of your heart!
The angels embrace you and you feel the power of
unconditional love flowing through you like warm, golden honey.
Then you sit down on the sofa together
and the angels ask how they can assist you.
Tell them where you need help, choosing one area of your life at a time.
The angels will come back to help you with
other issues, whenever you ask.
The Angels promise to assist you in any way they can.
You get a wonderful angel hug goodbye
and a promise that they will always be near you.
Give heartfelt thanks and return to waking reality.
Please remember to ground, attune and protect yourself.

Affirmations:

I acknowledge the existence of angels!
I open my heart and invite the angels into my life for guidance,
protection and support!
I am deeply grateful for the service of angels to humankind!

God-confidence

To achieve true self-confidence first acquire God-confidence!
Have faith in God and trust that you can rely on Him 100%!
God is omnipotent and omnipresent and you are made in His image!
Therefore, all God's abilities and qualities
are yours by divine decree, purpose and design!

Meditation:

Make God your confidant.
Bare your soul before Him and allow God
to transmute all your fears and feeling of lack.
Proceed on this path, step by step, handing over more
and more of your "luggage" to God, until the burden is lifted.
You are free and what is left of you is your God self!

Now you will finally be confident of who you truly are!

Affirmations:

My self-confidence equals God confidence!

I am made in God's image and all divine qualities
are inherent within me!

I am confident in my God-given talents and abilities!

Purity

Aim, above all, my beloved, for purity of mind!
For when your mind is free of false beliefs about
yourself and the outside world, then you are truly liberated!
Your unadulterated mind, like the mind of an innocent
little child, then becomes one with the divine mind.
From your pure mind will issue forth purity of speech,
and the purity of your deeds will be ensured from then on!

Meditation:

Ask the healing angels for assistance.
See yourself standing in front of a pond with a fishing rod
in your hands and a large empty bucket on the shore next to you.
The pond is representative of your mind.
How clear is the water in the pond?
How many bits of debris are floating in it?
You now decide that you are going to clear the pond
and you start to fish out all the bits with your rod.
Put all the debris in the bucket and when it has filled up,
hand it to the healing angels, who take it away
and transmute the negative energy for you.
Keep on "fishing" until the pond is clear.
Give thanks to the angels and repeat as often as necessary.
Please do not forget to ground, attune and protect yourself.

Affirmations:

My pure mind is one with the divine mind!

I am pure in thoughts, words and deeds!

I am pure in body, mind, emotions and spirit!

No regrets

Do not harbour regrets my beloved!
What you think you have lost, you will find
again, perhaps in a different form.
What you think you did wrong was not wrong, as your
perceived wrongdoing was also part of God's divine plan!
The opportunities you think you have missed,
will present themselves to you again!
And the loved ones you think you lost live forever in your heart!

Meditation:

See yourself working in a sweet-factory.
You are standing at a huge conveyer-belt,
packing the sweets as they come along.
To your great surprise, what comes along next,
instead of more sweets, is something you thought
you had lost forever, never to be seen again!
You are overjoyed at this gift from the universe
and this time you are able to keep it for good!
Give thanks to the abundant universe!
Please ground, attune and protect yourself.

Affirmations:

Loss is an illusion created by my mind!

The universe constantly provides me with new opportunities!

Love never dies!

Moving on

You will know in your heart, when it is time to move on!
Do not allow yourself to be held back in your spiritual
and worldly progress by feelings of guilt or uncertainty.
Guilt is a projected emotion!
Find out who or what is influencing you in
such a negative way, and untangle yourself from that situation!
Remember, my child, that the only constant in this life is change!
Be open to change as a means to learn and grow
and decide that uncertainties are just part of the process of change!

Meditation:

Take this into contemplation:
Ask yourself the question, from
which area in your life do you need to move on.
Ask the special team, the removal angels, for help
and see them drive up to meet you in a huge, golden removal van.
To start with, the angels help you to sort out the old,
all of which goes to a nearby heavenly recycling plant.
As soon as that is done you jump into the removal van together
with your angelic team and drive into a new and glorious future!
Give thanks.

Affirmations:

I let go of the old and invite the new into my life!

I allow the angels to help me with my transitions!

I am moving onwards and upwards!

Spiritual foundations

You build houses; you start businesses
and universities and start families...
But are you working on building spiritual foundations?
Go within your own heart, my dear child,
and seek to find the truth about this state of affairs!
God, the angels and the whole universe are at hand to help
you build strong, solid foundations, made from unconditional love,
peace, trust and unshakable faith in the divine within.
Accept their assistances and soon
your spiritual foundations will be unshakable!

Meditation:

What state are your spiritual foundations in?
Ask for a team of building angels to assist you
in strengthening, enforcing and enlarging your foundations.
Work together with the angels to achieve
a solid, strong spiritual foundation.
Pour love, trust, peace, contentment and lots of faith
and patience into the cement and see it
dry into a beautiful bedrock for your earth-mission!

Thank the building angels for their hard work!

Affirmations:

My spiritual foundations are rock-solid!

I base my whole life on the bedrock of love and light!

I am unshakable in my trust and faith of the divine principle within!

Obedience

Obedience to the divine laws governing this universe is a necessity!
Law and order are to be upheld at all levels of existence.
Align yourself with God's divine will and
your inner moral code inherent within you
from time immemorial, will show you the way without fail!
Stray not from the path when temptations test your faith.
Instead ask God and the angels to guide you every step of the way!

Meditation:

Although you may not enjoy having to learn the Highway Code,
it is still necessary to do so, to ensure safe driving
and the uninterrupted flow of traffic on the roads.
You, the driver, have to learn the rules
and take responsibility for your vehicle.
If you cause an accident, you put your own life
and other innocent people's lives in danger.
In the same, way the universal laws
are the Highway Code God has designed for you!
Your obedience ensures a safe, trouble-free
and speedy journey on your chosen path for you,
and for all your brothers and sisters on this planet!

Affirmations:

I am obedient to God's laws!

I comply with the laws of the universe!

God is my ultimate authority!

October 20

In-tuition

Intuition is the highest form of knowledge, my dear one!
You might be intelligent and learned, but your mind
is conditioned by what you have been taught and what
you have observed over many life times.
Now the time has come to link your mind with the universal truth!
This high state of being can only be attained through attunement
and meditation and by bypassing the lower-mind,
which constantly seeks to create new realities for you.
Your intuition teaches you the true reality!
Trust and listen!

Meditation:

Breathe in white light and let it flow through all your chakras.
See a silver cord connecting your crown chakra
with your higher self, your God self.
The silver cord is your "Intuition phone line".
When you are ready, make a call!
Ask your higher self a very simple question
to start off with, then be still and simply listen!
You will receive an answer!
Practise your intuition by guessing who will phone you next,
who will visit you next, what the weather
will be like tomorrow and so on.
As you go along step by step, with practice,
you will start to learn to trust your intuition!
Do not forget to ground, attune and protect yourself.

Affirmations:

I trust my intuition!

I use my intuition to attain higher knowledge!

My intuition is superior to my intellect!

Your inner light

As the year draws to an end and the daylight hours are beginning
to shorten, you will depend more and more on your inner light.
This inner light of yours, properly tended and cared for, will illuminate
the hours of outer and inner darkness which are yet to come.
You are the keeper of the divine flame!
Have faith and trust.
You are never alone!

Meditation:

Light a candle.
Sit comfortably in front of it.
Gaze gently into the flame for a while, breathing in the golden light.
Close your eyes.
The flame will appear within your third eye.
Hold it there for a moment.
Then allow it to drop into your heart chakra.
Breathe more and more golden light into it
and the light of the candle will grow and grow.
As the light fills the chamber of your heart to the full, let it wash
through you, cleansing, clearing and energising your chakras.
Then send the light in your heart out to all sentient beings
on this planet that come to your awareness at this moment.
Finally shrink the flame back into the centre of your heart,
where it will keep on burning bright!
Give thanks and make sure that you are grounded and protected.

Affirmations:

I am connected to the light of divine love at all times!

My inner light shines bright!

I am the light and the light is within me!

October 22

Time

Time, as you understand it on this earth plane,
does not exist outside your reality.
However, as you are living within the framework
of third-dimensional reality, make good use of
the time you have at your disposal in this present incarnation.
Focus on the here and now.
Allow expectations to gently leave your energy field.
Any attachments will burden you and so dilute the cosmic
essence of present time, which, my earth child, is so precious to you!
As you trust and surrender all to the divine,
much can be accomplished at "a moment in time"!

Meditation:

Start with breathing in timeless calm, as pure white light,
into every chakra, releasing stress and anxiety on the out-breath.
Start with the base chakra, breathing in white light,
releasing and letting go on the out-breath.
Then breathe the white light into the sacral chakra, the solar
plexus, the heart, the throat, the third eye and the crown chakra.
To end with, visualise your auric space
to be filled with cosmic white light.
Stay with this cosmic energy until
you begin to experience a sense of equilibrium.
Repeat often in times of stress and anxiety.
Do not forget to ground, attune and protect yourself.

Affirmations:

I now let go of all expectations about timing and of any time limits
myself or others have imposed on me!

I am always on time, and I have all the time
in the world available to me!

I am in the right place at the right time according to God's will!

Mystery

My beloved child, you are surrounded by magic and mysteries.
All God's creation is such. To learn about it, focus on the small.
Look and meditate on a flower, for example.
What a magical, mysterious thing a flower is!
From a minute kernel a beautiful, sweet fragranced
rose springs, truly a magical event for you.
God is within every one of these flowers,
and truly the flowers are also part of God.
So are you within God and God within you.
This is what you are: a perfectly
formed divine spark of consciousness!
Rejoice!

❀

Meditation:

Put a single flower in a vase in front of you.
Find a relaxed position.
Gaze at the flower;
concentrate on the form,
then on the colour,
then on the scent.
Ask to link up with the divine spark
within this flower, the plant deva.
Listen carefully to what she has to teach you!

Give thanks.

Affirmations:

From now on I will look for magic and mysteries in small things!

God's love is expressed in all creation and I am part of it!

I am part of God and God is part of me!

Your inner landscape

Take a look at your inner landscape,
the landscape that your soul inhabits.
As you know, it is housed in the chamber of
the heart and has a vista over your whole chakra system.
From there it views a lot of clutter and debris,
unsightly boulders in the landscape.
Make it your first and foremost business
to clear away such cumbersome blockades.
When the view is clear and the inner light is shining bright,
you have indeed succeeded in your chosen task of self-illumination.

Meditation:

Breathe in the pink ray of self-love.
Repeat seven times through all the chakras.
Put your awareness into the base chakra,
look around in this chakra and send all debris to the light.
Repeat this within all the chakras.
Return to the heart chakra, the seat of your soul,
and place a red rose, the symbol of the Christ, within it.
Allow the energy of this rose to accompany you
through the days, months, and years to follow.
Give thanks.
Remember to ground, attune and protect yourself.

Affirmations:

My mind controls my experience!

My higher self is in control of my mind!

I use my mind to my highest good, governed by the divine wisdom of
my higher self!

One-ness

My child, you, and all of creation, experiences a great yearning,
the yearning for one-ness, which is the yearning to be loved.
You share this feeling with all your brothers and sisters.
However, you are often not aware.
Many times you feel that your fellow brethren want to harm you.
Look within if you have these feelings.
They are only a reflection of the harm
you are currently doing to yourself in your own life.
Clear away these feelings and you will find people
coming into your life who are wholly loving and accepting of you.
By loving the troubled part of yourself, you have not
only allowed people around you to grow and heal,
you have also broken down the barrier of "mine" and "thine".
You have truly been a light-worker and co-operator with God!

❀

Meditation:

Breathe soft pink healing light into all your chakras.
Then put your awareness into your heart centre.
Become aware of a beautiful seed, your soul seed.
This seed glows intensely and magically.
Watch this seed sending out electric love rays.
First they fill your heart; then they fill your whole body.
Then they fill the room you are in; then the house, beaming
into the hearts of all the people who live in it; and then they fill
the town or the village you live in, sending the light to all inhabitants.
Then the rays fill your country and the light fills
the hearts of all the people who live in it.
Then the rays fill the whole world
and all of its inhabitants with that beautiful healing light.
When you have done that, draw the light back in, where it will stay.
Please ground, attune and protect yourself.

❀

Affirmations:

You and I are one!
I love all creation totally and unconditionally!
I am wholly accepting of my fellow brothers and sisters!

October 26

Truth

Do you resonate with the "one and only truth", the absolute or divine
truth, the one reality that transcends time, space, and all barriers?
At first this will feel very uncomfortable.
It is as if a high-powered drill is blasting
away debris from your emotional and mental bodies.
It really hurts, and at this point you will often resist the divine truth.
The flow of change has brought all this debris to the surface
and it is being chipped away with the help of your higher self
and all your guides, your masters, your guardian angel,
the healing angels, and all the other divine helpers.
Trust, surrender. Do not resist this process.
If you do trust, you are surrendering the fear also.
As fear, pain and suffering leaves your body, they are immediately
replaced by the vibration of divine truth and love, which allows you, at
the end of this process, to know finally with absolute certainty who you
really are: a wonderful divine spark of our Father- Mother God!

Meditation:

Breathe in love and light and on the out-breath think
of letting go and releasing. Do this three times.
Then visualise a beautiful golden Buddha,
a symbol of self-knowledge, sitting in your third eye.
Gently keep this image there. Connect with it.
Allow the essence of the Buddha to infuse your energy field.
Allow the essence of the Buddha to speak to you,
may it be in words, may it be in pictures,
may it be in sounds of music, may it be in thought patterns.
Absorb the sublime knowledge and holy essence of the Buddha.
Remind yourself to ground, attune and protect.

Affirmations:

Only the truth shall set me free; therefore I align myself with the divine
absolute truth in any situation I find myself in!

I am now in my highest truth!

I shine and radiate with the energy of absolute truth!

Power

What is the nature of power?
When you feel powerful, where does this energy actually come from?
True power should flow from the heart – love power.
A strong combination indeed.
Sadly this is not so with the majority of humankind.
Their seat of power is the lower self, the solar plexus, the ego self,
which is power as a defence system, a form of attack, born of fear.
Only if you are able to release these fears will you
experience true power, the power of unconditional love,
which comes from the heart, the seat of the soul.

✿

Meditation:

Take three breaths of healing white light.
Then allow your awareness to drop from the top
of the crown chakra down into the solar plexus area.
Ask the fearful parts and aspects of your self
to talk to you, to tell you what they are afraid of.
Ask them what you can do to help them overcome their fears.
Then centre yourself in your heart chakra and send
a beam of unconditional love down into
your solar plexus area until it feels still, calm and relaxed.
Repeat as often as necessary.
As the fears are released true power,
governed by the heart, will reign supreme.
Remember to ground, attune and protect yourself.

Affirmations:

I am one with the power of God!

I am an all-powerful being!

I am affirming my power in alignment
with divine will, divine law and divine purpose!

October 28

Brotherhood/Sisterhood

Human brotherhood/sisterhood brings all
your brothers and sisters "under one hood".
This "hood" is the mantle of God, the God within.
It is for you to extend your heart and hold your mantle of
unconditional love over your brothers and sisters on this earth plane.
There is no separation, you are all brothers and sisters, my dear one.
You all have the choice to enter into the oneness of your being.

Meditation:

See yourself standing on a hilltop.
You are wearing a golden cape.
Now breathe in white light and fill your heart with it to the brim.
Allow the energy to overflow from
the heart into the palms of your hands.
Open your arms wide.
See yourself feeling the healing light of God around you,
extending itself farther, bit by bit, until it wraps itself
magically around the whole world, giving love
and light to all humans and sentient beings on this earth.
As you do this, many brothers and sisters, and also animals,
will seek shelter under your golden cape of unconditional love.
Always ground, attune and protect yourself.

Affirmations:

I love all my brothers and sisters as best I can!

I am willing to overcome, through the powers of unconditional love,
all separations of race, colour and creed!

I realise now that we are all children of God and,
as such, we are all one!

Abundance

If you are still bound up in feelings of lack:lack of money, lack
of health, lack of power, lack of love, this is a sorry state of affairs.
Why is this so, my dear child?
It is because you are still listening to what the world at large
would want you to believe, that there is not enough for everyone.
Hence, human beings put up borders, enforce laws
and trade embargoes, and so this sad tale goes on.
Please reconsider for a moment, be still, and go within.
There within your core is a wellspring of power,
the power of unconditional love, a source of energy
that will never, and can never, dry up.
Tap into this energy.
It will bring you a true abundance of all you desire.
When you desire from the heart, it will be given to you.
There will be enough, not only for you, but also
for all your brothers and sisters to share, and,
last but not least, the more you give the more you will receive.

❈

Meditation:

Go and look at the stars at night, or if this is difficult,
visualise in your third eye, a beautiful starry night.
See how many stars there are in front of your eyes.
Dwell on this, concentrate on it.
This is true abundance; there are billions of stars in the universe!
And as there is this abundance above,
so it exists below on our beloved earth plane.
Now think of the trillions of pebbles on beaches
around the world, of the trillions of blades of grass…
What a wonderful abundant planet we inhabit.
Rejoice and feel your heart being filled with love for all creation.

❈

Affirmations:

I believe that there is health, wealth and love in abundance!
I believe that I am worthy of receiving it!
I believe in abundant love, health and wealth!

Humility

What does it mean to be humble?
It means to love all and serve all, at all times and any situation.
Serve all; they may be children, teenagers,
adults or elderly people; scholars or peasants; rich or poor.
Give of yourself whenever the need arises
in another person or situation.
Share some of your divine love energy, and share it freely!
Do not force yourself onto anyone or anything,
but humbly offer what you want to share or give.
Your gifts are unique!
Remember this!

Meditation:

Breathe in the golden healing light.
Breathe it three times through all the chakras.
Then breathe in the blue light of the Archangel Michael
and again breathe it through all your chakras three times.
Then humbly ask for all pride to be released.
Ask humbly for all intolerance to be released.
Ask humbly for all judgement to be released.
Ask humbly for all criticism to be released.
Let it all go.
Now breathe in beautiful pink unconditional love energy
and fill yourself with the power of unconditional love.
Remember to ground, attune and protect yourself.

Affirmations:

I am a humble servant of God!

I love all and serve all!

I am happy to share my gifts with anyone in need!

Patience

Are you a patient being, or do you operate on a level
where you want to have things done yesterday?
Or maybe you are somewhere in-between.
Why do you find it so hard to be patient with yourself and others?
The answer to this riddle is that deep down, that is, within the ego part
of you, there is a need to control all the goings-on in your life.
If all is not going according to plan, that is your lower ego's plan; you
become instantly impatient, as you subconsciously fear
losing control of the outcome of the situation.
Of course, many times things do not work out the way you wanted
them to and sometimes they only work out because you force the issue,
thereby working directly against your own highest good.
If you hand over the need to control every aspect of your life to
God, the God within, you slot automatically into a divine time frame.
Everything will happen according to divine timing
for the highest good of everyone concerned.
Let go, let God!
Sit back and watch your life unfold like a beautiful flower!

Meditation:

Connect to the golden healing light
and breathe it in three times through all of your chakras.
Visualise your chakras as little closed rosebuds;
then see them very gently open one by one.
Breathe the golden light of wisdom
and patience into them until they radiate brilliantly.
Then close your chakras down to form small buds once more
and seal each with a golden cross enclosed by a circle.
Please ground, attune and protect yourself.

Affirmations:

I know deep in my soul that everything in my life is in divine order!

I am abundantly gifted with all the patience and trust I need!

I trust that all I need will be given unto me!

Blessing for the month of
November

Rejoice

Accept your divine inheritance now!
Claim your birthright and rejoice in
the fullness of creation
May you rejoice in who you are!
May you rejoice in what you are!
May you rejoice in what you have!

May you rejoice in the limitless blessings
of the universe yet to come into your life!

Inner Strength

In your daily life, my beloved, you are faced with many challenges.
To cope with all of these you need inner strength.
How do you acquire access to this inner strength?
Why do some people seem to have more of it than others?
First you must find the true source of this inner strength,
which lies deeply embedded within your own spirit.
When some of your brothers and sisters have lost all will
to live or have become depressed, it is said that their spirit is broken.
This means that they have lost their strength, the strength
that comes from the ego self, the strength that depends
on the lower nature for sustenance.
It is by accessing your higher spiritual self
that you develop true inner strength.
Use your will in alignment with divine will and simply state
that you want love and light to flow abundantly through you.
Within love and light all properties such as strength,
endurance and courage are contained.
You ask and you shall receive.

❁

Meditation:

Visualise a beautiful golden lotus representing
your higher self above your crown chakra.
Ask to connect with it mentally.
Soon you see the petals opening slowly and a ray of light and love flows
from the centre of the lotus into your crown chakra.
First it gently flows through the third eye, then down to the throat,
into the heart, into the solar plexus, then into the sacral and the base
chakras, and it fills them with beautiful golden light with the purpose of
imparting strength and courage for your chosen tasks.
Finally, see the lotus closing and give thanks.

❁

Affirmations:

All my needs are met by my higher self for my highest good!
I ask and I shall receive!
I am at all times totally self-sufficient

Creativity

If you want to live this life God has given you to the full,
you will need to develop the creative aspect of your self.
This is a very important step on the spiritual path,
a very important part of your development,
for you are striving to become a co-creator with God.
It is a very simple process.
By connecting to the Mother Earth energy and infusing it
with the Father heavenly spirit energy a divine spark is ignited.
This is the start of creativity flowing from your base chakra up into
your heart, where you then use this energy, fused with love, to create.
Thus you have become a co-creator with God!

Meditation:

Grow golden roots into the earth.
Ask Mother Earth for some of her energy.
Feel this energy flow into your
lower chakras and up into your heart chakra.
Ask God the Father for the divine spark of creation to enter you.
Feel a beautiful beam of golden light entering your
crown chakra and flowing down into your heart chakra.
As soon as it arrives there, a bright spark
of energy ignites, and begins radiating from your heart.
Now use your will, in alignment with
your higher divine will, to create what your heart desires.
Do not forget to ground, attune and protect yourself.

Affirmations:

I have within me the source of all creativity!

I have within me endless possibilities and opportunities!

I am working for the highest good of humankind and all sentient beings
on this planet earth!

Never a victim

Before you incarnated into this physical body,
you chose a "karmic deal" for the earth life you are currently in.
Therefore you are never ever a victim!
On the higher levels of existence you
chose the experiences by pre-birth agreement.
All souls involved in this agreed with unconditional love to
"serve karma" to you, and you agreed in return to "serve karma" to them.
Now make the best of the life you have been given
and be mindful of your reactions to the actions of others.
All the God-given power is within you; you can access it at any
time through a simple prayer, asking for help in any given situation.
God will never fail you.

❁

Meditation:

Breathe in love and light.
On the out-breath, think of letting go.
You become aware of the many chains knotted all around
your body and realise that they are all victim thoughtforms.
Now get hold of a pair of big golden shears and cut away the chains
one by one, chakra by chakra, each time releasing
all the negative thoughtforms which have been stored
in the chains attached to the chakra you are working with.
Soon you are victorious over the thoughtforms
and not a victim any more.
Please ground, attune and protect yourself.

❁

Affirmations:

I have the power of divine love within me!

I am totally in charge of my life in accordance with divine law!

I am free to follow my dreams and higher aspirations!

November 4

Acceptance

Often, my dear child, you find acceptance difficult,
not only acceptance of the bad in your life but also the good.
Anything and everything that happens to you
on your earthly journey will serve you.
Dwell on this truth.
Be attentive not only to the grand, but also
to the minuscule occurrences in your day-to-day living.
Embrace each and every challenging situation so that
you learn the lesson it is imparting to you to its fullest,
and when good fortune comes along, welcome it with open arms.
Do not be shy or feel unworthy of it.
God's greatest joy is to bestow His gifts on you in great abundance.
Alas, all too many times you are the one who prevents
this from happening by declaring yourself to be unworthy.
Open your heart and mind.
You are the child of God and worthy of all the riches the world
has to offer you and, most of all, the greatest gift of all, God's love.

Meditation:

Breathe a pink ray of love into your heart centre.
Repeat this three times.
Feel the pink ray expanding, feel it radiating,
feel it charging up your whole being.
Carry on breathing in the pink light until you feel
totally enveloped in this energy and totally, completely loved.
Accept this love as a gift from God!
Give thanks.
Make sure to be grounded, attuned and protected.

Affirmations:

I joyfully accept all the good that comes to me!

I am a child of God and I deserve the best!

I accept all, I embrace all!

Love is never lost

When you lose your nearest and dearest or a beloved pet, you often
feel that you have lost that love and grieve for it to come back to you.
Rejoice, for in truth that love has never been lost
and it has never left you.
Love is beyond time and space and, once expressed,
is never lost, but absorbed into every fibre
of your being, right into the depths of your soul.
So even when you leave this mortal coil you will take all
the true love that was ever bestowed onto you into the higher realms.

Meditation:

Breathe in love and peace.
Visualise everyone you have ever loved around you.
Become aware of a beautiful pink ray of light
that links all your hearts together in perfect harmony.
Feel this beautiful connection of unconditional love flowing between you.
Give thanks, and let everyone go.

Remember to ground, attune and protect yourself.

Affirmations:

I give and receive love freely and unconditionally!

Love and my loved ones reside within me!

Nothing can ever be lost!

The light

What is "the light"?
The light is pure unconditional love,
containing within it all the knowledge there is.
When you have finally absorbed the light into every cell of
your physical and subtle bodies, you have truly become enlightened.
In order to come to recognise the light, you have
to have experienced the dark in every aspect:
physically, mentally, emotionally, and spiritually.
"The dark night of the soul" is an expression
used frequently on your earth plane.
So your dark hours have served you well,
my dear child, for without them you would indeed
not be aware that you are walking in the light, right now.

Meditation:

Feel and visualise yourself surrounded by twelve bright suns.
Take in the rays of every one of them.
Each sun will give off a slightly different colour or hue.
Surround yourself with a mantle of blue and then of golden light.
Give thanks.
Remember to ground, attune and protect yourself.

❋

Affirmations:

I am open and willing to receive the divine dispensation
of light into my being!

I am the light!

All I need to know and experience is contained within the light!

Your heart's desire

Are you listening to what your heart is trying to tell you, my child?
Or are you denying yourself your heart's desire?
Listen carefully to what the heart has to communicate to you,
for the heart is the seat of the soul, and emotion is the soul's language.

Be still and go within, and all will be revealed to you.

Meditation:

Breathe the light of golden love into all your chakras.
Put your awareness into your heart chakra.
Gently ask your soul to speak to you of its dreams, wishes and desires.
Now listen intently…
Make a mental note of what your soul is saying to you.
Promise your soul that you will take
appropriate steps to fulfil its wishes and dreams.
Please ground, attune and protect yourself.

Affirmations:

I am in constant communication and communion with my soul!

From now on, I listen to my heart's desires"!

I love my life with heart and soul!

Joy

Where does the emotion of joy come from?
How does it manifest itself?
You may believe that lovers, children, gifts, success, vacations
and so on and so forth will give you joy, which at times may be true.
However, the joy brought to you from the outside is
not a lasting one, as it depends on external sources
over which you have no control, no matter how hard you may try.
True, everlasting joy is found within, where it dwells at
all times; only you are not aware that it is available to you always.
You can access your divine birthright to everlasting joy and
happiness simply by acknowledging its existence as an outgrowth
of the divine love of God, dwelling within your very own being.
Lift the veil of ignorance, the false belief that your joy and happiness
depend on the outside world, allow this gift of God to light up your life.

Meditation:

Breathe in love and light; centre yourself in your heart chakra.
As you do this, you become aware that your heart is covered by many
old layers – layers of expectations, unfulfilled dreams, pain and past
hurts. See yourself peeling them away one by one. All are coming off
until you are left with a clean, smooth heart.
As you arrive at this point your heart begins to open and starts to
radiate pure joy; you can feel this energy flowing out from your heart
and energising your whole being.
Remember to ground, attune and protect yourself.

Affirmations:

I have an everlasting wellspring of joy within my heart!

I will now allow this joy to flow freely!

I am light and love and joy!

Grace

My child, the infinite grace of God is available to you at all times.
God is always ready to shower you with this divine gift.
However, you are sometimes not ready and willing to receive it.
You prefer to give yourself a hard time,
as you say down on this earth plane.
Why, my dear one, do you judge yourself so harshly?
Why are you so critical of others and yourself?
All of this is an unfounded figment of your social conditioning.
God loves you unconditionally; He does not judge you, but until
you have made some headway towards accepting yourself as a child
of God, He is, by the law of free will, not able to bestow
grace onto you in as great an abundance as He would wish.

❀

Meditation:

See yourself walking through a beautiful meadow,
full of wild flowers, little birds and colourful butterflies.
You come to a beautifully lit grotto and, as
you walk towards it, a being of light emerges from it.
The being welcomes you with open arms.
As you stand eye to eye, and the eyes are the windows
to the soul, you feel the beautiful energy of grace flowing
from the being of light into your very being.
You allow this process to take place.
Thank the light being, who returns back to the beautifully lit grotto.
Walk back again through the same meadow
until you arrive in your own space.
Have you grounded, attuned and protected yourself?

Affirmations:

God's grace is truly available to me!

I am gratefully accepting God's grace for now and forever more!

I allow the state of grace to become a natural part of my life!

Simplicity

What does it mean to you, my beloved, when you
read spiritual teachings that ask you to lead a simple life?
You, whose life is complex indeed.
So many layers, so many facets.
Indeed, many times you don't know what to make of your life.
"What is wrong or right for me?" you ask.
So many choices are available to you; too many, maybe.
The answer to this dilemma in itself is simple;
if your heart feels lifted when you contemplate
an action or a deed, then you are on the right track.
When your heart sinks, you clearly are not.
Emotion is the language of the soul
and this is the key to simplifying your everyday life.
Listen to your soul and allow your soul to speak to you.

Meditation:

Allow your main concern or problem at this
very moment to show itself to your mind's eye.
Now ask for assistance from your higher self.
Become the observer and ask the worry or concern
what it wants from you, or if it would like to impart
some lesson, knowledge or wisdom to you.
You may receive pictures or just
have a conversation going on in your mind.
One way or another the essence or root cause
of your problem will be perceived and will reveal itself to you.
Thank your higher self for its co-operation.

Affirmations:

My life is simple and easy!

I stand in my own truth and I am guided every step of the way!

I embrace my life, which provides me with effortless
focus and endless opportunities!

Life's purpose

Ask yourself today what is your life's purpose in God's creation?
Is it to rush out and make lots of money,
have many children, collect many friends?
Or is there a deeper purpose behind your existence?
Deep inside none of these achievements
or any others are truly fulfilling you.
You are running on empty.
Allow God's love, which is all around you, in the centre
of a flower, in a bird's song, in a whisper in the wind, to reach
deep within your heart, igniting the love for the self, awakening
you to the divine love which slumbers within you.
Once awakened you will feel a quickening;
you will start to feel a passion for life.
You will overflow with unconditional love from your own heart,
so igniting the hearts and souls of your fellow
humans and in this alone lies the purpose of your existence.

Meditation:

Breathe in the pink ray of love.
Fill your heart chakra to the brim with this ray; then see
yourself giving everyone you know a wonderful heart-to-heart hug.
As you do this you notice their faces lighting up
and when they walk away from you, you can see
a ray of pink love emanating from their own heart chakras.
They have caught the "love bug" from you!
Be happy, you are a wonderful co-worker with God.
Do not forget to ground, attune and protect yourself.

Affirmations:

By being happy I am fulfilling my purpose for this lifetime!

God's purpose of existence is to love me and I love God in return!

I am fulfilling my divine purpose by loving and accepting myself!

Flow of life

Allow yourself to go with the flow of life.
Do not struggle against the tide.
Be attentive.
The universe gives you pointers at every turn of your chosen task.
You may receive these signs via friends, family or your
work colleagues, through reading a book or watching a film.
You may indeed find that Mother Nature delivers insights to you.
Be open; look and listen.
All the answers are right where you are!
So the more you watch out, listen and learn to read
the signs, the easier and more free-flowing your life will be.

Meditation:

See yourself sitting in a canoe floating down a beautiful river.
Enjoy the ride; enjoy the scenery.
Take in all around you: the sky,
the water, the trees, plants, birds and fish.
Realise that the universe supports you.
Realise that life supports you.
Keep on floating, drinking in this feeling
of being loved and steered by the hand of God.

Please ground, attune and protect yourself.

Affirmations:

I am capable of reading the signs the universe is offering to me!

I am effortlessly flowing with life!

I am gratefully embracing all which life has to offer me!

Trust

You distrust so many things, people, events and happenings.
You never feel totally optimistic about the outcome of any situation.
All of this is going on around you because you
have not addressed the lack of trust in yourself.
God loves you unconditionally.
All that happens to you happens for your highest good.
Remember, you are not the body, you are not the mind, you
are not the emotions; you are a spirit and therefore indestructible.
You can and will not be harmed.
At all times you are connected with
the divine part of the self via your intuition.
Use it.
If things feel right and lift your spirit, then they
are right, and you are acting in alignment with divine will.
Surrender yourself and trust will follow.
God loves and trusts you 100%, so love and trust yourself 100%.

❊

Meditation:

Think of a task you would like to achieve,
but you have never trusted yourself to do so.
Now breathe in love and golden light and visualise
yourself carrying out this task with ease and grace.
Repeat until you have achieved this in real life.
Give thanks.

Affirmations:

I trust my inner judgement!

I trust that God loves me unconditionally!

I trust that the divinity within me will guide and protect me at all times!

November 14

Insight

Many times you pray to be given insight.
This is a gift that is not conferred lightly.
You have to make an effort yourself to look inside of things.
In accordance with divine law, only if your intent is
clear and focused and you are engaged at all levels, physically,
emotionally, mentally and spiritually, in the process of looking within
will the gift of insight be bestowed onto you.

Meditation:

See yourself walking into a large mansion.
First you step into the hall and you see a door.
Above the door there is a sign and you see written
on it the precise problem you want to have an insight about.
Now ask your the angels and your higher self to help you
focus your mind on the task ahead; state your intent to find
out about this problem and, when you are ready, open the door.
You enter the room.
In it you will find all the answers and the solutions you will need.
Give thanks.
Walk back out again into the hall, out of the front door,
back into the place of your meditation.

Do not forget to ground, attune and protect yourself.

Affirmations:

I am guided at all times to ever-increasing knowledge and insights!

I look within, where I gain true "in-sight"!

I am eternally grateful for the gift of insight!

Peace

"I want peace," you shout many times on your earth plane.
You frantically search for peace all around you,
but peace eludes you every time.
Why? Because it cannot be found in the outside
world, in other people, places, objects or circumstances.
Peace can only be found on the inner planes,
the world deep within your heart.
Hand over all desires, all expectations, all worries
to the God within and you will find that peace will make
itself at home in the chambers of your heart.

Meditation:

Imagine yourself in your favourite surroundings,
maybe a beach, a forest or a green meadow.
Feel the beautiful energies around you; feel also
the connection with your true self, your God-self.
A feeling of peace and tranquillity will
spread from your heart through your whole body.
Allow yourself to bathe in this beautiful energy as long as you like.
Then walk from your favourite place back
to the room you are currently in.
Remember to ground, attune and protect yourself.

Affirmations:

I am at peace with myself and the world around me!

I am at peace on the inside and therefore I inspire peace
and harmony on the outside!

Peace dwells within my heart always!

November 16

Inner Eden

If you love others as your sisters and brothers
then you surely are opening the gates of Paradise.
The Paradise I am talking about is the Garden of Eden that
exists within your own heart, the dwelling place of your divine self,
a place where light and love exist in great abundance,
radiating forth into the world at large.

Meditation:

See yourself holding hands with people of different races,
creeds and colours, your earth brothers and sisters.

You are forming a circle; the circle keeps
expanding until it embraces the whole globe.
At the moment it does, the circle becomes a circle of pure light
and this light radiates through every sentient being on planet earth
and you see yourself as being one with all!

Affirmations:

I am deeply connected with all sentient beings on this planet!

I am radiating love and light freely to all!

I am one with my brothers and sisters!

Friendship

How happy I am when I see you, my child,
join hands with others in friendship.
Value your friends, my dear one, as you do need them on
your side, holding your hands for a little while along your path in life.
Cherish them and tell them often how much you love and honour
them and, of course, in return, be the best friend you can be.

Meditation:

Centre yourself in the heart chakra and thank all
your friends for what they have done for you.
Send love and light to all of them in return.
Do this often.

Please remember to ground, attune
and protect yourself always.

Affirmations:

I am grateful to my friends for their love and support!

I am lovingly affirming the bonds of friendship I already have!

I love my friends and they love me in return!

November 18

Surrender

You do not easily surrender yourself to God, my child.
Indeed, most of the time you try to hold onto
to the reality you have created for yourself out of fear.
Fear of lack of money, fear of your own power,
fear of the future, fear of love itself.
Please, dear one, do not dwell on this reality any longer.
Surrender all your fears to the Creator, God.
He will take care of you and will
furnish you with everything you need and more.
Through the act of surrender you will feel much lighter;
you will have unburdened yourself of the old reality
and be ready to receive the new and light into your life.

Meditation:

Breathe in love and light into every chakra;
then see yourself throwing all your
worries, fears, and anxieties into a big golden dustbin.
As soon as the bin is full two angels appear and wheel it away
to the recycling centre, where the energies
will be transmuted into more light.
Fill as many bins as necessary and thank
the angels for assisting you with your task.
Do not forget to ground, attune and protect yourself.

Affirmations:

I now surrender all that is not love!

I am surrendering the old and accepting the new gratefully,
by the grace of God!

I gently surrender my old beliefs and invite the love and light of God!

Inner Guidance

When you follow your inner guidance,
wondrous things occur, my dear child.
New opportunities arise seemingly from nowhere
and problems are resolved as if by magic.
By following your inner guidance, you align yourself physically,
emotionally, mentally and spiritually with God, your own divine self.
You thus allow the light, which in itself contains not only
unconditional love but also information and wisdom,
to flow freely into your energy field.
So, my child, take heart and always allow yourself to be guided
this way on your path to enlightenment.

Meditation:

Gently relax and ask yourself what you need guidance on.
Now visualise a movie screen within your third eye.
Connect with your higher divine self and then
ask for a solution to be shown to you on the screen.
Sit back, relax, and watch the show.
When you are ready come back into your daily life.
Remember to ground, attune and protect yourself.

Affirmations:

I am guided at all times by my divine self!

My inner guidance never fails me!

I am divinely guided, protected and loved at all times!

Choice

How many times do you say, "Oh, I had no choice in this, it was
all somebody's else's fault, the matter was taken out of my hands".
No, it was not, my child; you always had a choice,
which is at many times not apparent, of course.
Stand up for yourself; you are a child of God, you deserve the best.
Stand back, detach yourself; contemplate
or meditate before you make any decisions.
Let your higher self guide you to the
right choice in accordance with divine law.
It may seem the tough choice at the time but when you finally see
the overall picture you will know why it had to be the tough choice.
God always chooses right for you.

Meditation:

Contemplate your situation or the problem in hand.
Visualise yourself standing outside the library.
This is a library of infinite knowledge.
Enter into the hall; focus again on your problem.
Now you see three doors in front of you; behind every one of
those doors is a different possibility for dealing with your problem.
Enter the doors one by one, exploring the possibilities.
When you have done so, you walk out into another part of the library,
where you see a fourth door; written on it is the word "solutions".
You then enter the fourth door,
where you find the solution to your problem.
Walk back out the way you came in.
Have you grounded, attuned and protected yourself?

Affirmations:

I am free to make my own choices at all times!

I let my higher self guide me to choose what is best for me!

When I am standing in my truth, I am making the right choices!

Joy, play and fun

Are you having enough fun?
Do you enjoy yourself often?
Do you take time out to play?
Not enough, my dearest one. Not enough.
It is not frivolous to be joyful; it is not selfish to take time out to play.
Being joyful is a blessing; it is food for the soul.
Allow yourself to express the needs
of your inner child or inner teenager; have fun and play.
As you merge with the child within,
you become a balanced, mature and joyful adult.
To be happy is your birthright.
Do not wait for long; do not waste any more
of the precious time you have in this earth body.
Go forth and claim your birthright now, my dearest one.

❀

Meditation

Breathe in the pink ray of love and joy.
See yourself surrounded by a group of jubilant angels.
They dance around you and ask you to join in.
You do so, and dance the dance of angel-love with them.
You twirl and twirl, and with every movement you let go
of the negative energies stored up in your energy bodies
and start to feel lighter and lighter.
Soon you feel like you're floating, just like the angels do.
Carry on as long as you like and give thanks.
Please ground, attune and protect yourself.

❀

Affirmations:

It is my divine birthright to be joyful!

I am entitled to fun and playtime in my busy schedule!

God is joy and so am I!

November 22

Be kind to yourself

Be gentle on yourself, dear one.
You are often rather harsh with yourself.
You treat others kindly, why not yourself?
You do deserve it, you know.
Being soft and gentle with yourself is one of the first
important steps of learning to love yourself, to cherish yourself.
Tenderness starts in the heart and spreads out
through your body, creating balance and harmony,
and thus affecting also everyone around you.

Meditation

Breathe golden light all through your chakras.
Now visualise yourself in a luxurious Roman bathhouse.
You wander in and then you take off all your old clothes
and you walk into the perfumed waters of this beautiful Roman spa.
You relax, breathing in the scents of rose and geranium.
When you come out, you find your old clothes have been replaced
with the most beautiful new robes you have ever set eyes on;
you also find the softest white towels with which to dry yourself.
After you have dried yourself you set your
eyes on an amphora filled with aromatic body oils.
You gently rub the oils into your body and then put on the new robes.
As you walk out of this luxurious bathhouse,
you walk past a full-length mirror.
You catch a glimpse of yourself in this mirror
and what you see is a magnificent, radiant being — you!
Do not forget to ground, attune and protect yourself.

Affirmations:

I am treating my body, mind, emotions, and spirit with gentle kindness!

I love and cherish myself!

I am kind in thought, word and deed to others and myself!

The gift of healing

You have the gift of healing.
Every human being has, my child.
Develop it – use it.
You do not need to become a healer.
You are a healer.
Decide in your heart right now at this
very moment that this is who you are.
This is how you want to express yourself in your life from now on.
Channel God's love freely and you will find that
a little will always stay back for yourself.
Become a witness to divine love in action
and grow with the experience.

Meditation:

Grow golden roots through the layers of the earth.
Breathe in golden light.
Breathe the golden light into each of the chakras one by one.
Ask the healing angels to connect you with your higher self
and offer yourself up to be a channel for the divine healing light.
You will feel an increased energy flow.
Allow it to energise your whole body.
When you feel this process has been completed,
give thanks, withdraw your roots and close down your chakras.
Now you are ready to go out and radiate beautiful
healing light from the centre of your being – your heart.
Give thanks.
Make sure that you are grounded, attuned and protected.

Affirmations:

I am a wonderful clear channel for the healing light of God!

I wholly embrace my God-given gift of healing!

Through healing myself I act as a catalyst for healing others!

November 24

Inner child

Nurture your inner child, my dearest one,
for it is longing for your love and attention.
You have an inner child within you that is lonely and unhappy.
Heed it and fulfil your role as a parent to your
inner child by passing on the divine power within you.
Channel this power into healing your inner child.
You will be guided in this process at all times by your higher divine self!

Meditation:

Breathe in the pink ray of love.
Allow this energy to flood your whole
energy system, all your chakras and your auric field.
Then breathe the pink ray three times into your heart chakra.
Now visualise your inner child right in front of you, sitting on a chair.
It is crying.
Greet it and ask it what it would like from you.
Your inner child will tell you what to do.
Follow the process through.
Promise your inner child you will come back to visit it often.
Give it a big bear-hug before you leave.
Repeat this exercise as often as necessary and one day when
you find a very happy inner child sitting on the chair in front of you,
you will know that a positive outcome has been reached.
Please ground, attune and protect yourself.

Affirmations:

I am the perfect parent to my inner child!

I am nurturing and caring for my inner child!

I am embracing the hurt of my inner child
and showering it with divine love!

Inner guidance

Follow your inner guidance, my dearest one.
Don't let others persuade you otherwise.
Your soul is communicating with you
through the language of your emotions.
When you receive this inner guidance take heed;
then decisions and actions will simply feel right.
If something feels wrong, you cannot fail to notice it.
You will be acutely aware of it.
Your whole being will tell you that something is not right.
Surrender to the wisdom of your whole self
and allow yourself to be guided.

✿

Meditation:

Ask your guardian angel to help you with this meditation.
See yourself sitting in your favourite surroundings in a natural setting,
whether it be the beach, a forest or a meadow,
choose any place you feel really at home.
Look around you and marvel at the beauty of the place.
Fill it in your imagination with all you love and cherish.
You will then have created a sacred space
in which you feel safe, happy, and relaxed.
As you gently relax within this sacred space, a beautiful being
of light appears to you and introduces itself as your higher self.
You sit down together and you ask your higher self for advice.
When you have received the advice you need to thank your higher self.
Your higher self invites you to come back any time you need advice.
Give thanks and return from your sacred place to the room you are in.
Remember to ground, attune and protect yourself.

✿

Affirmations:

My inner guidance is available to me at all times!

I value the wisdom of my inner guidance and invite it often!

I trust my inner guidance!

God loves you unconditionally

God loves you unconditionally.
He never judges you.
As you go through life His love is always available to you.
God never withdraws His love
because of what you may have done wrong.
In His eyes there is no right or wrong.
Things just are as they are.
God is total love, therefore He is total acceptance.
If you are a saint or a sinner His love for you will be no different.

Meditation:

Breathe in golden light, gently allowing it
to flow through your chakras and your energy bodies.
See yourself walking in a light-filled landscape; it is very beautiful.
Ahead of you, you see a golden building; you enter this building
and within you find a light being which represents Father-Mother-God.
This being welcomes you with open arms
and tells you how much He/She loves you.
You are given a gift and invited back any time.
Wander back exactly the same way you came, and give thanks.
Always ground, attune and protect yourself.

✿

Affirmations:

God is unconditional love!

God's love is available to me at all times!

I allow God's love to flow through me!

Inner tools

God has given you all the tools you need
to accomplish whatever you need to do in this present lifetime.
These tools are within you.
You do not need to go and look for them in the outer world.
You have been given everything necessary, my beloved child.
There is nothing you cannot do or achieve.

Meditation:

Visualise a fountain of brilliant yellow light above your head.
As you breathe in, this clear, bright, yellow light flows
through all your chakras and through the layers of your auric field.
Visualise yourself in front of a
television set that at the moment is switched off.
Now hold the present situation you need
an answer or solution to in your mind.
Ask your higher self to show you a solution or
an answer on the television screen as soon as you switch it on.
After a little time you turn the television on; immediately coloured
pictures, words or sounds will appear relating to your question.
Watch carefully.
Switch the television off when you feel
you have been given all the answers.
Now come back into conscious awareness.
Do not forget to ground, attune and protect yourself.

Affirmations:

God provides me with all the tools I need
to lead a happy, successful life!

I have all the tools I need for my life journey within me!

I am gifted with all the inner knowledge I need to be successful
in this present incarnation!

The spoken word

Watch your speech, my dear one.
Let love flow from your lips.
Be aware and truly be in awe
of the spoken word, as it is very powerful.
Choose your words wisely, slowly, carefully;
do not judge, do not criticise, do not condemn.
Instead, encourage, uplift and enlighten your
fellow brethren with your softly spoken words of love.

Meditation:

Visualise golden healing light flowing into your third eye chakra.
On the in-breath think of releasing and letting
go of all negative thoughts you have about yourself.
On the out-breath release and let go of all of them.
Then again breathe in the golden light into your third eye chakra
and, on the next out-breath, release and let go of all critical
and judgemental thoughts you may have about other people.
Release. Then again breathe in another wonderful ray of golden
healing light, and now, on the out-breath, think of releasing
and letting go of all negative thought projections
that you feel might have been directed against you.
Now with the next in-breath of wonderful golden healing light,
fill your throat with thoughts and words of love.
Repeat this process often, particularly if you have a sore throat
or a cough or a tickle in your throat, all of which are signs
that there are issues with speech that need to be healed.
Please always ground, attune and protect yourself.

Affirmations:

I speak words of love, truth and wisdom!

I am love in action through the power of my spoken words!

I choose my words with love and careful
consideration for others and myself!

The perfect you

Be you, be truly yourself.
Stand in your own light.
You are perfect in every way, as God created you in His image.
There is no flaw in this sparkling jewel you are.
It is in your perception of yourself wherein lies the fault.
You see yourself as the sinner, as unworthy.
Change your mind about how you think you are.
You are not the sinner, the unworthy servant,
the lowly student; instead, you are one with God and His glory.

Meditation:

See yourself as a diamond with many facets.
Can you see a dull facet?
It may be the facet of willingness, loyalty or trust that needs polishing.
Polish this facet with a cloth made of light and unconditional
positive regard for the self, and with as much
unconditional love for the self as you can muster.
Repeat on many occasions until the whole diamond,
the whole of you, truly sparkles with divine love and light.

Remember to ground, attune and protect yourself.

Affirmations:

I am one of God's creatures and therefore perfect in every way!

I am a sparkling diamond radiating unconditional
love and light all around me!

I perceive myself as a perfect, flawless diamond
in God's crown of glory!

Laughter

Laughter is the best medicine; this is a certain truth, my child.
Laughter is also a spiritual medicine.
It transmutes negativity and sets you free
from cumbersome physical, emotional and mental conditions.
Do not take yourself so seriously.
Make light of the situation you find yourself in and you
will find that life flows easier when you apply such medicine.
Trust and believe in your own sense of humour and practise it often.
Laughter is infectious and you will want
to infect as many of your brothers and sisters as possible.
Laughter equals light, equals good feeling and "God-feeling".

Go forth, my child, and laugh heartily as often as you can.

Meditation:

Breathe in pink light, filling all your chakras
and all the layers of your auric field.
Now visualise yourself in front of a mirror.
Look into the mirror; first you look quite serious, your normal daily self.
Then you start to laugh.
The more you see yourself in the mirror laughing,
the more laughter will come naturally.
You laugh and laugh, and you really are now "tickled pink".
Carry on as long as possible and repeat often.
Do not forget to ground, attune and protect yourself.

Affirmations:

I invite laughter, fun and humour into my life!

I can easily laugh at myself and not take myself so seriously!

I apply the bandages of laughter with caring and respect for my fellow
soul brothers and sisters in need!

Blessing for the month of

December

Release

The time has come to release the old
and make space for the new!
Let go of anything, that is not love!
That way you are prepared to receive
the miracles of the new year to come!
May your thoughts be pure and kind!
May your speech be pure and gentle!
May your deeds be pure and good!

May you be showered with abundant blessings always!

December 1

Acceptance

Accept yourself as you are right now, at this moment in time.
You are made in the image of the greater God and,
as such, you are a perfect child of God.
Allow this reality to filter through from the higher self to the soul
level and then into your mind, your emotions and your physical body.
Allow yourself to feel that you are perfect as you are.
As you embrace this reality with all your heart,
a great healing will take place from whence you will
emerge feeling much more in touch with who you really are,
a spark of the divine enclosed in a human body.

Meditation:

Visualise a mirror image of yourself sitting opposite you on a chair.
Say "hello" and ask why you are not being more accepting of yourself.
Allow the mirror image, which represents your lower self, to air all its
grievances and talk things over, if possible in great detail.
Then get up and give your mirror self a big hug and say,
"I love and accept you just as you are. You are a beautiful being."

Do this as often as necessary; you will find success.

Affirmations:

I accept myself unconditionally!

I love and accept myself in all I do, in all
my thoughts, feelings and actions!

I accept that I am perfect as I am!

Wisdom

You are a seeker: a seeker for divine wisdom.
You look for it everywhere, in foreign scriptures,
in lands far away, and in hearsay too.
All along divine wisdom has eluded you as you were looking
for it outside yourself in gurus, priests, preachers and other folk.
All along it has been sitting right there within you,
deeply buried for many, many lifetimes.
Allow the angels to connect you to your own divinity,
through allowing yourself access to the divine wisdom within,
the answer to all your questions.

Meditation:

You are surrounded by golden light.
In front of you, you see a heart-shaped
golden book, ornately decorated.
You become aware that this book symbolises your heart chakra,
the seat of your soul, the container of divine wisdom.
Meditate now on any question you need answered. Hold the question
in your mind and then see yourself opening the heart-shaped book.
The answer to your question will be right there
in front of you on the page you have just opened.
Contemplate this answer and then close the book,
give thanks and return to the here and now.
Please remember to always ground, attune and protect yourself.

Affirmations:

I am the receptacle of divine wisdom!

I hold all the secrets of the universe within me!

I am able to access divine wisdom freely and effortlessly!

Loving Kindness

Practise loving-kindness.
To succeed with this task you must first of
all start to practise loving kindness with yourself.
There seems to be great difficulty in that for you.
It is so much easier to be loving and kind to another being.
Do you feel you do not deserve it for yourself?
Yes, this, my child, is the root of the matter.
Take heed and listen, give yourself this gift.
Give it often.
You do deserve it a thousand times.
All God wants is for you to be content and when you
are loving and kind to yourself that is what you will become.

❀

Meditation:

See yourself in a beautiful Turkish bath; the basin is decorated
with exotic tiles, the air is filled with fragrance and soft music.
You walk into the pool and relax deeply.
Let the water carry you.
Feel all negative energy draining away from you.
As you step out, a beautiful being of light gives
you a heavenly massage and dresses you in your new robes.
The light being says goodbye and tells you to
come back as often as you like for this heavenly treat.
You thank the being of light and return to waking consciousness.
Please remember to ground, attune and protect yourself.

❀

Affirmations:

I am now taking care of myself in a gentle, kind and loving way!

I am as loving and kind to myself as I am to others!

As I love myself more, I feel more at peace with myself!

New Beginnings

Every day is a new day, my child; as the sun rises,
fresh opportunities, new beginnings await you.
Every hour, every minute, every second, you can make
conscious choices, fresh starts, based on truth, integrity, love,
and the understanding that power lies in the moment, in the now.
Seize it, shape your future, take charge of your becoming,
and you will be acting as a co-creator with God.

Meditation:

Visualise the rising sun glowing in front of you over a calm lake.
The sun's rays, the rays of the solar angels,
shine straight into your heart chakra.
You are infused with solar energy, feeling first warmed
and soothed and then more and more uplifted and inspired.
Take in as much solar energy as you want
and then thank the solar angels.
Repeat as often as you would like.

Do not forget to ground, attune and protect yourself.

Affirmations:

I am in charge of my life!

Every day, every hour, every minute, every second of my life
provides the opportunity for a new beginning!

With every choice I make in love and in truth, I co-create with God!

December 5

Time to play

You have forgotten how to play, my dear one.
You think play is being idle.
"It is not a spiritual thing to do", you say. Nonsense.
Play is vital to your spiritual development and well-being.
In fact, it is an integral part of your spiritual path.
Play nurtures the soul, the spirit,
the mind, the emotions and your physical body.
Every physical and etheric part of
your being is being energised with fun and play.
Those higher vibratory notes thus uplift your whole being.
As this is so, my child, could taking out time
to play and have fun be the waste of time you thought it was?

Meditation:

Visualise yourself in one of your childhood playgrounds;
all your favourite friends and toys are there.
Watch yourself as you play and have fun, observing
closely that the more fun you have, the more uplifted you feel.
Now move on to a different playground and see yourself
playing with the toys you never had when you were a child.
Then, when you feel you have played with those toys and taken
pleasure, you move on to yet another playground where you play with
the friends you didn't have but would have wished for as a child, maybe
friends who were not reachable through circumstances at the time.
Now see yourself walking home as a happy, happy child
and return back to the here and now.
Please ground, attune and protect yourself.

Affirmations:

I am arranging my life so that I can fit in
regular doses of fun and play!

Life is fun and I live it to the full, effortlessly!

I honour and nourish my inner child by letting
it have fun and games whenever it wants.

Surrender

Surrender, my dearest one, surrender to the divine within.
Allow your mortal ego self to dissolve and your divine self to shine.
Let go of fears, false promises, hopes and expectations.
Offer it all up on the high altar of love and forgiveness,
and in return, you will receive freedom and great blessings.

Meditation:

Ask for the assistance of the healing angels.
Focus your mind on surrendering everything that is not love.
Raise the white flag of surrender to the healing angels.
The angels greet you now with open arms
and are thrilled at your surrendering.
Then just think of letting go and surrendering everything
that is not love, and let the angels take care of the process.
When you have finished this process, you will feel much lighter.
Give thanks to the healing angels.
Do not forget to ground, attune and protect yourself.

Affirmations:

As I surrender to my divine self, I set myself free!

I am aware that the healing angels are by my side at all times to assist
me in the process of surrender!

I am grateful for the assistance I get!

December 7

Listen to your soul

Listen, my dear child, to the whispers
of your soul for it has much to tell you.
Your soul has travelled countless times through time
and space, incarnating in different bodies on different
planets and in other galaxies.
Through this, your soul has become rich in experience
and carries all previous knowledge with it every time it incarnates.
You may draw on this storehouse of the insights gained any time;
for all you need to get by in this, your present,
incarnation lies safely stored within your soul.
Meditate or contemplate often, so that your soul
is given the opportunity to pass on this knowledge learned
with so much effort through the aeons of time.

Meditation:

Breathe pink light into your heart chakra; focus your awareness on it.
Ask your soul to show itself.
Communicate your deepest thoughts to your soul.
Your soul thanks you for making contact and asks you
to repeat this wonderful experience as often as possible.
Give thanks.
Always ground, attune and protect yourself

Affirmations:

I am one with my soul!

I embrace my soul and thank it for all the work it has done for me!

I have all the wisdom I need stored within my soul!

Live life to the full

Live life to the full, my child, do not fritter away
precious moments of it through mindless pursuits.
Instead, honour yourself by partaking of enriching activities.
Feed your body, emotions, mind and spirit
with high doses of love, light, humour and noble aspirations.
Make all this your goal.
Set this goal for yourself, hand it over to the divine
within you and go out and live a beautiful, fulfilled life.

Meditation:

You wander through a forest; soon you arrive at
a magical spring surrounded by flowers, birds and butterflies.
This is the spring of life.
Next to it is a golden goblet.
You fill the goblet with the water of life
and drink the wonderful energising fluid.
You do this three times.
Then you walk away feeling re-energised and rejuvenated.
Thank the devas of the forest and the water.
Walk back the way you came and give thanks.
Remember to ground, attune and protect yourself.

Affirmations:

I am honouring myself by nourishing
my body, emotions, mind and spirit!

I am overflowing with love, light and energy!

I drink from the wellspring of life and live life to the full!

December 9

Thank you, earth

Take good care of Mother Earth, your home.
She is the one who nourishes and sustains your physical vehicle.
She lets you use her resources for your personal disposal.
You eat her food, drink her water and breathe her air.
Without her you would be nothing.
Remind yourself often of this truth.
Honour the earth and what she is offering you.
Be kind to her, be gentle to her.
Offer something in return for her sacrifice.

Meditation:

Visualise the earth as a globe suspended in front of you.
It is turning slowly and you are able
to see all the land and the waters and the mountains.
Now place your awareness into your own heart chakra.
Radiate beams of golden light and love towards
the earth from your heart; concentrate on places of great need.
Finish when you feel that the earth now has a nice golden glow.
Finally thank Mother Earth for all she is providing for you.

Do not forget to ground, attune and protect yourself.

Affirmations:

I am deeply connected with Mother Earth!

I show the earth my gratitude by honouring her in many different ways!

I am part of the earth and the earth is part of me!

The animal kingdom

All animals on this planet are your brethren, my dear one.
Whether they roam the forest, swim the seas or fly through the air
they are all your brothers and sisters of the animal kingdom.
Sentient beings they are and, as such,
treat them with reverence and respect.
If you feel you must consume them to sustain yourself
make their deaths painless and thank them for their sacrifice.
Take heed, my beloved.
Your destiny and theirs are intertwined so what will
happen to them will surely, in time, also happen to you.

Meditation:

Centre yourself in your heart chakra and send a beam of healing light
to all wild animals, all farm animals, all pets, all animals in
experimental laboratories and all animals about to be slaughtered.
Now visualise all the animals on this planet
as one happy, healthy family.
Then thank the animal kingdom for their sacrifices.
Do this meditation often, as it is very much needed
at this moment of time on planet earth.
Please ground, attune and protect yourself.

Affirmations:

I love, honour and respect all sentient beings!

I deeply honour all of God's creatures!

The animal kingdom is part of myself and I am a part of it!

Divine timing

Human timing is not always divine timing, dear child,
but this subject is the cause of many tears,
fears and disappointments in your current earth life.
You feel that events should happen right now.
That is not always so; it may not be
for your highest, absolute, greatest good.
Unfortunately you are not able to see
the bigger picture to make this judgement for yourself.
Therefore please hand the timing of events over to God,
or your higher self; then you are able to transcend the ego self and
allow what is best for your highest good to happen in divine perfection.

Meditation:

Hold the timing issue in question in your mind;
then mentally hand it over to your higher self and let go of it.
Relax for a little while; you will find that within
a short period of time you will have an inner knowing
of the divine time-scale of your issue.
Thank your higher self for the co-operation.

Affirmations:

I now let go of my earthly concept of timing and allow
divine timing to take place!

I am aligning myself with divine timing!

Time is always on my side!

Living in the here and now

Live every day like it is your last day on this earth.
Dwell not in the past or project your desires into the future,
for either will rob you of precious life force,
which will leak from you into the past or future dimensions.

Stay in the very moment, cherish it, and see it as a gift from God.

Meditation:

Breathe seven breaths of blue light into your brow chakra.
Gently allow all thoughts of past and future to drain away from you.
Now centre yourself in your heart chakra; ask your soul
what it would like to communicate to you right here, right now.
Listen attentively; everything that your soul has communicated
with you will reach your conscious awareness.
Give thanks.
Always ground, attune and protect yourself.

Affirmations:

J am dwelling in the present moment!

J am free of thoughts relating to the past or the future!

All my energies are focused totally in the here and now!

December 13

Develop compassion

Make haste to develop your compassionate nature.
Move beyond reacting to apparent behaviours.
Behind every angry, aggressive attack
lies a wounded human being, a soul in pain.
Reach out with your heart to your fellow brothers and sisters.
Your compassion will ease the pain and healing will take place.

Meditation:

Remember the last time you were attacked by someone.
See this person in front of you.
Now link your heart with theirs;
ask their soul for an explanation of their destructive behaviour.
You will be given this information instantaneously.
As you now understand the pain or despair behind this attack,
you are able to send love from your heart centre
to the other person and forgive them.
Ask for blessings and repeat this process
with everyone with whom you feel you have discord.
Do not forget to ground, attune and protect yourself.

Affirmations:

I am a compassionate being!

I know that pain and despair are at the root of my fellow brothers'
and sisters' destructive behaviour!

I am healing myself and others through the act
of compassionate forgiveness!

Helping hands

Allow those around you to give you
a helping hand, to love and support you.
Let go of the notion that you have to do it all alone, all by yourself.
When you go it alone, you are shutting out the hand
of God, which operates through your fellow brothers and sisters.
Accept the offers of help graciously, and, in doing so,
you give others the opportunity to show you their love in return.

Meditation:

Breathe in pink light.
Ask your higher self to help you to release all sense of pride;
feel it literally draining away from you.
Now see yourself at a party with friends or at a family function.
Visualise your friends or family showering
you with gifts and acts of kindness.
You see yourself accepting all gifts graciously, hugging and kissing
your friends and family, and they are radiating with the joy of giving.
Repeat this process until you feel at peace
with your friends and family in the acceptance of their love.
Remember to ground, attune and protect yourself.

Affirmations:

I allow my friends and family to love me as much as I love them!

I am open to love coming to me from different
sources and different people!

I fully exchange unconditional love with all sentient beings!

Abundant Universe

The universe is abundant; there is
a limitless amount of energy available to you.
All you have ever dreamt of, or can
ever dream of, is available in vast quantities.
God is limitless in His giving; you can have all you want,
providing what you want is in alignment with your highest good
which is why at times your desires are not fulfilled right there and then.
As you truly honour yourself and your needs,
you are magnetising yourself to the gifts of the universe.
God wants so much to bestow these gifts onto you.
Ask and you shall receive.

Meditation:

Go within and ask the healing angels to take away all notions of
"I do not deserve"– a new car, new house,
new dress, new friends, new job, success, love…
Release and let go; then visualise what you want
in accordance with divine law and ask for it to be brought to you.
Give thanks.
You may have to repeat this often.

Affirmations:

I now accept all the gifts the universe has in store for me!

I am a perfect child of God and deserve all
the good the world has to offer me!

I am a limitless being in an abundant universe!

Mind clearing

Purify your mind, my child.
To do this you must first find out what is on your mind.
Become the observer and watch your thoughtforms.
You will be surprised at what you will find.
Most of it you will want to release, as it is of
a negative nature and therefore detrimental to your development.
Once you have become aware of the content of your mind,
you will be in control of it, rather than it being in control of you.

Meditation:

Make sure you observe your thought forms while doing
mundane jobs like ironing, washing up, washing your car.
Note on a piece of paper the themes of these thoughtforms.
Now pick out the pattern that recurs most often.
Sit comfortably, relax, and take this pattern into contemplation.
Ask your higher self to show you the root of the issue.
You ask and you will receive, and you will soon
get a feeling or a thought about the root cause of this issue.
Once you have found it, hand it over to the healing angels to be
taken away, returned to source, and transmuted back into light.
Then you can work through all of your issues and release them.
Give thanks to the healing angels.

Affirmations:

I am in control of my mind and perfectly capable of locating and
releasing all negative thought patterns!

I choose to focus my mind on love and light!

My mind is a powerful tool with which to achieve enlightenment!

You are a gift

You are God's gift to the world.
You have within you many answers, many pleasures to give.
Some are still buried under the burden of hatred,
fear, self-criticism and many other unreleased emotions.
However, once you begin to give your gift you will find that,
through the joy of giving, great healing will
take place for yourself and others.
You are very precious to God, so treat yourself
and God's other gifts, namely your fellow human,
animal and plant brothers and sisters, kindly.

Meditation:

Breathe into your heart chakra;
visualise it as a beautifully wrapped parcel.
Now start to unwrap it slowly and carefully; inside
you will find a special gift your soul has to give to this world.
See yourself fulfilling this task of giving your gift
through a variety of actions, maybe through your work,
or through playing, or through the arts.
Finally, once you have achieved this, give yourself a hug.
Always ground, attune and protect yourself.

Affirmations:

I thank God for my gift of life!

I honour and cherish this gift!

I hold the precious gift of unconditional love in my heart
and give of it freely to all in need!

Pleasure in small things

Find pleasure in small things, my child.
All too often you feel that only great events, special performances,
luxurious gifts will give you the pleasure you so strive for.
That is not so.
Often these grand things require continued efforts, and the enjoyment
you get out of them is rarely as great as the joy of the expectation.
The end result is disappointment.
There is pleasure to be had 24 hours a day.
Just learn to look for it, for God has implanted it everywhere:
the light of day, the smell of a rose, the song of a bird,
fresh wind on your cheeks, the voice of your beloved.
Take pleasure and delight in all of those.
The more you find pleasure in the small stuff of life,
the more it will become apparent to you that there is beauty
and joy to be found everywhere and in every thing.
What a great gift from God to you.

✽

Meditation:

Play your favourite music.
Now breathe it in…
Now drink it in…
Now be immersed in it…
And, finally, become the music…
You are the music!
Enjoy.

✽

Affirmations:

I delight in God's creation!

My eyes are open to the wonders of God's creation
and I am ready to enjoy them!

I look at the world with the eyes of love and see love
in everybody, in every thing!

December 19

The light within

As the nights are drawing in, do look for the light within.
You light candles and sit by the fireside for Christmas cheer.
My child don't forget that the inner light,
the light of your soul, is the most important one to be burning bright.
Do not be fooled by pomp and tinsel, and false illuminations.
All of these will only be meaningful if tended by a loving soul.

Meditation:

Concentrate on the heart chakra.
See a small spark igniting in its chambers; it grows into a bright flame.
Watch over this flame until you see it burning brightly.
Sit with this flame for as long as you like.
When you feel your body, mind, emotions and soul are truly
illuminated and you are saturated with this bright light, start
to radiate it out through your own home, through the community
around you, and, finally through the whole world and the universe.

Please make sure that you are grounded, attuned and protected.

Affirmations:

I am the light!
I carry the light of God within me!
The light of my soul radiates out into the world.

A vessel for love

See yourself as a vessel, a vessel
containing never-ending amounts of unconditional love.
Even if you feel empty and sad, just ask God
to refill this vessel within you with love.
Whenever you or one of your human or animal
brothers and sisters need a dose of love, just turn on the taps,
the compassion in your heart, and out pours unconditional love
for all in great abundance.

Meditation:

See your heart as an ornate, bejewelled container.
God's love keeps pouring into it through
your crown chakra in a never-ending stream.
As the vessel overflows, direct the energy
to anyone you know with need of it.

Give thanks and close down your chakras.
Please ground, attune and protect yourself.

Affirmations:

I am an instrument for God's unconditional love!

I am filled with God's love and give it away freely to anyone in need!

The love in my heart is eternal!

December 21

Honour your parents

Honour your parents, for they fed, kept,
clothed and brought you up to the best of their abilities.
Forgive their shortcomings for they did not know what they did.
Their actions were based upon the understanding gained
from their upbringing, and, if they did not experience love,
then they did not know love, and so could not pass it on to you.
Harmonise your mind with a compassionate heart towards them.
Ask for blessings and allow all that was
not love to go out of your childhood memories.
Rejoice, look for and honour the divine spark
within your father and mother.

Meditation:

Visualise both your parents, whether they are still with you or in spirit.
Forgive them what there is to forgive and thank them
for all the gifts, lessons and blessings they have bestowed on you.
Ask the angels to bless them and yourself.
Give thanks.

Make sure that you are grounded, attuned and protected.

Affirmations:

I thank my parents for granting me the gift of life!

I thank my parents for the opportunity to learn and grow!

I love and honour my parents!

Believe in yourself

Believe in yourself.
You are a true child of God.
Within you is slumbering the awesome power of creation.
Believe yourself to be one with this power,
not just a little part of it, but all of it.
Believe in the power of one, the non-existence of separation.
Do not be fooled by the illusion of your third-dimensional experience.
Merge yourself into that vast, infinite oneness,
that sea of infinite bliss. Wholly become one with it.
Peace, love, harmony and endless bliss await you.

Meditation:

Breathe golden light into your solar plexus and then ask the
healing angels to help you identify your negative beliefs about yourself.
With the help of the healing angels those patterns
will now surface in your conscious awareness.
Acknowledge them, own them and then ask
the healing angels to take them away for you.
Repeat often, thanking the healing angels for their assistance.
Have you grounded, attuned and protected yourself?

Affirmations:

I believe that I am part of the one!

I believe in the power of unity in love!

I believe in myself and all that I do is in alignment with divine will!

December 23

Open doors

When one door closes, God will open another one for you.

Do not despair or be impatient and try to push through
the closed door, for you are not to experience what lies behind it.
There is no need to be involved with whatever
awaits you in the reality that lies beyond it.
When a door closes in your life, then first
take stock of the circumstances that led you
to this point; "how did I get here?
Why?"
Then you take the situation into contemplation,
taking guidance from your divine self.
Ask the angels for patience in this process.
Another door will open for you,
and you will step through it with ease and joy.

❀

Meditation:

You wander along a road that leads through beautiful
poppy fields in full bloom; soon you come to a crossroads.
The road to the left leads to a life of natural abundance;
the road to the right leads to a life of emotional fulfilment;
the road in the middle leads to enlightenment.
Follow whichever road appeals to you at this moment in time;
walk along it and find what it will bring for you.
Remember to ground, attune and protect yourself.

❀

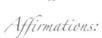

Affirmations:

I walk with ease and joy through the doors God has opened for me!

I trust my inner guidance to walk my chosen path!

I am aligning myself with divine will and the doors
of heaven on earth will open for me!

The God self

You are the God self.
The gift of "God consciousness" is within you.
You will connect to your God self by releasing
all which is not love, thus surrendering your lower ego self to it.
Your soul will rejoice in the vibration of
perfect harmony with the divinity within.
Allow God and the angels to assist you in this process.
Demand their help and guidance at all times.
State your intent clearly and firmly.
You ask and you shall receive all the love, light
and support you will require on your journey to the God self.

Meditation:

Visualise a golden cross as the symbol of
the crossing out of the I, the ego, the lower self.
Hand over your ego desires to God, your divine higher self!
As you do this, the cross slowly dissolves and changes
into a beautiful rose, one of the symbols for God.
Take the rose and plant it firmly into your heart;
then thank the angels for their support and assistance.
Please remember to ground, attune and protect yourself.

Affirmations:

God is within me!

I am within God!

I hold within my heart God's light of love!

December 25

Forgiveness

Remember, from the act of forgiveness springs liberation.
Forgive and you shall be set free.
When you so forgive yourself and others,
you release the negative bonds that so far
have tied you together, and gain instead the blessings
of God and the angelic realms, substituting darkness with light.
With every bit of forgiveness, your soul's load lightens a little more,
until your soul will be without burden and so it will be free to
permanently dwell in the heavenly realms.

Meditation:

Connect to your higher divine self
and breathe three times into your heart chakra.
Then ask for all the people you need to forgive to be shown to you.
Forgive, and let them go and ask for all bonds
to be released by Archangel Michael.
Finally, ask the healing angels for blessings.
Repeat this, forgiving yourself also.
Give thanks.

Do not forget to ground, attune and protect yourself.

Affirmations:

I attain perfect freedom through the act of unconditional forgiveness!

I forgive and I am free!

I forgive and I am free to give and experience unconditional love with
all of those whom I have forgiven!

Limitless Strength

Deep within your own soul lies the source of
unlimited strength, the belief in your own divinity.
You are able to draw all you need from that source within you.
From that point of divine power, strength pours forth, the very
strength you need to carry on your divine mission on this earth plane.
Trust you are a child of God, believe in your divinity, for so it is.

Meditation:

Attune to love and light, which is all around you,
and then bring your awareness into the chamber of your heart,
the chamber that is the seat of your soul.
Within you, to your surprise, you find a spring, bubbling beautifully.
This spring of divine energy is constantly filled
by God's grace with unconditional love.
You now walk up to this spring, you kneel by it and,
with a golden chalice you find next to it, you draw
the precious liquid of life force from the spring.
As you drink it, you feel the divine life force
strengthening, rejuvenating and uplifting you.
When you feel low, visit this source of limitless supply of divine energy.
Please always ground, attune and protect yourself.

Affirmations:

I am always connected to the source!

I believe in my own divine strength and limitless energy!

I am at one with the source of all love, light and power!

December 27

Attunement

You desire divine guidance, but how often
do you practise the art of attunement my child?
In receiving clear guidance from the source
of your higher divine self, clarity is of utmost importance!
To achieve this clarity you must strive for attunement.
Develop this spiritual discipline
and the rewards will be worth your while.
Through the state of attunement divine guidance
will be able to reach you in it's purest form, namely in
the form of unconditional love and light!

Meditation:

Take three deep breaths, releasing all emotional
and mental worries, fears and anxieties on the out-breath.
Now send golden roots into the earth
from the soles of your feet and ask
Mother Earth to ground, balance and nurture your whole self.
Then ask God to connect you to the heavenly source of all that is.
As soon as you ask, you feel pure white light pouring
in through your crown chakra, flowing through all your
chakras and filling the seven layers of your auric field.
Give thanks, make sure to close your chakras
and leave your roots a few inches in the ground.

Make sure that you are grounded, attuned and protected.

Affirmations:

I am in perfect attunement with Mother Earth and God!

I am connected to the source of all that is!

I receive clear guidance whenever I am in need of it!

Nature

Listen closely to what nature has to tell you, my beloved!
The great spirit of this earth, Gaia, is in despair!
Her seas are polluted, her mountains bare,
the trees felled and her body mutilated.
You seem to have forgotten that you breathe "courtesy of Gaia",
that what you eat is a gift from her and that the water
you drink is her "blood", which she gives willingly to you
to sustain you throughout your human experience.
As you have angered and abused her, volcanoes
are erupting, tornadoes are creating devastation
and floods are covering many miles of land.
It is time to honour and respect Mother Earth!
Stop polluting her body; she has sacrificed
herself for you for millions of years!
Pray for Mother Earth and most of all
thank her daily for her great service to you!

❀

Meditation:

Centre yourself in your heart chakra and send a beam
of golden light from your heart to encompass the whole earth.
Then visualised a completely healed earth with
an abundance of trees, wildlife, clear lakes,
sparkling seas and rivers and unpolluted fresh air.
Give heartfelt thanks to Mother Earth for her sacrifices to you!
Remember to ground, attune and protect yourself.

❀

Affirmations:

I thank Mother Earth daily for sustaining and nourishing me!

I love, cherish and honour her!

As a guardian of this earth, I pledge to look
after her to the best of my abilities!

December 29

Hand over your fears

My beloved child!
It is time to hand over all your fears to God!
For they are nothing but a misconception on your behalf.
Fears arise when you allow the little
lower ego-you to create your experiences!
Let go of this erroneous self-concept
and let God, or your divine self, "do the doing"!
Let go and let God; trust and you will never be afraid again!

Meditation:

Breathe white light into all your chakras.
Now you become aware of a knot
of dark energy sitting in your solar plexus.
These are your fears.
Take a deep breath in and visualise the white light,
like a sharp laser beam, bombarding the knot of fears and anxieties.
Soon the knot disintegrates and as you breathe out
you release and let go of it once and forever!
Next take a deep breath of golden light, allowing it to flow through
all your chakras and your auric field to sooth and re-energise you.
Give thanks.
Repeat successively until a "light feeling" in your solar plexus pervades.
Remind yourself to ground, attune and protect.

Affirmations:

I hand all my fears over to God!

I am not body, mind or emotions!

I am spirit incarnate!

Spiritual food

First and foremost find spiritual food to feed your soul!
Then you will find that you will not need
to consume so much earthly food.
When your soul is fed, it will be happy and content
and material needs will be much less important.
When your soul infuses your emotional body with unconditional love,
your emotions will be much les starved and your need
for earthy food, which primarily feeds the emotions, will diminish.
So will the need for many other pleasures that come out of need.
They all will be transmuted into joy by your ever-loving soul!

Meditation:

Visualise the chamber of your heart, the seat of your soul.
The room is infused with a beautiful, luminous pink light
and you notice that it is a vast storeroom!
Everything you need is stored there.
All the "soul food" you will ever need is to be found in this space.
You are very happy to have found this treasure trove of
unending supplies and rejoice in the knowledge
that you are totally provided for!
Remember to ground, attune and protect yourself.

Affirmations:

I am nourished by my soul!

I have a limitless supply of all I need within!

All I need is love and I have it right within my soul!

December 31

Renewal

As the last day of the old earth year dawns,
prepare to set your intentions for the new year to come!
Align yourself according to the divine will,
the divine plan and purpose, in perfect divine timing.
First, spend some time in meditation or contemplation
so that your soul has the opportunity to transmit
to you the intentions which need to be set for the year ahead.
Then you will be ready to start to create your intentions, which are
now in perfect alignment with the plans God has in store for you.
Fuel your intent with passion and compassion and the divine plan will
work out perfectly for you and for all around you in the coming year!

Meditation:

Visualise yourself in a golden temple of learning.
As you look around, you see a huge map on a wall near you.
Your name is written on it in golden letters.
You walk up close to the map and find
that it clearly charts the year which lies ahead of you.
The major points of your journey
are clearly mapped out for you by God!
Study it as long as you wish and return anytime you like.
Do not forget to ground, attune and protect yourself.

Affirmations:

The new is constantly available to me!

I intend to follow the path that is mapped out for me by divine design!

I intend to be a vessel for unconditional love!

Spiritual and Personal Self Development:

Bailey, Alice A., *Education in the New Age*, Lucis Press, ISBN 0-85330-105-0.

Bailey, Alice A., *Glamour: World Problem*, Lucis Press, ISBN 0-85330-109-3.

Bays, Brandon, *The Journey*, Harper Collins, ISBN 0-7434-4393-4.

Brennan, Barbara A., *Light Emerging: The Journey of Personal Healing*, Bantam, ISBN 0-553-35456-6.

Gardener, Mike, and Barbara Gardener, *Sathya Sai Baba and You: Practical Spirituality*, Wisdom Works Press, ISBN 0929839005.

Hay, Louise L., *You Can Heal Your Life*, Hay House, ISBN 0-937611-01-8.

His Holiness the Dalai Lama, *The Art of Happiness*, Hodder and Stoughton General, ISBN 0-340-75015-4.

His Holiness the Dalai Lama, *Advice on Dying: And Living a Better Life*, Rider, ISBN 0-7126-6223-5.

Krystal, Phyllis, *Cutting the Ties that Bind*, Red Wheel/Weiser, ISBN 0-87728-791-0.

Myss, Caroline, *Anatomy of the Spirit*, Bantam, ISBN 0-553-50527-0.

Myss, Caroline, *Why People Don't Heal and How They Can*, Bantam, ISBN 0-553-50712-5.

Tolle, Eckhart, *The Power of Now*, Hodder & Stoughton General, ISBN 0-340-73350-0.

Walsh, Neale Donald, *Conversations with God*, Hodder Mobius, ISBN 0-340-69325-8.

White Eagle, *Gentle Brother: The Power of Love in Your Life*, White Eagle Publishing Trust, ISBN 0-85487-112-8.

White Eagle, *Heal Thyself*, White Eagle Publishing Trust, ISBN 0-85487-107-1.

Yogananda, Paramahansa, *Where There Is Light*, Self Realization Fellowship, ISBN 1-59467-438-8.

Yogananda, Paramahansa, *Scientific Healing Affirmations*, Self Realization Fellowship, ISBN 1-5659-178-3.

The Chakras and the Auric Field:

Brennan, Barbara Ann, *Hands of Light: A Guide to Healing Through the Human Energy Field*, Bantam, ISBN 0-553-34539-7.

Johari, Harish, *Chakras, Energy Centres of Transformation*, Destiny, ISBN 0-89281-760-7.

Leadbeater, Charles W., *The Chakras*, The Theosophical Publishing House, ISBN 0-8356-0422-5.

Spiritual Healing:

Angelo, Jack, *Spiritual Healing: Energy Medicine For Today*, Element, ISBN 1-85230-219-4.

Bek, Lilla, and Philippa Pullar, *The Seven Levels of Healing*, Century, ISBN 0-7126-9473-0.

Bradford, Michael, *Hands-On Spiritual Healing*, Findhorn Press, ISBN 0-905249-92-5.

Brofman, Martin, *Anything Can Be Healed*, Findhorn Press, ISBN 1-84409-016-7.

Edwards, Harry, (the founder of the National Federation of Spiritual Healers, England), *The Power of Spiritual Healing*, Jenkins.

Furlong, David, *The Healer Within*, Piatkus, ISBN 0-7499-1877-2.

Meditation:

Caddy, Eileen, *Opening Doors Within*, Findhorn Press, ISBN 0-905249-68-2.

Caddy, Eileen, *The Living Word*, Findhorn Press, ISBN 0-905249-69-0.

Harrison, Eric, *How Meditation Heals*, Piatkus, ISBN 0-7499-2109-9.

Main, Darren John, *The Findhorn Book of Meditation*, Findhorn Press, ISBN 1-84409-005-1.

Trungpa, Chogyam, *Meditation in Action*, Watkins. ISBN 0-7224-0105-1.

Angels:

Cooper, Diana, *A Little Light on Angels*, Findhorn Press, ISBN 1-899171-51-7.

Lawson, David, *A Company of Angels*, Findhorn Press, ISBN 1-899171-02-9.

Virtue ,Doreen, *Healing with the Angels*, Hay House, ISBN 1-4019-0422-X.

Earth Healing:

Lovelock, James, *Gaia: A New Look at Life on Earth*, Oxford Paperbacks, ISBN 0-19-2862-18-9.

Stowe, John R., *The Findhorn Book of Connecting with Nature*, Findhorn Press, ISBN 1-84409-011-6.

Pogacnik, Marko, *Christ Power and the Earth Goddess: A Fifth Gospel*, Findhorn Press, ISBN 1-899171-92-4.

Pogacnik, Marko, *Earth Changes Human Destiny: Coping and Attuning with the Help of the Revelation of St. John*, Findhorn Press, ISBN 1-899171-53-3.

Pogacnik, Marko, *The Daughter of Gaia: Rebirth of the Divine Feminine*, Findhorn Press, ISBN 1-899171-04-5.

Pogacnik, Marko, *Healing the Heart of the Earth: Restoring the Subtle Levels of Life*, Findhorn Press, ISBN 1-899171-57-6.

Pogacnik, Marko, *Nature Spirits and Elemental Beings: Working with the Intelligence in Nature*, Findhorn Press, ISBN 1-899171-66-5.

Roads, Michael J., *Talking with Nature*, H.J. Kramer Inc., ISBN 0-915811-06-5.

Roads, Michael J., *Journey into Nature: a Spiritual Adventure*, H.J. Kramer Inc., ISBN 0-915811-19-7.

Stowe, John R., *Earth Spirit Warrior*, Findhorn Press, ISBN 1-84409-004-7.